S. A. SEMENOV

Prehistoric Technology

an Experimental Study of the oldest Tools and Artefacts from traces of Manufacture and Wear

TRANSLATED, AND WITH A PREFACE BY M. W. THOMPSON

MOONRAKER PRESS

© Copyright 1964, 1970, 1973, 1976 by M. W. Thompson
SBN 239 00029 3
First published in Russian in the USSR in 1957
English translation first published 1964
Second impression 1970
Third impression 1973
Fourth impression 1976 published by
Moonraker Press, 26 St Margarets Street, Bradford-on-Avon, Wiltshire
Printed by Redwood Burn Limited, Trowbridge & Esher
Bound in Great Britain

Contents

Illustrations

Translator's Preface

THIS BOOK IS THE RESULT of some twenty years of microscopic research on prehistoric stone and bone tools, which has shed a flood of light on both their methods of manufacture and use. Various practical difficulties have had to be overcome, notably that of rendering flint opaque so that it could be examined in reflected light under a microscrope. The most important discovery has been that during use microscopic striations ('linear marks') were produced on the tool's surface by friction. The striations reveal the direction of movement of the tool during use and so allow its purpose to be identified with fair confidence. This in its turn throws a sidelight on the way of life of the people who employed the tool.

Apart from the new technique used in the work the book draws together a great mass of scattered information on experimental work in making and testing tools, and also ethnographic parallels that by comparisons throw light on prehistoric tools. Comparisons with modern techniques—as steel burins in metal industry or the way a modern bricklayer cleaves a brick—are rarely adduced in this type of study, but as used by the author here relate ancient to modern techniques as well as making the description more vivid. The book therefore will serve both for reference and as a manual or textbook.

Prehistoric Technology (*Pervobytnaya Tekhnika*) appeared in 1957 as number 54 in the Materials and Researches on the Archaeology of the U.S.S.R., published by the Institute of the History of Material Culture of the Academy of Sciences of the U.S.S.R. Since this series started in 1940 over 100 quarto volumes have appeared and have earned it a place among the leading world publications on archaeology. The volumes normally deal with special periods or areas and quite often are monographs, as in this case. The Russian edition has been out of print for several years.

This English edition is virtually a complete translation of the Russian edition with the exception of the description of Russian instruments in parts 5 and 7 of section one and another minor omission on page 59 made on the author's instruction (at the translator's suggestion). Omissions in the text have been marked with an asterisk. A list of illustrations and an index, not included in the original, have been added to this edition. In the footnotes titles of articles have been omitted, but the titles of journals given in full, in order to avoid the need for a list of abbreviations. Footnotes concluded with the letter T have been interpolated by the translator. The format is broadly similar in both Russian and English editions.

Dr Semenov has most kindly made available either the prints used in the original edition or (in a few cases) substitutes. A few poor or damaged prints have been omitted, but with the exception of the colour plate in the Russian edition the illustrations are substantially the same in both books. The quality of reproduction is better in the English edition, which also contains one print of high magnification (fig. 47). Scales are not always given in either edition and where they are should be regarded as approximate.

*

It is hoped that the translator will be excused for introducing a personal reminiscence of how he first became interested in Russian work on this subject.

In connexion with a doctoral dissertation I wished to make some antler harpoon heads for experiments. It seemed to be worth while to use actual palaeolithic techniques.[1] Reindeer and red deer antlers having been obtained

---

[1] See Appendix iv of my dissertation *Some Mesolithic Cultures of the Iberian Peninsula* (June 1953) typescript at the Cambridge University Library.

from Finland and Scotland and flint flakes from the Brandon flint-knappers, a difficulty at once arose: how to make a burin. The Brandon knappers averred that it was physically impossible by flaking, and so rather than waste time several 'burins' were cut with a diamond cutter. After prolonged softening of the antler by soaking, it proved fairly easy to cut grooves along the full length of the beam and extract the necessary antler strip. Several harpoons were made, mainly with steel tools, but in one case using one of the burins as a chisel. The rough tools could then be ground smooth with sandpaper. The main failure in the experiment (and perhaps the reason why it was never published) was the ineffective nature of the 'burins'. In cutting the grooves in the antler a long flint flake was used, partly wrapped in cloth and held in the closed fist, and then dragged with the full strength of the body along the beam. The flake was not held like a knife (Gerasimov's method in fig. 78.1), but at right-angles to the groove, so that to the accompaniment of a loud squally shriek antler material was torn off each side of the groove, the waste being rather like sawdust. The movement is identical to that described by Semenov for a burin, and no doubt the explanation for the ineffectiveness of my 'burins' was not so much that they were diamond-cut as that they were too short. The tool must be held in the fist, not between the forefinger and thumb, because the secret of the operation is simply brute force; the whole strength of the trunk and shoulders must be brought to bear.

This digression brings us to a cardinal point of Semenov's book: in modern experiments one can do practically anything with flints; the only reliable guide to the original purpose of a tool is the traces of wear that it bears. As described in the Introduction the study of function can be envisaged as a sort of trident; the central and main prong is analysis of traces, the two auxiliary prongs are practical experiment and ethnographic parallels.

The first section on methods is divided into seven parts, the last three of which deal with the technical problems of microscopic research. The first three deal with natural changes and processes of wear on stone and bone, while the fourth describes the kinematics of working with the hand. We have to be clear in our own minds how tools are moved in different operations, so that the microscopic striations which reveal the direction of movement can be interpreted in terms of function.

The main part of the book which deals with stone is section two. Three introductory parts give a valuable table of stones used arranged according to the smoothness of fracture surface, an account of obtaining material, and—the most interesting—Semenov's views on the extent to which the quality of tools depended on the properties of available material. The case for a decisive influence is very strongly put, particularly the beneficial effect of chalk flint in those limited areas where it occurs. The translator would certainly agree with most of this cogent section.

Parts 4 and 5, both divided into numerous subsections, deal with the manufacturing of stone tools and identification of their function respectively.

As he is dealing with techniques—in this case percussion—the author does not separate core-tools from flake-tools, a distinction which underlies so much western thinking on the subject. On blade-making, he is not able to offer any final solution of how blades were made, although he believes that the tip of the presser was made of flint. Semenov regards bone and wood as having played a much smaller part in primary working than is generally believed in the west. Perhaps the most remarkable theory is that Solutrean surface retouch was merely a technical device for removing the natural curvature on the blade, very necessary in projectile heads. By the same token we might argue that the Magdalenians abandoned Solutrean retouch because they made their projectile heads of bone. This curvature on the blade is regarded by Semenov as one of the main snags arising in the use of blades, and for this reason he regards segmentation, the manufacture of microliths by dividing the blade and inserting them into a haft, as the logical culmination in the evolution of blade industries. This view should help to raise mesolithic industries in our esteem! Burin-spalling by a vertical blow the author regards as used not only for making burins, but also as a method of blunting a sharp blade-edge for holding in the hand or hafting. The subsections on pecking, grinding, sawing and boring—predominantly neolithic techniques—are extremely clear and thorough, and should be of great help to the student.

A point that inevitably comes to mind is how far can the 'neolithic revolution' be regarded as a technological revolution in terms of stone-working. The late Gordon Childe used the word 'revolution' to connote a social or economic transformation, the change from hunting to agriculture as the means of subsistence. Practically all the techniques of stone-working enumerated by Semenov were known by mesolithic times; what was new in the neolithic period was the massive application of slightly used techniques to new materials, more particularly grinding previously used on bone now used on granular rock. The eighteenth-century Industrial Revolution was, after all, largely a matter of employing old techniques, like the water wheel, in new ways and on a larger scale. As Semenov says, the technique of grinding brought into use a new range of raw materials which made possible the colonization of large, previously uninhabited areas.

In part 5 we come to the heart of the book, the identification of the function of stone tools from traces of wear on them. The results are not entirely at variance with previous ideas, but rather clarify and make more precise our existing notions. Side-scrapers (from one example) are identified as a tool used in a two-way movement for primary cleaning of the underside of the skin, while end-scrapers were used with a one-way movement for secondary scraping, softening by rubbing. Burins are identified without hesitation as used for grooving ivory, bone and antler, the burin angle acting as a sort of saw-tooth, removing bone pulp from the side of the groove. Two new types of tool identified by Semenov, and only recognizable by microscopic traces, are meat and whittling knives. A moment's reflection will show that in the sort of life led in upper palaeolithic times knives of this kind must have been indispensable. An important discovery is the identification of a flint axe from Kostenki I, regarded by Semenov as used primarily for chopping mammoth tusk. This may provide an origin for the axes which play such an important role in post-glacial industries. The accounts of the use of ground axes and adzes and the traces on stone sickles are a particularly welcome addition to our knowledge. The reasons put forward by the author for the lop-sidedness of neolithic axes, like those for the lop-sidedness of end-scrapers, carry complete conviction, for the translator at least. The final subsection on the abrasive instruments from Verkholensk is a very fine piece of detection.

The third section on bone lacks some interest for the western reader, because it does not deal with the wide range of tools of reindeer antler found in the French Magdalenian sites. However, against this it does give us much information about the use of mammoth ivory on Russian sites, where it is, of course, much more common than in the west. Of particular interest is the notching technique for severing tusks, using an axe, chisel or burin. The longitudinal division of ivory tusk closely resembled the removal of strips from antler already mentioned; with this difference, that ivory has no soft spongy centre, so that strips could not be snapped out, but had to be struck free with a chisel. Semenov has some very sensible things to say about softening bone, and the translator has added some additional information in the footnotes.

Part 3 deals with Eskimo bone tools and their origin. The curious feature about these has always been that the earlier the industry the finer the bone tools appear to be; it now seems reasonably clear that the ingenious toggle-head harpoons used for seal-hunting (upon which the winter survival of the Eskimos depends) could not have been made without metal. Eskimo life therefore, like buffalo-hunting on horseback by the prairie Indians, ultimately owed its existence to borrowing from a much more advanced culture.

The parts on handles, burnishers and mattocks are of especial interest. It is reasonably clear that a burin required some sort of handle, because of the force used and the danger of lacerating the hand. The mattocks were essential tools for the upper palaeolithic inhabitants of the Russian steppe in order to dig their well-known semi-subterranean houses. Part 5 describes the use of long bones on later Classical and medieval sites. The 'skates', which are also found in England, are identified as used attached to the feet, not for skating, but for thickening cloth.

The book ends with an essay on regularity in the development of tools in the Stone Age which it would be impertinent for the translator to attempt to summarize. Western archaeologists tend to regard stone tools as type fossils and not to seek underlying evolution throughout this vast period of time. A technologist like Semenov understandably is not interested in cultural divisions, which in any case in the Stone Age are not very meaningful, and seeks to find the technical improvements that the changes imply. While we should be hesitant of seeing 'laws of development', that a Marxist desires to find, nevertheless the sort of underlying changes described by Semenov seem to be real and helpful to our understanding of the subject.

*

Such is the gist of the book without doing justice to the cogency of the argument, clarity of thought and prolonged research on which it is based. There are, however, two criticisms which in fairness to the reader ought to be made.

Firstly is the foreign work that is ignored, probably due to the difficulty of obtaining the books in the Soviet Union. In a book that very largely deals with upper palaeolithic industries it is surprising that there is no mention of Mount Carmel or Parpalló. The segmentation of blades is described without reference to microburins, while in describing the longitudinal cutting of ivory no reference is made to the analogous method used on antler in western Europe. Such examples could be multiplied, and, while they do not vitiate the argument, the reader should bear this fact in mind.

The second criticism is of the method. We are told how tools were selected for micro-analysis by fairly obvious signs of wear. It would inspire more confidence if a fixed sample of tools had been taken and record made of how many did or did not bear the given traces of wear. For example the marks of a stone presser-tip on the platform of a blade or core are described by Semenov, but he says that in numerous cases there were no marks (p. 53). This might mean that the blade came off at the first exertion, but it might mean that the presser-tip was of a softer material, such as bone. No doubt the explanation is that with a very laborious process like micro-analysis it would not be practical to attempt it unless there were obvious signs of wear on the tool, but nevertheless the reader should bear in mind the selective nature of the samples.

These criticisms in no way detract from the translator's warm admiration of this very fine book which undoubtedly marks a major step forward in the subject. It only remains for the him to record the pleasure the translation has given him, and his gratitude to Dr Semenov for supplying the original prints for the figures. Warm acknowledgement must also be made to the publisher, Mr Anthony Adams, whose idea originally it was to publish a translation, and to Miss Sarnia Butcher, who has most kindly read and made many corrections to the typescript.

M. W. THOMPSON
Wimbledon, February 1963

Introduction

IT is well known what significance the study of tools and the history of manufacturing has for historical science.

Marx stated the necessity for the creation of a history of the development of manufacturing tools and wrote: 'Darwin directed attention to the history of natural technology, that is to the formation of plant and animal organs, which play the part of manufacturing tools in the vegetable and animal kingdoms. Does not the history of the creation of the productive instruments of social man, the history of the material basis of each entity of social organization, deserve the same attention from history? And would this not be the easier to write since, as Vico put it, precisely what distinguishes human history from natural history is that the first is made by us while the second is not. Technology reveals the active relationship between man and nature, a direct process of his existence, consequently of the social relationships of his life and so of the spiritual phenomena that arise from them.'[1]

The present study is devoted to the problems of the history of the oldest working tools.

For the study of prehistoric technology archaeological investigation of the remains of the working activity of man of the Stone Age has provided great opportunities, in particular in the palaeolithic period, researches into which began with the discoveries of the 'first tools' (Chellean hand-axes) by Boucher de Perthes in France. However, in studying very ancient technology scholars have encountered great difficulties. Tens and hundreds of thousands of years separate contemporary tools from palaeolithic ones, so not much can be understood by simple observations and comparisons.

Investigators studying the Stone Age have not infrequently attempted to prepare ancient tools with their own hands out of flint and other material, and so by experiment, not only to test their effectiveness and reliability in work, but also to find out the functions they fulfilled in the hands of prehistoric man. Boucher de Perthes, J. Evans, E. Lartet, G. de Mortillet, L. Capitan, L. Leguay, E. Piette, A. Vayson de Pradenne, L. Pfeiffer, V. A. Gorodtsov and many others by means of actual experiment have achieved solutions to problems of this kind to a greater or less degree, believing this to be the simplest and most straightforward way of doing it. Experimental work in the study of the most ancient techniques of working stone has continued more recently through the efforts of such scholars as: L. Coutier, F. Bordes, A. Barnes, D. Baden-Powell, J. Reid Moir, F. Nowells, and L. Leakey. Several of them have carried out experiments over the course of many years. A film has been made of the work of L. Coutier.

However, although there have been several essential discoveries relating to the method of preparation of stone tools these workers have achieved hardly any success in the elucidation of their function. Even when it was possible to carry out a definite type of work with this or that tool there could be no certainty that prehistoric man employed it for exactly this purpose. Experience showed, for example, that a flint blade can cut meat, or dress skins, or whittle wood; that a burin will incise bone and wood and even bore through these materials; that a point can be mounted in a stick and used as a dart or serve with or without a handle as a knife.

L. Pfeiffer experimenting with an end-scraper found that its circular retouched end worked equally successfully for scraping or cutting, if held at right-angles to the working surface, and several functions have been assigned to the end-scraper on the basis of those experiments.

It is very probable that in the time of prehistoric man there was not a rigid division of function between the various categories of tools; sometimes several functions were fulfilled by one tool, or one and the same job was done by different tools. But all the same prehistoric man had a varied inventory of utensils, not contenting himself with just a few forms.

Thus the experimental approach cannot serve as an independent method of study of the function of tools; precise evidence is required of what was the real purpose of the tool in each specific example.

There is yet another weak aspect to the experimental

---

[1] K. Marx, *Capital* (Moscow, 1951), I, 378. (G. V. Vico, 1688–1744, Italian jurist and philosopher. T.)

approach to the solution of the problem of the purpose of a tool. It is very difficult to re-create the actual conditions of work of prehistoric man and devise in a contemporary laboratory experiments with these objects, used just as he would have done. The palaeolithic hunter worked with stone burins on mammoth tusk and deer antler, with flint side- and end-scrapers he dressed skin, and with knives he disembowelled animal carcasses or cut up meat. Working processes of this kind cannot easily be re-created with the precision necessary for experiment without the replacement of proper objectives by substitutes and direct courses of action by indirect ones. The amateur nature of the experiments and doubts about the results is the reason why the majority of archaeologists leave their work unpublished. We know about them only by brief references in archaeological publications.

It would be a serious error, however, to reject entirely the part of experiment in this matter of studying the function of tools. As an auxiliary method to confirm or make more precise deductions made from the traces left by wear direct experiment is undoubtedly useful. Nevertheless its full-scale application is only possible in those cases which are accessible to us, as, for example, working stone, bone, wood, skin, soil, and other materials, the introduction of which into the practice of the experiment is less difficult than other objects of a hunting culture.

Experiment is important (apart from testing the mechanical properties of ancient tools) for the physiological experience of really assessing the nature of the working skill of prehistoric man, of the live sensation of the expediency of form of a stone tool, and so on.

Checking by experiment is important in study of the efficiency of work of ancient tools. Experiments to test stone sickles, neolithic axes, bows and boomerangs from ethnographic and archaeological collections, carried out in Czechoslovakia, Denmark, Brazil and other countries are by no means valueless. Thanks to experiment it has been possible in a number of cases to assess with an appropriate example the efficiency of implements about which information was inaccurate, due to faulty ethnographic description or prejudiced opinion, casually given by certain ethnographers and archaeologists.

Ethnographic materials play a vital role in the study of the function of ancient tools and the establishment of the techniques of manufacture. However, evidence for techniques of manufacture among backward tribes of Asia, Africa, America, and Australia is far less satisfactory than information about art, customs and beliefs, kinship and social relationships. At the time when the backward tribes of these countries still preserved their technology and economy there was no deep interest among the majority of ethnologists and travellers in the 'prosaic' side of the life of the societies they described. Nowadays these societies have either perished as a result

of the brutal colonial policy of imperialist governments or exist in conditions where to all intents and purposes their original economic life and tools no longer survive.

Ethnographic evidence, either in museums or from field study, in spite of its inadequacy and sporadic character, still retains a great deal of value. As a basis of of comparison it is very useful in the investigation of ancient manufacturing.

In the study of the technology of the earliest stages of human development, when the tools commonly are of puzzling shape, giving rise to different opinions and controversy, we have worked out our own method of study. This is based on the fact that tools, independent of the materials out of which they are made and the shape they have been given, bear characteristic macroscopic and microscopic marks which are traces of work. There are two categories: (1) traces of wear and use, (2) traces of manufacture. Traces of wear make it possible to define what work was done with a given tool, that is how the object being studied was used and on what material. Traces of manufacture can explain with what tools and by what means the given object was made.

Traces of work are very valuable documents, as they allow us to understand the whole range of variety of tools in the light of the distinct functions and working activities to which man subjected them.

Traces of manufacture on ancient tools have occupied the attention of archaeologists for a long time. Observation of these traces played a decisive part in the study of the preparation of tools in the palaeolithic and neolithic periods (percussion, flaking, retouch, grinding, sawing, boring and so on), although the evidence of ethnography and, to some extent, experimental work have made no small contribution. By study of the surface of clay vessels it has been possible to distinguish wheel-made as distinct from hand-made pottery. In 1828 Tournal, one of the first defenders of the thesis of the great antiquity of man, put forward as proof of his theory the traces of work by sharp tools surviving on the bones of extinct animals in the Grotte de Bize (Aude) in France. Later, traces of use of sharp tools on bones served archaeologists as quite definite evidence of the contemporary existence of man and mammoth. E. Lartet and G. de Mortillet drew attention to the way such traces could be distinguished from others left by the teeth of animals, notably beavers.

Study of traces on ancient tools was one of the tasks of the Laboratory of Historical Technology in the State Academy for the History of Material Culture in the first years of its existence. N. P. Tikhonov wrote: 'This comprises study of the technique of manufacture beginning with the extraction of the material and going right up to the final division into different shapes and forms. It is necessary to study with the microscope and spectroscope the appearance of the surface, to discover the traces of instruments and means of boring, grinding, etc., and so by analogies with contemporary traditional methods in the same regions re-create the technical environment in which work took place.'[1] All the same, such laboratory work never took place. Nor did studies of the traces of wear on tools ever materialize, although various archaeologists retained their interest in the subject. In particular P. P. Efimenko in 1934 selected a number of flint tools from Kostenki I with traces of wear from use in the form of polishing on various parts of the surface, which formed the material used in our own first researches.

The credit is due to G. A. Bonch-Osmolovsky for correctly identifying the dents on the fragments of long bones from the cave of Kiik-Koba (Crimea) which made these objects recognizable as retouchers. Previously the view of H. Martin had prevailed among western archaeologists that the traces, well known on long bones from palaeolithic sites, were due to use of the bones as anvils.[2] Bonch-Osmolovsky, studying the traces of work on bones, in particular cuts on the epiphyses of bones of domestic dog, rightly concluded their origin as due to the use of this animal as food by the mesolithic hunters of the Crimea. He wrote: 'We can confirm from these examples that material from palaeolithic sites is by no means so dead as is often thought; it is the object-seeking, formal typological approach, carried to the point of dogma, which kills it.'[3]

The same worker first put forward an important argument in favour of a functional approach to the material. Using the experience of his own observations, he stated: 'Completely different types of tool of the lower and upper palaeolithic periods had one and the same purpose. This proposition is an essential blow to the formal typological treatment of the industry from a site which indissolubly binds each different shape to a function and almost turns this into a fetish.'[4] Our researches on materials drawn from several periods fully support this contention.

The work of M. V. Voevodsky on traces on clay vessels of their method of manufacture, as well as the investigations of G. G. Lemlein on the techniques of manufacture of ancient stone beads from the evidence of perforation, grinding and polishing, were begun at about the same time as our work.[5]

The remarkable method of B. A. Rybakov used in the study of the artistic metal objects of medieval Russia deserves special mention.[6] It is based on detailed study of the surface of the jewellery and the recognition of identical marks left by jewel-workers from which we can define the centres of production and the market areas.

Important observations about the technique of manufacture of the log coffin from Pazyryk (Grave. 1) were made by M. P. Gryaznov from study of traces left on the wood by metal adzes.

The first stage of our work (1934–8) was confined to a narrow range of problems; methods of study of traces of wear on palaeolithic flint implements were worked out. Predominantly upper palaeolithic material (from Kostenki I, Timonovka, Malta, and so on) was employed. It was quite evident from the beginning that few traces of wear on tools of such a hard material as flint would be distinguishable with the unaided eye or with a simple magnifying glass, but normal microscopic examination by means of a monocular instrument would not allow inspection of the multiplicity of things desired. By use of a binocular lens with maximum magnification of $45\times$ a start could be made with the first microscopic research on surfaces of ancient stone implements.

Rubbing or polishing was adopted as a basic criterion of wear on a flint tool. Rubbed parts on a flint vary in degree of shine, shape, and size. Even a comparatively trifling mark due to insertion in a handle has produced valuable evidence. Above all, the number of tools with evident traces of use was significantly increased. Besides this the examination of a large number of those flints which we are accustomed to call flakes and regard as waste products revealed examples that bore traces of use, showing that they were tools.[7] Concurrently with working out a means of selecting tools with traces of use, the peculiarities of these traces were closely studied in order to distinguish marks due to the action of natural agencies, as well as false traces arising from deliberate or accidental interference by contemporary man. Study of this entailed the examination of the micro-structure of flint on a fracture face, inquiry into the effect of patination on traces of use, attention to signs of submersion in rivers or desert sands, and also, an extremely necessary matter, study of the distribution of the traces of use in relation to the overall shape of the implement. Such observations were necessary to identify the working part of the tool with precision, and differentiate it from the area of marks left by friction of the skin of the hand when the tool had been used without a handle.

[1] N. P. Tikhonov, *Reports of the State Academy for the History of Material Culture*, 11–12 (1931), pp. 44–45.
[2] G. A. Bonch-Osmolovsky, *Palaeolithic Period of the Crimea, I, The Cave of Kiik-Koba*, Quaternary Commission of the Academy of Sciences (1940), p. 17.
[3] G. A. Bonch-Osmolovsky, *Reports of the State Academy for the History of Material Culture*, 8 (1931), p. 27.
[4] ibid., p. 26.
[5] M. V. Voevodsky in *Ethnography*, 4 (1930), pp. 55–70, and *Soviet Archaeology*, i (1936), pp. 51–79.
[6] B. A. Rybakov, *Handicrafts of Ancient Russia* (Moscow, 1949).
[7] S. A. Semenov, *Short Reports of the Institute for the History of Material Culture*, 4 (1940), p. 23.

In perfecting the method it was important to distinguish traces of wear on palaeolithic tools which are visible to the eye as chips and dents on the edge. These marks of use are often hardly different from light retouch employed intentionally to sharpen a blunted edge or blunt too sharp a one.

In the first period of our micro-analysis of palaeolithic tools we made an observation whose significance has only been given its proper weight in the last decade. We established that almost all tools with signs of wear, besides gloss or polish, bore striations in the form of minute lines, scatches, or grooves showing the direction of movements of the tool and its position on the object being worked. Striations from wear were found especially on the working edge of end-scrapers from the palaeolithic site of Timonovka.[1] These marks can be examined in this case with small magnifications and normal sources of light. Striations from wear seem the most important key to discovery of unknown functions of ancient tools, for they allow us to establish the kinematics of work in the use of these tools.[2]

The study of traces of wear on flint tools both in respect of size (micro-topography) and linear direction (micro-geometry) required a graphic method of recording the evidence by means of drawing and micro-photography. Great difficulties were encountered in the recording of traces of wear by means of micro-photography, since an attempt to reproduce the size of these marks is limited by the degree of possible enlargement. These difficulties have only recently been partly overcome by the use of stereo-photography.

The first stage of research on tools concluded with a successful experiment on the neolithic materials from the graves on the River Angar excavated by A. P. Okladnikov. Here the work was not merely to determine the function of the different categories of tools, for to some extent it shed light on the whole branch of an economy based on fishing.[3]

In the last ten years we have transferred our methods from stone tools to the bones in the archaeological material. Bones, teeth and antlers of animals were often used by man after a very small amount of treatment or sometimes even in an unworked state. Commonly therefore quite a series of unexplained bone objects present themselves not only from the palaeolithic period but even from the quite recent past.[4] The sole reliable source of information about their function is the traces of use they bear.

The functional analysis of bone objects has its own special features and required different methods of work to settle new problems. Among these we can count: (1) recognition of the traces of human use among the traces of natural agencies; (2) study of the plastic and structural characteristics of the different kinds of bone (ivory, long bones, antler); (3) experiments on the processes of wear of bone and on the processes of working it with stone and metal implements.

Through the study of traces of working on long bones, ribs, broad and flat bones, ivory and antler, many of the most elementary devices of palaeolithic technique, hitherto unknown or unexplained, were discovered.

Simultaneously with the work on bone we carried out studies on tools and objects of palaeolithic and neolithic times of mineral and rock (obsidian, nephrite, slate, quartzite, and rocks of volcanic origin) to which we had previously given very little attention. Traces of use and working on these materials also have their own peculiarities. By explaining and interpreting the marks we made intelligible the great nameless mass of river pebbles and sandstone and slate plaques, used as striker stones, retouchers, pestles, mortars for grinding colours, sharpeners for knives and axes, and other material needs of prehistoric man.

It is important to note that on the new materials (bone and different types of stone) the striations mentioned above continued as the leading feature. Together with these, traces of use of a micro-plastic but non-linear character were found in significant quantity. These have no common characteristic and consist of holes, chip-marks, effaced projections, scars, cracks and so on. Particles of material (colouring, chalk, silica sand, resin, metallic oxides, etc.) were observed on the tools' surfaces.

Remains of mineral colouring matter were generally found in the pores of rough stone surfaces. In palaeolithic sites where colouring so often occurs in the cultural layers its traces were often found on the objects, but this as a rule must have arisen accidentally; prehistoric man sometimes left colouring matter scattered about his hut, or sometimes it was brought by water into the layer.

The combination of wear and colouring matter on a tool deserves attention. Red or brown colouring matter (ochre) tends to be concentrated on working parts of the tool. This is the case particularly with stone pestles and slabs or flags used in the pounding and grinding of mineral colouring materials. Less often we find these tools made out of bone. Commonly the investigator first notices colouring on a tool of this type, and then signs of wear in the form of scars or striations from friction are identified afterwards. Sometimes, on the contrary, the colouring matter is only found with a magnifying glass, because it is deeply concealed in the

---

[1] S. A. Semenov, *Bulletin of the Commission for the Study of the Quaternary Period*, 6–7 (1940), pp. 110–13.
[2] Kinematics—'Science of motion considered abstractly without reference to force or mass'. Concise Oxford Dictionary. T.
[3] S. A. Semenov, *Materials and Researches on the Archaeology of the U.S.S.R.*, 2 (1941), 203–11.
[4] S. A. Semenov, *Short Reports of the Institute for the History of Material Culture*, 15 (1947), 138–42.

crevices, while the wear is visible to the naked eye. The presence of colouring on the surface of pounders, plaques and flags in conjunction with striations is a very reliable clue for identifying these tools, even although we are only dealing with the usual river pebbles and lumps of paving-stone type without any traces of preliminary shaping or dressing. Moreover, the presence of colouring prevents us confusing pestles and mortars with identical tools used for the mincing-up of food, on which as a rule colouring does not appear.

Rubbing tools used on skin and fur also sometimes bear colouring. Some bone burnishers of palaeolithic times made out of animal ribs have coloured, spatula-shaped working ends. In all probability these were used on skins that had already been coloured or the colouring matter was rubbed into the skin with them. It is known from ethnographic evidence that colouring matter was mixed with animal or plant fats, and applied to skin to make it impermeable and more lasting.

On stone and bone tools of later periods particles of other materials have been observed. In the Classical town of Tyritace in the Crimea two large flat pebbles weighing 400–600 hg were found in the excavations in 1947–8 by V. F. Gaidukevich. On one side each pebble bore marks of prolonged friction. On the less flat side of one pebble were remains of ochre, and here faint traces due to a circular movement of the pebble were visible. the surface being rubbed almost to a shine. The second pebble was quite flat with straight, fine striations all running in one direction. In addition, on the edge of the flat side was a small hollow scar retaining an appreciable amount of a hard, shiny mass, consisting of grains of sand and lime. It appears that this was an instrument for smoothing the plaster on the walls of buildings. The first pebble evidently was a burnishing stone for polishing the plaster to provide a surface for colouring.

For more detailed study of traces of use on tools of flint and other glasslike minerals and also on ground tools (neolithic and early metallic periods), in the second period of our researches we used a binocular microscope with a maximum magnification of 180× natural size and a monocular microscope, with binocular attachment, which gave even greater possibilities. The first result of our researches with the new devices was the identification of a palaeolithic axe from Kostenki I and of ancient stone sickles from Luka-Vrublevetskaya.

In the course of the work new difficulties arose with the techniques of investigating the surfaces of stone tools. The translucency of the glasslike mass of flint, rock crystal, chalcedony, agate, and other similar minerals of the quartz group was a serious obstacle in studying the surface of tools at high magnifications in reflected light. This required a special treatment of the surface with magnesium powder, the application of a thin layer of diluted Indian ink, or colouring with methyl violet or a metallizer. Magnesium powder and metallizers had already been used in micro-photography; colorizers were first employed in photographing surfaces of stone and bone in our own work. The peculiarities of the archaeological material and of the problems involved did not allow us just to copy the methods of microscopic analysis employed in other sciences. In particular the well-developed method of slicing used in the study of minerals and rocks is completely impracticable in the study of the function of stone tools. On the other hand, stereo-photography and micro-stereo-photography, otherwise very little used (in mineralogy, metallurgy and biology), have a vital importance in the study of traces of work on tools and artefacts of ancient man.

Microscopic observation on jewellery of coloured metals, bronze, silver and gold, has yielded quite fruitful results. The opaqueness of metal, its solidity and plasticity, together with the quality of retaining even slight changes on its surface, have favoured the study and micro-photography in reflected light of traces of techniques of hot and cold working on metal objects. However, work in this field began only a few years ago and its results will be published later on, as well as our work on ornament on clay pots and on techniques of working wood.

Recently we have put together our researches on the techniques of working stone in the palaeolithic and neolithic periods from traces of work. Methods of stone-working have always attracted the attention of scholars, just as originally they were used as a basis of the divisions into periods of the Stone Age. Microscopic studies of stone tools, for instance of the pressure areas on cores and prismatic blades with traces of work, adornments with traces of sawing and perforation, and so on, have provided corrections to previously held views about the working of stone at that time.

Have these traces such clear differences from each other that they definitely show the different functions of tools and methods of work?

The method of study of functions by traces of work is based on the kinematics of working with the hand, the special features of which are expressed in the striations due to wear (geometry of traces). In addition the size of the traces of wear indicates the character of the material being worked, its structural and mechanical properties (topography of traces). These two types of evidence, geometric and topographical, when analysed, are related to the form of the working part of the tool, its general shape, dimensions, weight, and the material of which it is made. All these matters taken into account together supply a solution to the question of the purpose of this or that tool.

Research on methods of making tools is based on study of traces surviving on the surface of the object from the action of other tools on it. Traces of manufacture indicate the shape of the working part of the implement, the angle of the movements used and other peculiarities of the process of manufacture. The results of observation on the traces of manufacture on tools have fully borne out the evidence yielded by the study of traces of wear.

The functions of implements can be determined in relation to the basic characteristics of the economic activity of ancient man. As essential work we may list: (1) shaping wood by whittling and chopping with a knife, axe, adze and chisel; (2) digging with a stick, mattock, scoop, etc.; (3) dismembering the carcasses of animals and cutting meat with a knife; (4) treating skin with side- and end-scraper and burnisher; (5) perforation of skin and fur for sewing with stone or bone awls; (6) boring wood, bone, and stone with drills of various kinds; (7) dressing stone with striker-stones and retouchers of stone and bone; (8) working bone with a burin; (9) grinding and polishing stone with various abrasive agents; (10) sawing stone with stone saws; (11) pounding, crushing and trituration of grain, colouring matter and so on by means of pestles, mortars, plaques, querns; (12) reaping with stone sickles, and so forth. Tools with relatively prolonged use of this kind bear its traces of wear. Accidental, auxiliary and supplementary functions had no great significance in the life of man and are only attested if the new traces are sufficiently strong to replace the old ones. Some neolithic axes and adzes that went out of use were employed as hoes or scrapers, or bear marks of blows by a hard object, but the signs of secondary functions are quite obvious.

Thus study of traces of work allows us to speak about ancient tools and their functions not conditionally and approximately, as we do with the typological method, but makes it possible to explain the actual and concrete purpose of each tool, as it was when in use.

Precise definition of function of ancient tools has allowed us to recognize certain branches of manufacture. Thus, for example, when we knew that in the palaeolithic period a bone mattock fixed in a handle was employed as a striking, earth-digging tool, we began to understand the methods of construction of the semi-subterranean houses of that period. The basement of such a house up to 25 cubic metres in volume dug in thick loam, as at Kostenki I, would have been very difficult to excavate using a simple sharpened stick, but became feasible with the help of a bone mattock. The old theory about the use of pit-traps for catching large animals by palaeolithic man now has a much more real basis, since we know that earth-digging in this remote epoch was carried out with far from primitive equipment. If we may be allowed the comparison, the heavy bone mattock with broad blade, the type found at Eliseevich, was as much more effective than the simple

stick in earth-digging as the axe was more efficient than the knife in dealing with wood.

Traces of work that have been identified by analysis will become characteristic signs for the definition of categories of tools and thus greatly simplify the recognition of the latter in sites of different countries and of different dates. Then implements would not be distinguished one from another by form or material but by whether they had one and the same function, like, for example, a stone hoe from neolithic China, an Eskimo mattock made of walrus tusk, and the iron hoe of a Nigerian cultivator. They will have uniform signs of wear which cannot be confused with traces of wear on other tools. Of course, these traces will not be identical, for the types of mattock, the material out of which they are made and even the ground which is being worked are different. Yet allowing for all these differences there will be no fundamental differences of wear on the tools.

Nevertheless not all implements from antiquity can be subjected to analysis with equal success. Stone, bone and metal objects whose surface has not survived in the condition it was left by man cannot be analysed. So stone tools rolled in a stream, weathered bone objects, bronze and iron objects that have suffered from severe corrosion, can be studied by their shape only. Even then some evidence about the purpose of the object can be elicited if its surface has not been entirely destroyed and some small parts survive in their original state.

The identification of function is more difficult when the tool is represented not by a whole series but by a single example. Marks of wear vary in their degree of clarity, and preservation is an irregular matter. In the case of a single implement marks of use may appear feebly or be quite covered over by other marks. The latter may arise when the tool was not used for its proper purpose, as not uncommonly happened in antiquity, just as in life today. In a series of objects the shape of the tools has to be considered, but the important matter here is the great possibilities for analysis that the surfaces have. Not perhaps on all but on one or another of the specimens the investigator will see not only the primary but also secondary traces of use, which will play no small part in the recognition of the implement's function.

The study of the function of some tools presents difficulties in spite of clear traces of wear, a range of material, and complementary signs of definite use by man. Deductions that emerge from an analysis of traces sometimes seem unexpected even for the investigator himself and so need support from ethnographic evidence. For example, such peculiar instruments as the bone rasps from Olbia demand research over a long period of time. Even after a correct identification of function, there will still remain a number of unexplained details.

From what has been said it follows that the study of traces of wear and manufacture is not a means entirely free from error for settling all problems arising from ancient manufacture, of explaining all difficulties and of disposing of existing controversies. This method deepens archaeological perspective by employing a new source of knowledge about the activity of ancient man, permitting us not only to have a more accurate definition of the material to hand, but also to grasp something about those things which have not survived. The method under discussion, of course, does not exclude other methods of research on the archaeological materials.

Combined study of the shape and material of ancient implements as well as of traces of wear on them has brought important accessions to knowledge about the characteristics of the construction of the hand and fingers of prehistoric man,[1] about methods and habits of work, and about the origin of right-handedness, and so on. Theories of comparative chronology and division into periods can sometimes be altered by the study of the technology of ancient manufacturing, since this allows us to differentiate traces of work by metal instruments from those left by stone tools, and so to find evidence for the use of tools not themselves present in the archaeological site.

---

[1] S. A. Semenov, *Reports of the Institute of Ethnography of the Academy of Sciences of the U.S.S.R.*, 11 (1950) pp. 70–82.

Section one | Methods

1. Surface changes on stone and bone tools due to natural causes

PATINATION is the most characteristic change which flint and similar stone undergo through natural agencies. Normally black or grey flint turns cream or porcelain colour through patination. Patina can not only cause deterioration in the surface but also deeply penetrate the rock and even quite alter it. Such completely altered flint objects of palaeolithic age weigh less compared to fresh flint and show white in a break.

Patination is produced by an exogenous chemical process from the action of sunlight, weathering and other factors, as a result of which the stone is dehydrated and its colouring matter broken up, forming cachalong, a mineral of the opal family marked by its crystalline softness. It may be noted that shallow patina hardly changes the micro-relief of the surface of the flint and so does not affect traces of use on the tool.

Besides patina palaeolothic flint tools commonly have a shiny surface; the origin of this and its extent is variable. Flint tools of the lower palaeolithic period (Chellean and Acheulian, named after western European sites but also known by material in the Soviet Union) are found in the majority of cases in secondary contexts. Changes in the original surface have been produced by erosion from rain and river water, and, as is well known water erosion is due as much to the movement of the water as to the sand that it carries. The flint's surface is gradually polished under the simultaneous influence of these two factors. The stone's surface can be polished without the action of water if sand-laden wind is the chief agent; we know that flints of quite recent time (neolithic and Bronze Ages) are found with quite a smoothed appearance on sand dunes.

The degree of brightness of a flint's lustre is obviously not dependent on the duration of the erosion alone, so, just as with patination, this is not a reliable criterion of age.

The formation of gloss on a flint is also related to the quality of the stone. Flint of chalk origin polishes the quickest to a smooth glass-like surface. The light dull shade (micro-granularity) which chalk flint shows in a break (fig. 2.3) quickly vanishes, but limestone flint with a hard, rough break-surface, quartzite, and chert polish more slowly. All the same, the appearance of a gloss on a flint surface can in some measure arise without the participation of water, wind or sand. For example, flint objects from undisturbed upper palaeolithic levels in many cases do not preserve their original micro-relief with the characteristic dull break-surface. Observations on material from the Kostenki-Borshevo region, from Gagarino, Timonovka, Eliseevich, Malta and other sites have shown flint objects that were covered by a light gloss almost all over their surface.

The origin of the gloss on flints in undisturbed cultural levels is unexplained, but in all probability it is not connected with patination. Patinated flints from Kostenki I found in the bottom of an earth-house in many cases had just this gloss like all the rest. It may be assumed that the gloss is due to chemical action on the surface from the surrounding materials. If these natural changes on the flint surface have been severe, it not only makes micro-analysis very difficult but renders observation on traces of work quite impossible. Several upper palaeolithic sites (Pushkari I) give just such material. Severe gloss has in this case covered and even quite destroyed traces of use on the tool.

Besides a general weak gloss on some surfaces, different shiny parts can sometimes be observed which attract attention by their brightness. They look like single or groups of scintillations, sharply defined stars or luminous veins. Their origin still remains unexplained.

Sometimes patches that have been polished by sand, water or wind are visible on tools. Commonly in making his tools ancient man used pebbles gathered on river banks or lumps of flint that had lain exposed for a long time. Remains of such pebble surfaces survive on tools with this origin, the shiny unworked parts standing out not only by the sharpness of their edges but also by their colour and relief.

Natural changes in surfaces of tools made of volcanic rocks (granite, diorite, diabase, andesite, sienite and so on) sometimes show themselves in destruction of the rock itself by weathering. In such instances the outer surface breaks up and crumbles first.

During our searches with the binocular microscope for traces of striation on the surface of tools of flint, chalcedony, quartz and obsidian we often noticed, and were delayed by, lines with a stepped or rib-like relief (fig. 2.4 and 5). The dimensions of such rib-like lines were very varied. On some tools they were sufficiently large to be clearly visible to the eye, but quite commonly they could only be detected by magnification. These lines have nothing in common with traces of work, but are a characteristic peculiarity of fracture of certain rocks. With a little practice they are easily distinguished, but they have a nuisance value for the researcher hiding the real traces of work, or impeding observations of the latter when mixed up with them.

In the study of traces of manufacture and use on bones it is essential to distinguish every kind of alteration on the surface of the bone tools and objects caused by the surroundings in which they occur. Let us list here eight types of change which have to be taken into account:

(1) General destruction of the bone and loss of its original form due to physical and chemical processes in the soil (temperature and dampness, action of natural solvents). Such bone even when collected by the analyst himself is quite useless.

(2) Destruction only of the object's surface, its shape being retained. This also has no value for research.

(3) Partial decay of the bone, which we often come across. This has not lost all value for the investigator, if traces of work fully or partially survive. It is very important to note that a working surface rubbed from use is less liable to decay, as the compressed bone texture will resist the destructive action of natural forces for a longer time.

It is not without interest to point out that an analogous fact has been established for this condition in polished metals. On a surface of finely worked metal as a result of adsorption a thin film of physico-chemical character is formed which protects the metal from decay. V. A. Barun said of this fact: 'The less rough the surface, or, in other words the smoother the worked surface, the less influence the surrounding conditions seem to have, and less corrosion takes place.'[1]

(4) Deformation of a generally intact bone, which happens if the bone has been wet and swollen. Later the damp evaporates, but the dried-out bone is not able to return to its original shape.

(5) Traces of plant roots on the bone surface. The organic acids secreted by plant roots eat into the surface of the bone, leaving grooves in the shape of curved, intricately etched lines often reminiscent of worm holes.

(6) Impressions of canine teeth of carnivorous animals and incisors of rodents on the bone surface. These traces are encountered less frequently, and are distinguished readily by the disposition in pairs of the impressions.

(7) Rolled bones. Bones found in a layer moved by water, which have been thoroughly rolled, can be distinguished by the uniform smoothness both of projections and hollows on them. Bone of this type does not require specialist analysis. In examining partially rolled bones (from a washed-out layer) suspicion can arise that traces of use are present, especially if a sharp projection of the bone has been abraded. But a current of water even with sand rarely produces striation traces, as the mechanical pressure of the sand is slight. If such traces are encountered, they are not always on the working part of the tool and do not give a kinematic picture characteristic of human work.

(8) Surface alterations due to atmospheric action prior to its burial in the cultural layer (weathering). In such cases the surface is cracked or even exfoliated, and also has a lighter hue than bone which has not undergone this.

The alterations due to natural agencies enumerated above do not finally exhaust all eventualities which the student may encounter. Several changes still await explanation. Quite commonly undoubted traces of work are found on objects, but as it were partially veiled over; the contours of the object are softened, the corners missing, and there are outlines of inexplicable traces. Whether this is the result of brief weathering or biochemical reactions it is difficult to say.

Still allowing all cases of damage to the surface of bone remains, traces of human work on them are numerous and varied, and of these we can speak with full confidence as a source of archaeological evidence.

---

[1] V. A. Barun, *The Micro-geometry of a Worked Metal Surface and its Measurement* (Leningrad, 1948), p. 21.

2. Basic traits of manufacture and wear on stone implements

CONTEMPORARY views about the stages of development of material culture in the palaeolithic and neolithic periods are based for the most part on the study of the techniques of manufacture, on the alterations and elaborations of the methods of manufacture of stone tools. Observation shows that the oldest of these tools were made in the simplest way—percussion (*obbivka*), that is by blows with one stone on another. The characteristic trait of such work by strong blows on flint or quartzite nodules are the large scars left on the surface by the detachment of the flakes. If a number of scars should occur in a certain combination on the stone, then this is sufficient for the archaeologist to be able to speak of traces of human activity and not of natural agencies. On flakes the marks of working are the bulb of percussion and retouch, and on upper palaeolithic blades, where the edges give the form of a prism, burin scars and flat, small and steep scars from pressure retouch. On neolithic axes, chisels and knives, besides the traces of manufacture already mentioned, the archaeologist notices a new trait, a ground surface on which even the unaided eye can observe a mass of tiny parallel wear scratches, that is traces of the action of an abrasive agent. Sawing and boring produce so great an alteration of the object worked that not only the method of work is visible but also the nature of the movements, and even the form of the instrument used. The so-called pecking technique on stone, that is striking off tiny chips, can be recognized easily by the rough, bumpy surface of the object.

Together with these visible signs of manufacture there are also microscopic traits on stone tools and objects. These are the tiny holes, 'peepholes' and cracks, which appear on a flinty material from blows and pressure by a hard instrument, that are not visible to the naked eye. Especially important are the scratches and striations that should be seen on the pressure platforms of cores, blades and other parts of stone objects where pressure flaking or retouch has been applied. They not only betray the direction of the instrument's movement but also some of the characteristics of its material. Sparkling, crushing of the edge and projections, starring of the surface, micro-retouch, hardly detectable abrasion and so on: these are all traces of manufacture from which the peculiarities of ancient technology can be identified.

The character of wear on a tool during work depends on various conditions. One of these is the quality of the material of which it is made, its less or greater degree of resistance. The wearability of a tool can depend both on the shape of its working part (angle of sharpness of the blade edge or tip) and on the length of time it is used on the work.

An obsidian knife wears more quickly than a flint one, as on the hardness scale obsidian is more than one point lower than flint. Given a uniform use a flint axe with a working edge of 50° shows a greater degree of wear than another with an edge of 60°, because the blade of the first bites deeper into the wood and so encounters resistance over a larger area of its working part than the second one.

Much depends on the human force applied. There will be quicker wear on an axe relatively if at each blow a force of 15 instead of 10 kilograms is used. Neolithic man took time to work out a rational edge angle of the blade of his adze for the various operations of woodworking: rough dressing of tree-trunks, hollowing out dug-out canoes, fine face-working of objects, or cross-cutting felled timber. Commonly he made a squarish adze with working edge angle of 75°, which required great kinetic effort, so that the tool wore severely and had a poor coefficient of useful work.

Other important factors that influence the degree of wearability of the tool are the speed of work and also the working position of the tool (angle of cutting, angle of striking).

Naturally even sharper differences of wear are due to different properties and characteristics of the material that is itself being worked. More wear on stone and metal tools is produced by working stone, than by working the ground where the wear depends on the nature of the soil. Later on, still within the subject of prehistoric technology, we shall say something on working in bone, wood, skin and meat.

Wear as a physical process is divided into two basic types. The first type is the very rough forms of deformation of a tool during the work. This comprises all kinds of alteration that arise in the course of blows that damage the working part by the dislocation of comparatively large pieces, discoloration, shatter, creation of scars, dents, notches, cracks and so on. The second type comprises the less noticeable manifestations of deformation in the tool which we can call microdeformation. The latter is observable in those very frequent cases when wear arises from friction between the tool and the object of the work.

Evidence of friction can be very distinct, ranging from the wear of a flint knife in cutting up meat to the friction of a bone or wooden hoe through a sandy soil. The intensity of wear, the degree and character of deformation of the tool are far from uniform. It is well known that even the most yielding material, showing not the slightest resistance to a tool made of the hardest material, with the passage of time will erode the tool's surface and even alter its shape.

In practice we can distinguish three degrees of wear on a tool from friction on another object: (1) *polishing* (small specific pressures with dispersion of minute particles and micro-plastic alterations of the surface), (2) *grinding* (higher specific pressures with dispersion of more substantial particles), and (3) *rasping* (large specific pressures with macroscopic destruction of the surface).

In the process of wear another fact has to be kept in view. In real conditions friction on another object never takes place on ideally clean surfaces. Besides atmospheric conditions with varying degrees of moisture and chemical agents, physical agents constantly intrude themselves between the tool and subject of work; dust, fat and sweat excretions from the hand, quartz grains and other hard particles, which in an unnoticed way act as abrasives. Even in the formation of polished surfaces by friction due to very slight specific pressures (for example, the pressure of a stone knife on the flesh in cutting up an animal, or in the palm or fingers of the hand pressing the tool) these particles constitute supplementary (intermediate) agents of destruction, strengthening the process of dispersion of the particles and alteration of the surface.

Strictly speaking, all aspects of wear on a tool can be reduced to a twofold change: the tool is altered in shape and reduced in volume. These alterations take place predominantly on the working part (butt, tooth, edge, blade, point). The non-working part suffers very slight wear except in those parts which were gripped with the hand or the handle, which caused some friction.

The most widespread mark on stone tools, which is noticeable before all others, is rubbing or, as it is usually called, polishing. On knives a gloss as a rule extends along the blade-edge, reaching from the edge of the blade inwards on to one or both faces depending on the nature of the work. The width of the polished part on the knife blade usually depends on the angle made by the blade to the treated object as well as on its physical properties. Naturally in a soft material the cutting instrument penetrates deeper and traces of work are more widely spread over the working part. With burins, borers and pointed knives gloss caused by use is found on the points, precisely because this part met the greatest resistance from the worked object.

Besides the places mentioned, gloss from use is found on a wide range of angles, points, edges and projections which were used in one or another way in the work.

No less an important mark of work is the shape of the polished area. Generally the lustre caused by use dims and weakens gradually towards its periphery and finally vanishes altogether. This fact is evidence of the direct part played by the live human hand, and shows the vibration of this resilient limb during the course of the work.

In studying gloss due to work it is important to note the nature of the retouch facets on the working part of the tool. The concavity of the facet is usually also polished from close contact with the worked object if this was of plastic texture (meat, skin, soft plant fibres).

However hard the stone, traces of rubbing by the hand were usually left on it, if the tool was used without a handle. Friction of flint against the skin, particularly when dusty and covered with sandy particles, gradually polished the stone surface. The gloss on flint produced in this way is different from other forms of polishing produced by friction with an object in work; its edges lack definition. A medium lustre here becomes weak and vague, which sometimes is reminiscent of gloss from use by a tool on a soft material, for example, in the cutting of meat. The shine extends not only over the projecting points, being quite strong on ridges and angles, but also into cavities, where it weakens.

In the majority of cases this type of rubbing is recognizable by careful analysis. Areas of strong gloss due to this are distributed around the flint, covering several facets which commonly indicate the method of grasping the implement. Moreover, this gloss usually occurs on that half of the implement which could only exceptionally have been the working part of the tool, since the sharp edges have been blunted with steep retouch or removed by a burin blow. The extensiveness of this glossed part confirms that it served as the handle.

Striation traces are rarely found on the handle part of the tool and, an important point, they do not have a definite orientation where they occur.

Traces of use in the form of lustre, or polishing, of different intensity, produced as a result of friction against meat, skin, wood, bone, antler and the hand, are characteristic not only of flint but of tools of other minerals of the quartz group (agate, chalcedony, jasper, hornstone and others).

In some instances when the tool has been used on hard materials the traces of wear have the appearance of dull patches that look ground. On flint saws for sawing stone or hard snail shells, on the working ends of borers for boring in the same material, and on burins for working bone, traces of wear in the form of grinding can often be seen. The appearance of such traces on the end of a burin indicate the great physical force concentrated in a small area of the working part of this tool.

Traces of use in the form of grinding are the most characteristic peculiarity of wear on obsidian tools. A glassy shine is the natural lustre of obsidian, but by friction in the process of work its surface becomes dull and even rough to the touch. This characteristic is due to the exceptional brittleness of the mineral. Under the action of rolling by water and weathering obsidian also loses its natural glassy shine, and forms a dark grey porous crust recalling pumice. The alterations on the surface of obsidian therefore are quite the opposite to what we have seen in tools of flint and kindred rocks.

Obsidian tools, which are softer and have glassy shine on fractured surfaces, retain traces of work carried out for even a short time. So obsidian is in a real sense a rewarding material for micro-analysis, if it occurs in an undisturbed level.

Grinding and polishing are not the only traces of wear on stone tools due to surface attrition, for there are also striations. Use on hard and very unyielding material, for example stone, creates such traces which are usually sharp and can sometimes be detected even with the unaided eye. When the tools have been used on bone, wood and skin the presence of striations in the majority of cases can only be established with the help of magnifying devices.

The formation of striations as scratches, lines, grooves and furrows on tools of such a hard stone as flint, when used on softer materials, takes place because of the accidental introduction into the pores of the worked material and on the tools themselves of small sand grains, the presence of which, particularly in the conditions of primitive techniques of production, can be readily understood.

The clarity and intelligibility of striations depend greatly on the character of the surface of the tool, its material composition and its degree of wearability. The striation lines are best seen and the direction of movement of the tool most clear on smooth level surfaces of chalk flint, even when the use has been of short duration, but hornstone, jasper, agate, chalcedony, quartz and other rocks with a smooth, glassy fracture, also retain striation traces on their surface very well. On a limestone flint with its rough and uneven fracture-surface, granular volcanic rocks, quartzites, sandstones and cherts the striations emerge much less clearly.

On retouched flint tools where the surface is broken by wavy rises striations can scarcely be detected, except for glimpses on small areas that project up between the edges of the retouch scars. Heavily worn blade-edges, blunted and polished to a shine, as, for example, on sickles, often have clear striations even on a retouched edge. In general the amount of wear on the working part of the tool influences the strength with which the striations are manifested. Granular rocks like granite, diabases and diorite become smoothed by prolonged wear, and the smoothed parts show the striations well. As already noted, on an obsidian surface so long as it retains its glassiness the striations show well.

Further use leads by attrition to a mat surface where the striations lose their earlier clear definition.

3. Traces of work on bone tools and artefacts

IN the economic activity of man in pre-metal times, together with stone, a remarkably important part was played by bone as a material for tools, weapons, ornaments and in the manufacture of objects of representational art. As opposed to stone the amount of study on bone has been very much less, and in particular in the palaeolithic field has been altogether weaker. The explanation of this is to be sought in the special character of bone. The methods of manufacture of stone tools—percussion, flaking, retouch and later grinding—required profound alterations of the natural form of material between obtaining the raw material and completing the work. Stone in an unworked or slightly worked form played a very minor part in the economy and was altogether a subsidiary matter.

Bone as a special material created by natural life and easily used by man for technical and domestic purposes required no elaborate treatment and was employed after partial dressing, or only slight alteration, or without any treatment at all. Pointed parts of antler, mammoth tusk or canine teeth are the natural tools of animals; the rod-like structure of ribs and long bones with their natural handles (the epiphyses in the latter case); the narrow section and strength of bones of small animals and birds; the cup-shape of skulls and pelvic bones of large mammals—all these considerably reduced human labour in shaping tools and objects for everyday use. So man was confronted with a wide choice of ready-made shapes from all the wide anatomical range of skeletal material from different species and individuals of different ages in the animal kingdom that surrounded him.

There are now grounds for believing that bone had a more varied application in manufacturing by ancient man than was formerly thought, not only throughout the Stone Age, but later, before the predominance of metal had been achieved.

The Stone Age might perhaps be called the Stone-Bone Age, for during this large period of time stone and bone were complementary to one another. Stone possessed hardness, bone plasticity but also firmness. These two separate essential qualities, hardness and plasticity, were brought together only in metals.

Bone tools in the mass do not lend themselves easily to differentiation and classification, and, often un-recognized, pass outside the researcher's field of vision or are put into the category of faunal remains.

Observation on traces of use reveals that Stone Age man employed all the bones of the skeleton of large animals and a good many from small ones. The bones can be divided into the following groups: (1) antler, ivory, tusk or canine teeth, teeth, and mandibles of carnivores with their canines; (2) long bones; (3) ribs; (4) wide flat bones (pelvis, shoulder, skull); (5) short bones (falanges and other bones of the paws and feet of large mammals).

Traces on bones and bone tools or objects revealing use by man can be subdivided into five basic categories, as follows:

(1) Traces of use on unworked or roughly shaped bones which yield evidence about the purpose of these bones in daily life.

(2) Traces of wear on worked bone tools showing the function of the latter.

(3) Traces on bones and bone objects revealing methods and devices of manufacture with stone tools, and also the level of technology in this.

(4) Cuts on bones made in cutting up the carcasses of animals and separating the sinews, traces of blows given in splitting bones to get the marrow, and so on.

(5) Traces of use of metal tools.

It should be remembered that if the traces are sufficiently well studied and deciphered they allow us not only to identify a tool's function, but also throw fresh light on an aspect of the life of the people who used it. So in the light of precisely defined function we can very often see the part played in the tool's manufacture by objects associated with it.

In the study of traces on bone tools we must bear in mind the qualities and properties of bone structure. The smooth surface of the external compact layer of bone has its own special micro-relief or micro-structure. Fairly light scratches should stand out sharply against the background of this relief under a magnifying glass. On antlers of animals like deer and elk we have to deal with a much more rugged surface.

The external compact layer of bone possesses a laminated structure and is composed of very fine lamellae, which are seen best in old dried-out bone. This second very important structural characteristic of bone allows us to identify wear from the kind of attrition that took place. The inner spongy matter showing through the compact layer is also an obvious mark of wear, provided all possible interference from natural causes have been taken into account.

Besides this we have at our disposal one proof of wear by attrition in the course of work. This is the alteration of the anatomical form of a bone, for each specie of animal has its own definite bone shapes.

Finally, striation traces showing direction of movements constitute by far the most important marks. Only in rare cases when the surface is damaged or obliterated during the work are there no striations. On bone the friction of even such a material as skin usually produces striations in the shape of slight scratches or even clearly visible channels that indicate the direction of movement.

On bone tools made by flaking or whittling traces of wear can be detected, firstly by marks of alterations on the worked surface, which has its own features and relief, and, secondly, by the degree of deformation of the artificially produced form, and thirdly by striation traces.

On traces of wear from friction we need not linger, because this is the most widespread type and shows an endless gradation in degrees of use on tools. These traces are the principal means of identifying different striking tools, such as bone mattocks, picks and wedges.

4. Kinematics of working with the hand and the formation of striations on tools

In the process of work man influences external nature not directly with his own limbs but through the intermediary of tools. Tools differ radically from human limbs. In a technical sense the more an advance the more really different are the physical properties of the material from which they are made from the organic material of living matter. Thus not wood and bone, products of organic origin, but stone and metal seem to be the most important materials for the manufacture of the leading and basic tools of work. With tools of these materials man could not only more successfully influence external nature, but also make other tools. With wooden tools it would have been impossible to work not only metal, stone and bone but even wood itself. As regards stone tools, with their help wood, bone and stone could be worked and even a start made with hammering metals; use of abrasion (grinding, sharpening) was already known. By the use of metals the working of all materials found in nature was put within reach.

Working tools are distinguished from human limbs not only by material but also by their purpose. Human hands are universally the same and their evolutionary origin is multi-functional. Tools were relatively all-purpose only in the early stages, for the origin of their development is specialization and the tendency towards a single function. This specialization achieved greater variety with each period of the history of manufacture. In this connexion there is yet one more very important qualitative difference between working tools and human limbs. The latter differ from tools by their structure; in them only to a very small degree are there the inherent signs characteristic of regular geometrical shapes and bodies. Tools by the nature of their work penetrate into other bodies, the objects of the work, and sever them, change their original shapes, and have a definite tendency to adopt all the more regular geometric shapes, especially in their working part.

All action of a tool on an object has as its purpose the alteration, the transformation of the latter into a form desired by man. Mechanical action, which is our main concern, leads to a transformation of the natural form of the object, to an alteration of its external aspect; the division of the whole object into equal or unequal parts, the separation of one or many small parts from the whole, that is fragmentation.

Through the action of the tool on the object of work one kind or another of friction is created. By friction due to the slipping or displacement of the working part of the tool against the object of work striation traces are formed on the tool. These are traces of the first order. They arise in the process of cutting, whittling, sawing, chopping, boring, drilling, piercing, grooving, grinding. Only a few kinds of action, such as blows or pressure, when the tool does not penetrate into the thickness of the object (shattering and flaking of stone, hammering of metal objects, stamping), which do not have the character of dragging or sliding, give traces of the second order (chip-marks, holes, roughening, dents).

The disposition of traces of the first order, to which as the most important marks we give our main attention, is a regular one. It is true that the human hand cannot in

general be compared to the arm of contemporary metal-cutting machine-tools with their rigid grip. The hand produces several weak movements relative to the working position of the tool and shows to some extent a flexible grip even when a hafted tool with its greater reliability is used. Movements of the tool in the hand are due not only to the weak grip but also to certain tactile sensations which affect our working limbs and which give them such delicate movements. All the same, traces of work as a whole regularly reflect the kinematic action of the hand, and striations represent parts of the path of the tool in its movement.

Observation shows that the basic working processes carried out by man have their own kinematic character. For example, in order to make a hole four different methods are possible: punching, gouging, piercing, or boring. The choice of one of these to make the hole depends on a series of circumstances, but first of all on the material to be perforated on the one hand and the material of the tool on the other. Each method of work has its own kinematic peculiarities reflected in the length of the line of movement and its shape (straight or curved). Essential kinematic differences come into the work of a knife in whittling wood, or skinning an animal, or cutting up meat, or gutting fish and its cleaning and filleting; different pictures of the hand-movements, positions of point or blade on the worked object, arise in each case.

The position of the tool in relation to the object of work, the angle of inclination of its working part, is very important in the formation of traces. It is essential to be able to distinguish such matters when the kinematic differences between the methods of work are slight. Into this category of movement falls work with the axe, adze and hoe. Thanks to some individuality of position in the working part of the tool relative to the subject of work striation traces from wear in the different processes do emerge with distinct differences. The differences consist above all in the special position of the lines of striation on the working surface of the tool. Each tool has its own disposition of striation lines on its working part. The lines may run parallel or at right-angles to the axis of the instrument, or to its blade, or diagonally to either axis or blade. They can go in one or several directions; that is they can run parallel or intersect, be straight or curved, continuous or interrupted. Moreover they have varied frequencies and length, as well as other characteristics.

Traces of work on contemporary metal tools (knives, axes, chisels, wedges, saws, needles, awls, razors, cutters, scissors and so on) give a clearer kinematic picture thanks to the plasticity, density and opaqueness of metal, and also to the geometrically regular form and smoothness of the working surface.

On ancient stone and bone tools in which shapes are less definite, hardness variable and surfaces rough, striation traces may be feebly retained and destroyed by the work. This is especially so with retouched surfaces of flint tools. In a number of cases the kinematic picture always remains vague because the lines are weakly retained and those visible give only the shape of the trajectory (part of the tool's movement) without information about the direction of the working movement. For example, striation traces of sawing may not show whether this was done in both directions. In such cases the character of the wear on the surface is a supplementary indication. The surface of a stone tool usually bears hollows (flake facets and holes) and projections (retouch arrises, various impurities and crystal grains) visible under a magnifying glass.

The tool's surface wear is indicated by micro-plastic changes on the edges of the hollows and sides of the projections from which we may assess the direction of movement, for it is precisely the projecting parts which are the points on the surface that suffer wear primarily due to friction on the worked material.

THE POINT OR AWL. Let us turn to the simplest kind of work, piercing with a pointed tool. Independent of the type of material worked on and the sharpness of the tool, its working part is worn by friction against the material into which it is thrust. *If the piercing is done by straight pressure of the tool (axial approach) the traces of wear arising from the movement will be straight lines parallel to the axis of the tool.* Deviations from this direction will show themselves in the disposition of lines on the point.

In practice piercing is not done by straight pressure but is accompanied by turns of the hand to right and left in a quarter or half circle. In this case the point's wear is influenced by two movements, a straight and a rotary one; traces on the point will reflect these two forms of movement. Lines parallel to the axis of the tool will be cut by lines going around it; that is at right-angles to its axis, if we think of it in section.

Experiments in piercing have shown a far from uniform clarity of striation traces on metal, bone and flint awls. While the point of the metal displayed all the peculiarities of the movement, on bone they were much less distinct and on flint scarcely or entirely imperceptible. When the kinematic picture is not clear, as on flint awls, it is possible to study the traces by changes in the irregularities of the micro-relief. The projections show polishing on the side of the point, the edge of the depressions on the side of the butt end.

THE DRILL. Piercing with a quarter or semi-circular rotation is the beginning of drilling. Hence it is natural to conclude *that drilling must leave on the working part of the drill only one form of traces—circular lines at right-angles to its axis as a result of the use of one movement only, rotation.* 'Rotary movement' may be regarded as a general kinematic definition of drilling.

Drilling can be done by hand or with a machine and includes interrupted rotation in one direction (one-handed drilling removing the hand each time), continuous drilling with alternating direction (one handed without removing the hand, two-handed rotation of the drill between the palms, drilling with bow and disk drill), continuous drilling in one direction (brace and bit, drill with toothed gear-wheels, mechanical drill). Each of these has its peculiarities that are reflected in the traces of wear. Hand drilling is usually done with a conical stone drill, machine drilling with a cylindrical one. In single-handed drilling a strong centralized force cannot be achieved, because the human hand is only capable of a semi-circular or at most three-quarter circular movement in a rotational direction. In order to make a full turn the hand has to be taken off the drill, change its position and make another half or three-quarter turn (interrupted rotation). This explains why one-handed drilling is nearly always done by alternating the direction of rotation (left to right and back again), as this is the only way of increasing the speed of movement. But in neither method, alternating or continuous, can one-handed drilling maintain a strong centralized rotation. The axis of the tool leans one way or another from the jerks of the hand. This is particularly evident with the alternating method. As a result a hole produced in this way is irregular in outline and has a greater diameter than the width of the drill. The wear striations do not lie parallel to one another, neither on the drill, nor on the sides of the drilled hole.

Two-handed drilling, done with continuous alternating rotation between the palms, gives greater speed to the movement. The hole produced by this has much more regular outlines. However, the axis of the drill with its long pivot also leans to one side during rotation. So the striation marks are not parallel on either the drill or the sides of the hole.

Traces of drilling with bow drill reveal a better standard of work; a hole produced in this way is regularly circular. Traces of drilling appear on the side of the hole as almost parallel circles corresponding to the traces of wear on the drill.

The regularity of formation of traces that has been mentioned is dependent not only on the means of drilling but also on the properties of the worked material. The softer the material the greater deviation in the shape of the hole and the less parallel the striations lie, and conversely the harder the material the less the deviation.

Flint drills, however hard, are brittle tools, and easily break from sharp turns and by leaning from the axis of rotation. So the slant that arises in hand drilling is only possible in the first phases of drilling, before the instrument deeply penetrates the material. Once it has penetrated, sharp turns on a leaning drill will easily break it. In a soft, yielding material like wood some variation in level rotation is quite possible, but in a harder material like bone deviation is more limited. With stone it is almost excluded or only slightly possible, so striation traces on stone drills, used for working on stone, have more regular geometric outlines. The rule just described tells us why bone and stone objects were drilled from both sides.

Striation traces from wear emerge fairly clearly on stone drills used for drilling stone, but with snail shells and bone the picture is less clear, and with wood they can only be detected with great difficulty. On the drill's working end only a vague gloss can be seen, study of which can reveal the direction of movement. If the drill was rotated from left to right, then projections will be more intensively worn (polished) on the right side, and the edge of the depressions on the left. If it was alternating rotation, then the sides of the projections and edges of the depressions will be worn uniformly left and right.

THE SAW. Dividing a whole object into parts along a straight line by alternate two-way movement (backwards and forwards) is commonly called sawing. The working part of the tool used for such work, the saw, is a flat blade. In the Stone Age from the palaeolithic period onwards flakes of flint, chalcedony, quartzite or obsidian with a toothed (retouched) edge served this purpose, and generally were used for severing bones into pieces by transverse cutting. In neolithic times they began to use laminated slate or sandstone saws for dividing stone.

Striation traces of sawing on sawing tools fully reflect the hand movements. *Traces of sawing in the form of straight scratches are always disposed on the side surfaces of the tool parallel to its working edge*. On the toothed part of the blade they are interrupted, but higher up more or less continuous, depending on the straightness of the saw and on the properties of the materials of which it is made. So long as the saw is at right-angles to the surface being worked *the striations from wear will be left uniformly on both its faces*.

Traces of wear on the toothed edge due to a two-way alternating movement, provided there is uniform pressure both backward and forward, differ essentially from traces produced by one-way sawing. In the former the teeth or projecting edges of the facets, if the blade is only retouched, will suffer attrition from both sides, in the latter from one side only. This difference will show itself in the micro-topography of the side surfaces within the toothed area. It shows itself in a different way by the slight wear of the holes (hollows) and attrition of protuberances on the side surfaces in a stone saw. *In two-way sawing the edges of the hollows are slightly worn and the projections worn down from both sides, in one-way sawing from one side (for example, the front side of the projection and the back edge of the hollow if the one-way sawing is done in a forward direction)*.

Traces of work on both faces of a saw show up as a more or less even band running along the whole length or the best part of it. On a flint saw used on bone this band has a polished or vaguely dull surface, on obsidian also dull, in flint saws for cutting stone also a dull shade. The peculiarities of traces on a saw face are dependent on form and material both of the saw and the sawn material.

THE REAPING KNIFE (sickle). Amongst the tools on which traces of use also occur as striations parallel to the blade-edge and on both faces we may place the earliest sickles, surviving in the form of flint reaping knives, which occur as slightly trimmed prismatic bladelets. They may be distinguished from saws by the fact that the worn part often has a different shape. The wear traces do not form an even pattern on the side, but instead are shaped like a triangle, one side of which is made by the cutting edge, while the hafted end, being embedded in the handle, remained unaffected.

The wear pattern on the surface of a reaping knife depends on its position in the handle. If the knife was set in a slantwise slot its end would suffer more intensive wear, as in this case the position of the knife is analogous to that of a tooth in the saw as it cuts deeply into the bundle of stalks pressed against it by the left hand. On the other hand, if the knife lies parallel to the handle set in a longitudinal groove, then the wear is distributed rather more evenly along the whole length of its blade. Just the same happens with composite sickles made up of a series of inserted flints. The micro-plastic features of the traces of work on a flint reaping knife or inserted flint of a sickle are of just that general disposition which so clearly illustrates the hand movement, one-way return movement ('towards himself'), as opposed to the sawing movements which are two-way alternating, or repeated forward movement ('from himself'). *On the blade of a reaping knife and sickle all the projecting points are worn on one side, that facing the operator. The wear at the edges of the hollows of these tools is also sharper on one side, not that facing the operator but on the contrary that away from him.*

THE BURIN. Incising comprises a very wide range of operations, but here the word burin is understood in the narrow sense applied to a tool whose incising part (edge or angle) has a very small area and whose axis is vertical or almost vertical to surface being incised. The angle of the axis varies between 80° and 90°. The working part of a burin consists of a single saw tooth, the cutting edge of which cuts a groove in the material by repeated one-way ('on himself') movements gradually deepening the groove. It is the cutting edge of the tool which mainly suffers wear, but due to its small area and the brittleness of the stone striation traces can hardly be detected there. *So the evidence of the line of movement of a burin is not striations on the cutting point but on the side edges. They*

19

are visible as lines parallel to the cutting plane, but at right-angles to the burin's axis.

THE SKIN-DRESSING KNIFE. The cutting-up of skin in the palaeolithic period was in all probability done with a flint knife whose working part was similar to that of the knife found fixed in a handle at Malta (Siberia). From the hafting of the blade we can judge the angle of inclination to the working surface at which it was held. Originally a returning movement ('on himself') was evidently normal with the palaeolithic dressing knife, but with the creation of a handle and the application of greater force the movement altered into a forward one ('from himself'). In this way (forward movement) the work was done with the neolithic elbow-shaped knife, known to us from northern sites, and so also in the contemporary use of the cobbler's knife. The expediency of this method can be explained, not only by the possibility of applying great force, but also by the circumstance that in the forward movement one can see the proposed line of cut and more closely guide the blade of the knife along it. Thus the movement in skin-cutting is still a movement in one direction.

Traces of wear on the working part of a skin-dressing knife, as with a burin, are found on both side surfaces, not at an angle of 80°–90° but of 45°–90°, for the angle of inclination of the axis of the knife to the cutting surface depends on the shape of the cutting part.[1]

THE WHITTLING KNIFE. Work with this knife gives rise to wear on one side of the blade only. This is produced at a working angle of 25°–35° to the worked face, and as a result the side of the knife facing the object suffers attrition, but the opposite face only suffers wear from parings. The greater the angle of the cutting edge the smaller the paring is, and conversely a reduction of this angle gives a larger paring. In stone whittling knives the blade-edge angle averages 35°–40°, but in metal ones 12°–13°. From this it follows that the back face of a metal knife suffers more intensive wear than the back face of a stone whittling knife, because the thicker paring in the former case causes more wear on its back face. A thin paring curls up into a circle or spiral hardly touching the knife's back face.

Whittling of wood or bone with a knife can be done in two ways. In the first the working movement is backwards ('towards himself') and in the second forwards ('away from himself'). One can whittle with both methods with a metal single-bladed knife with low edge angle and without edge facets, that is both 'towards himself' and 'away from himself'. With a neolithic one-sided whittling knife which always has a facet on one edge one can only whittle in one kind of way, arising from the fact that the edge with facet cannot as a rule be placed downwards on the material, but has to lie face upward. So for whittling in both ways the neolithic craftsman had to have two single-edged knives with blades on opposite sides; looking from the butt end the facet edge was on the right on one, on the left on the other.

In palaeolithic two-edged knives, made on quadrangular prismatic blades, it would have been possible to use each of the edges for whittling by both means. Yet palaeolithic man rarely used both edges for whittling; most commonly he blunted the second edge with retouch or took it off with a burin blow, for resting his finger on, and worked with one edge.

Traces of wear on whittling knives, as already explained, occur on one side of the blade. The striations (very fine scratches and lines) are sometimes at right-angles to the working edge, but more usually somewhat inclined towards the working end of the knife, caused by the pressure of the human hand, which pushes the blade in a parallel direction to the whittling surface. In a number of cases there are even distinct lines parallel to the blade-edge, due to the fact that a whittling knife with a blunt edge is used in a saw-like movement on wood or bone in order to make it easier to penetrate the material. The flat unfaceted side was used for whittling with a neolithic knife, but with a palaeolithic knife the ventral side of the blade was normally the working side, as the facet closely limited the working edge on top. If the working edge of a whittling knife has undergone slight retouch, the latter is on the dorsal side and not on the under side, as retouch makes the working edge too rough, increasing its resistance to the material worked. During use the blade of the whittling knife may be chipped, shown by tiny scars on the under face, but these are unevenly distributed and so cannot be regarded as intentional retouch.

A MEAT KNIFE is distinguished by more complicated kinematic characteristics. It was used by the hunter for cutting up the carcasses of game, cutting the skin free, and cutting meat while eating. The movement of this knife and functions are much more varied than with other knives. The resistant materials of the animal's body, consisting of elastic fibres of skin, muscles, ligaments and cartilage, which bend and stretch under the pressure of the knife, naturally could not be severed at one particular angle, so there was not one but several cutting planes. At the moment of cutting open the animal's belly the knife movement could have been down and forward (ripping), when the axis of the tool would be inclined, or instead pressing upwards with a saw motion, just as a modern kitchen knife is used on meat. In cutting free and removing skin from the carcass and in dismemberment and removal of the intestines the knife was

---

[1] The palaeolithic knife from Malta has its blade inclined at 45° to 60°, while neolithic elbow-shaped knives have the blade inclined to the axis at an angle which varies from 45° to 90°.

almost completely buried in the body of the animal and in contact with tissue at all points on its surface. Consequently the working end of the hunter's knife is burnished and polished on all sides, the more so if it is pointed at the end (a point).

Research has revealed that in cutting meat palaeolithic man did not use just the knives, which we can call 'hunting' knives, that is blunt-ended or pointed knives, made from fairly long prismatic blades. In everyday practice he very often also used knives made of short blades, or even flakes, held between the thumb and first two fingers. The index finger pressed from above on the back, which was worked by retouch or a burin blow.

Traces of wear on meat knives present themselves as polishing on both faces, but also within the flake scars and hollows. Striations from wear on a meat knife only arose if some extraneous abrasive particles fell on the meat (quartz, felspar, lime, etc.). *On knives that had long use as meat knives striations have covered the polished areas and very often run almost parallel to the blade-edge on both sides, or commonly they intersect, especially noticeable on the ends of long hunting knives.*

THE AXE in use has a very marked linear form of movement which is therefore very well defined by striations. Seen sideways the axe's trajectory is curved, but from the front it is straight. At the moment of striking an object its axis is not vertical but inclined to 50°–60°. Consequently its blade (parallel to the handle in an axe) is inclined at a similar angle to the striking surface. *Striation traces on an axe therefore run diagonally and occur uniformly on both faces.*

THE ADZE is a cutting tool very similar to the axe in kinematic characteristics. Seen sideways the trajectory of an adze hardly differs from that of an axe, and in front view it is also straight. Even in its shape the neolithic adze strongly recalls an axe, differing only in its profile, where the working edge is asymmetrical, although this is not an absolute rule, for adzes with symmetrical profiles are also encountered. However, in its method of seating in the handle the adze is sharply distinguished from the axe, for the blade is at right-angles to the handle, which causes a different geometry of traces on the blade. *While on an axe the striations lie diagonally, that is at an angle to its axis, on an adze they lie vertically, that is parallel to the tool's axis. In addition, while on an axe traces of wear are disposed uniformly on both faces (cheeks) of the working part, on an adze they belong fundamentally to the forward face, although appreciably shorter striations and feebler wear occur on its back face.*

THE HOE has constructional and kinematic traits that are broadly similar to those of an axe and adze. Structurally the hoe is more analogous to the adze, also hafted with the blade at right-angles to the axis of the handle. The axis of a hoe or its digging-blade lies at 70° to 75° to the axis of the handle, but kinematically a hoe is closer to an axe. The line of movement of a hoe is curved, seen sideways, but from the front indistinguishable from that of an axe or adze. A hoe like an axe can fall vertically or inclined at a fair angle, when it is necessary to dig ground by side-blows with the hoe's axis inclined first left and then right. *Consequently on the digging blade of the hoe its front face, which encounters the main resistance from the dug ground, bears striations that lie at an angle and not parallel to its axis and that intersect with each other. If the front face of the hoe is convex, then the striations form a fan shape, and the intersecting lines are weaker. On the back surface of a hoe traces of wear are feebler, as the resistance of the ground is less.*

The peculiarities of the disposition of the traces of wear on hoes have a range of variations depending on the shape of the digging blade, force of the blow and consistency of the ground. Yet in spite of the discrepancies in the characteristic traces the most permanent and important functional criteria for a hoe are wear on both faces and intersection of the lines on both front and rear faces of the digging blade.

A SHOVEL differs radically from a hoe both structurally and kinematically. Shovelling earth does not require a blow and presupposes work on soft or loose soil by means of pushing or pressing. The working (cutting) part of the shovel consists of a blade, whose sharpness depends on the material of which it is made.

Metal shovels, of course, have a thinner edge than wooden or ancient antler shovels, like those from the Gorbunovo peat bog. Ancient wooden and antler shovels obviously were intended for use on very soft and loose soil or snow. In working any kind of hard or heavy soil this was first broken up with picks, hoes or pointed sticks, and shovels were only used to throw it up.

Although shovel blades suffered wear on front and back it was the back part that encountered the stronger resistance. Striations occur parallel to the axis of blade and handle, as the line of movement of a shovel at the moment it sank into the soil remained straight.

We have lain before the reader some basic and very elementary examples of the dependence of striation patterns of wear on the kinematics of working with the hand. This dependence holds good for tools of stone, bone, wood and metal of all periods, which bears witness to the fact that, while basic hand tools and their methods of use change with changing quality, strength and methods of manufacture, they alter in response to definable laws of movement.

5. Optical devices and sources of light for studying the surface of archaeological materials

RESEARCH on the surface of objects for traces of one or another human activity constitutes a special aspect of the micro-analysis employed in the study of functions of ancient tools and artefacts.

Initially this came down to the choice of optical instruments. Binocular optics with three-dimensional, stereographic vision seemed most suitable for this purpose. Without doubt binocular lenses reduce the possibilities of micro-analysis, for the powers of these instruments are limited; for example, a binocular magnifying glass gives a magnification of $38\times$, binocular microscope $180\times$. However, although the magnification of binocular lenses is not great, the limits seemed sufficient in the early stages and micro-analysis with them gave positive results.

With regard to simple magnifiers of one or several lenses enlarging from $2\times$ to $20\times$ in laboratory conditions only a glass with magnification of $6–10\times$ proved useful. More powerful (short-focus) lenses produce discomfort in the work, as they reduce the field of vision and give rise to eye-strain. Experience in research convinces one that the normal pocket lens is mainly useful for looking over and selecting material in the museum case, where it would be impracticable to take mechanical optical devices, or for the archaeologist under field conditions.

In a workroom for studying the tools in hand binocular lenses are essential, as well as a binocular microscope, specially set up to study surfaces in reflected light. As they give stereoscopic vision, they allow at comparatively small magnifications examination of objects both in the flat and in depth, a clear view of surface changes, detection of chip-marks, lines, scars and cracks, and comparison of worn and unworn parts of the surface. Moreover, through binocular lenses the object is not seen reversed as in the normal monocular microscope. Work with binocular lenses does not tire the vision, as the strain is shared by both eyes.

The construction of clamp-stands is very important in the use of binoculars in the laboratory when archaeological material is studied. When using either a lens or a microscope a clamp-stand with straight vertical column and heavy base is necessary, its horizontal bar movable up or down, backward and forward, and also around the column in a circle or transversely.

The fixing of optical instruments in the necessary position is done by means of screw-clamps on the sleeves with which the column and arm of the clamp-stand are firmly held. A stand of such construction allows

observation of the surface of large objects with the use of a small movable rest for the object, or with this held in the hands, as it is commonly necessary to do.

The binocular magnifier, owing to its large field of vision and good lighting, plays an important part in the preparatory study of the whole surface of the tool in the search for traces of use. In using binocular lenses, particularly those of small magnification, the object under examination can be held in the hand gradually moving and turning it about under the lens and a directed ray of light. This saves a lot of time that would be lost in setting up a circular rest and fixing the object to it. One should resort to the binocular microscope only when the tool's surface has been carefully studied with the magnifying glass and detailed analysis is necessary of the traces of work that have been detected, their configuration and direction.*

A rest with ball-joint is a crucial piece of equipment in microscopic research; without it the use of the microscope is impossible. At high magnifications even a slight jerk of the hands produces a sharp vibration of the image. A hinged stand can be made by the investigator himself by using the ball-head of a camera tripod. A ball-joint allows the object to be inclined in all directions up to an angle of $90°$ and also turned through a vertical axis. The main drawback with the ball-joint top of a camera tripod is the rough construction of its screw clamp, which produces sharp jerks during regulation and does not respond to the delicate adjustment that microscopic precision requires.*

In certain cases the observations require the use of a monocular microscope, the majority of which are mounted on stands designed for examining slides in a direct light. . . .* With the monocular microscope the investigator is interested above all in exploiting the possibilities which detailed examination offers of very small areas at magnifications of $300\times$ to $500\times$ or more. For this purpose the best instrument is a monocular microscope which has had binocular eyepieces fitted. In such a microscope observation is made through one set of lenses, but both eyes look into a dual eyepiece. . . .*

In practice the most important part of micro-analysis is lighting. Modern microscopy has a variety of illuminators or lamps for examining opaque objects through monocular microscopes at high magnifications. . . .* When the delicate structure of the micro-relief of a surface has to be studied a one-way illuminator is indispensable.

In studying the surface of a stone tool with binoculars

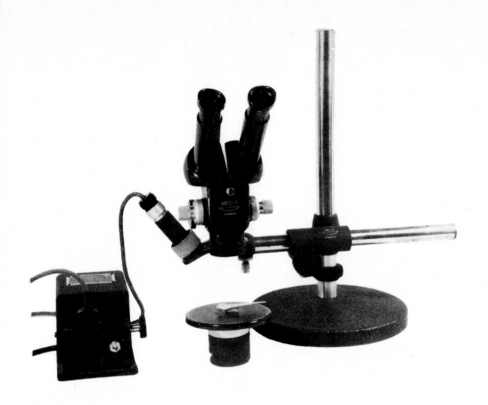

1 **Above.** *Binocular microscope MBS-1 attached to clamp-stand and lamp, with transformer and object on ball-jointed rest.* **Below.** *Metallographic microscope MIM-6 with camera, lamp and transformer.*

at relatively low magnifications one can in many cases do without special lighting. A medical lamp with metal hood and flexible spiral joint allows the lamp to be adjusted to any position and regulation of the amount of side-light to meet requirements.

Special illuminators are required for tools with weak traces of use when using the binocular microscope. It is necessary to resort to the latter very often, as traces of work on palaeolithic tools are in general elusive and difficult to recognize.*

Independent of the source of light, that is of kinds of illuminators and lamps used, the special devices for directing light are of great importance in studying microscopic objects as well as in micro-photography. As explained above, in practice only diagonally reflected light can be used in studying tools and other archaeological material. . . .*

23

6. Preparation of the surface of objects under examination

AN ancient artefact even after being cleaned, washed, labelled and placed in store still retains on its surface particles from the surroundings in which it lay for thousands of years. Examined under binoculars, one can always find loess, clay, black soil, charcoal, ochre and much else from the cultural layer.

In a good many cases these particles are of great significance in identifying the purpose of the tool. Perhaps therefore it would be advisable in general not to wash and clean finds on the excavation site, but to do this in the laboratory after their preliminary examination. However, in studying traces of work the tool must be free from extraneous matter, including lime concretion. The latter very often covers parts of tools and objects of stone and bone with a hard crust.

A hindrance to micro-analysis is the later handling of tools by the archaeologist which commonly gives them a deceptive sheen resembling traces of use. Sweat and fatty excretions of the hand mixed with dust leave a thin shiny film on the surface which covers parts of the tool important for research. So the surface must be cleaned with spirit or benzine and washed in hot water with a light application of soap. Only then can optical observations be carried out. If the traces are clear and can be clearly recognized, so that the functional interpretation raises no doubt, study of the surface can be confined to examination without special preparation, but such instances are not characteristic. For the most part the linear texture of traces does not clearly emerge even in the binocular microscope, because of the transparency, translucency or glassiness of the flint; the light which passes through it takes the contrast out of the image. On a metallic surface, for example, the micro-relief stands out more sharply under the binoculars than on flint, where it disappears, dissolving as it were.

A natural factor partially neutralizing the glassiness of flint and facilitating study of the traces of work is patination, which increases the definition. However, one cannot rely on patination alone to bring out the traces of work, especially if it is combined with a roughness of surface.

Flint is a rock of fine-grained structure, which causes the dull colour of its surface in a fresh fracture. If the flint tool has parts polished to a mirror-like shine, then with the light at a certain angle it will be possible to detect very fine striations, and ideally a smooth surface will give uninterrupted linear marks. If the tool only had short use and did not acquire a mirror-like shine but only some degree of polishing or burnishing in working on a soft object, the striations will be very difficult to detect. The traces will show as short cuts and stand out

as hollows that lose themselves against a background of small scintillations. To make them intelligible it is necessary to neutralize the flint's translucency.

In the study of traces on flint tools with an uneven surface it is impossible to find one angle of light which brings out the full picture; examination requires constant adjustment of the binoculars and ball-jointed rest. The general picture is therefore the sum of many images given by the instrument at different angles. This kind of analysis resembles study of the structure of crystals as done by petrographers with Federov's polarized microscope and rest.

Examination of the striations on the mirror-like parts is practical without the use of light filters. By inclining the horizontal surface of the rest in different ways and changing the position of the sources of light there will be a moment when the striations on the shiny surface will be visible if not wholly, then at least partially.

Spectrographic analysis in studying traces on a shiny area should be used only if the more rational methods of observation are impossible. Among the latter we may include devices for preparing the surface of the objects under study.

The translucency of flint can be neutralized by dusting with magnesium powder, when the flint surface is covered by a fine layer of white dust—magnesium oxide. However, quite apart from the disagreeable procedure of dusting in the flame of burning magnesium, such a method does not always give satisfactory results. The micro-relief of the surface is covered by a layer of magnesium oxide, and the finer texture of the traces loses its sharpness or may vanish beneath it.

A simpler method than magnesium dusting for reducing translucency is to treat the parts being studied with a colorizer. For this purpose black finely ground Indian ink is to some extent suitable. After careful washing the working part of the tool is covered by a solution of Indian ink. The film of ink must cover the flint surface evenly and with maximum thinness, within the limits of tenths of a micron. It partially holds back the rays of light and allows a better vision of the micro-relief and wear traces under the binoculars.

The advantage of Indian ink over other opaque pigments lies in the fact that it can be easily washed off the flint's surface. All that is needed is a small operation with an artist's paint-brush to produce a surface suitable for research. The necessity for careful washing with hot water and soap goes without saying, as the Indian ink will not lie evenly but collect in patches after spirit and benzine have been used on the surface. However, no formula for concentration can be given beforehand; it can be left to the student to observe and judge for himself on the concentration of the solution and the evenness of the film, and reach the desired effect by experience. The use of Indian ink improves optical analysis; streaks, lines and scratches will come out more clearly; traces that do not appear in normal conditions will emerge. The micro-topography of the surface becomes more accessible to our view.

The use of Indian ink for the purposes mentioned simplifies research on ancient stone tools, but it has a negative side. Ink is almost impossible to lay at the same time very thinly and in an even layer. Filling up the irregularities of the micro-relief, it covers them over and collects in patches. In studying the small part of an object it is necessary to wash off the ink frequently and apply another slip.

In practice the best results have been obtained by using chemical colorizers, especially methyl violet, which will in some measure chemically react with the

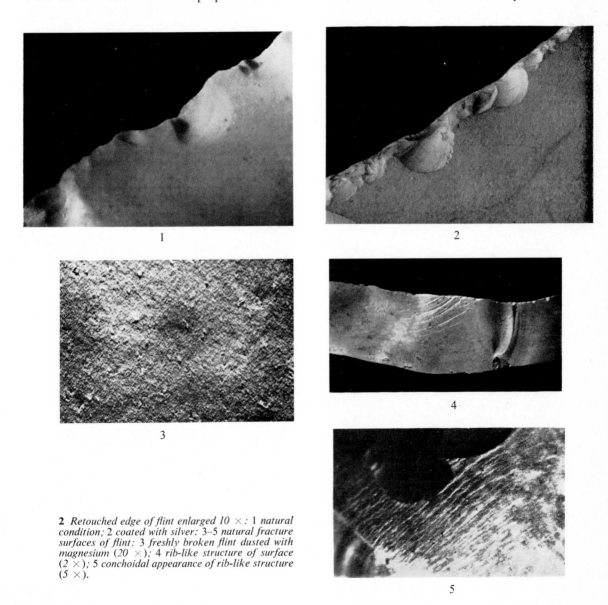

2 *Retouched edge of flint enlarged 10 × : 1 natural condition; 2 coated with silver: 3–5 natural fracture surfaces of flint: 3 freshly broken flint dusted with magnesium (20 ×); 4 rib-like structure of surface (2 ×); 5 conchoidal appearance of rib-like structure (5 ×).*

patina on flint. A weak solution of methyl violet dabbed on the flint surface with a paint brush can bring out very minute striations. After the colour solution has dried out it has to be wiped over with a cloth or rag of thin soft material, for example cambric.

Colouring with methyl violet is an effective way of studying objects of unpatinated flint and other rocks. In addition the surface under examination can be subjected to metallization with the aid of a vacuum machine (with silver, chrome, copper etc.), or silverized by applying a solution of silver nitrate. A very fine layer of silver completely eliminates the translucency of flint and gives definition to details of the micro-relief on parts of the surface not covered by silver (fig. 2.1 and 2).

Bone tools may also be coloured by Indian ink or methyl violet in weak solutions, if the surface of the working part is sufficiently well preserved, and especially if it has been polished by use.

7. Photography of traces of wear

IN the workroom exceptional importance is attached to the graphic presentation of the results and evidence of archaeological researches. Archaeologists have not yet introduced into their general practice all those means of establishing and documenting evidence which contemporary techniques place at their disposal. This is particularly the case in micro-photography, stereo-photography and micro-stereophotography which have been in use for some time in other spheres of knowledge.

Micro-photography now possesses its own methods and techniques and constitutes a regular branch of auxiliary science.[1] Without it laboratory researches could not be undertaken in biology, medicine, mineralogy, petrography, metallurgy and other branches of science.[2] Micro-photography should not be confused with micro-tracing. The latter is a laborious process requiring special skill and a markedly more elaborate method of documentation.

Taking micro-photographs in workroom archaeology for studying traces of work on ancient tools and artefacts has its own special requirements.

Undoubtedly in laboratory researches by archaeologists there is a place for the study of slides of different vegetable and animal remains, and also slides of stone, pottery and metal objects. Such work is gradually beginning to win a place for itself in archaeology. But here we have a practice already established in other sciences with its methods fully worked out. Research on traces of human activity on working tools is to a large extent a new field both in methods of observation as well as in documentation. Micro-photography of traces of work, which are three-dimensional, encounters greater difficulties as the need for greater magnification grows. It is true that this applies to all micro-photographic work, but with traces of use low limits of magnification are a more limiting factor than with flat objects.

Any archaeologist can carry out macro- and micro-photography with small-model, mirror cameras ('Exact', 'Praktiflex', 'Zenit' and others) with short focal lenses (1 : 3.5; f=50 mm.) with the use of one accessory, a supplementary tube. The latter is placed between the exposure chamber and the lens and acts as an extension to the camera bellows. The limits of magnification with a small camera with supplementary tube are not large ($2\times$ to $10\times$), but the prints can be enlarged up to $8\times$ to $30\times$, given a perfectly adjusted camera and enlarging apparatus.

The essential value of using a small camera with tube is that this simple device can be employed not only in the laboratory but on the excavation site, where the necessity to record various details of the object directly in the cultural layer, and even of the layer itself, may arise. The small camera, moreover, makes it possible to take pictures of objects as a whole or even groups of objects, if the number of rings in the tube is reduced, or if it is taken out altogether.*

In all major work when microscopic documentation goes hand in hand with micro-analysis apparatus of more complicated type is required. In this case it is micro-photographic eyepiece attachments and universal micro-photographic stands that are the two most suitable pieces of equipment.*

In all photography, including micro-photography, lighting plays a crucial part. We have already described the lamps used in micro-analysis of traces of work and their methods of use. The same lamps are suitable for

---

[1] L. I. Tsukerman, *Practical Guide to Micro-photography* (Moscow, 1950); C. Shelaber, *Micro-photography* (Moscow, 1951).
[2] Professor S. M. Potatsov, *Legal Photography* (Moscow, Leningrad, 1948); N. V. Terziev, B. R. Kirichinsky, A. A. Eisman, E. B. Cherken, *Physical Researches in Criminal Law* (Moscow, 1948).

micro-photography. We should note that in the micro-analysis of traces of work lamps can be used with or without filters.* Essentially short-wave radiation is preferable in the practice of micro-analysis, because the defining power of the lens is greater the shorter the wavelength of the light falling on it.

Therefore in micro-photography methods of work with blue and violet light filters have been in use for a long time, but recently ultra-violet lamps have been introduced permitting examination of a larger number of details on an object.[1]

In the photography of traces of use on stone and bone objects another important matter besides light filters is the proper preparation of the area being photographed. Just as in analysis the colourless translucent surface of flint (and to the same extent the surface of bone) tools requires dusting with magnesium, or colouring with a metallizer, or smearing with Indian ink, so as to give definitive light and bring out the linear outlines of the traces.

In field as in work-room archaeology stereophotography and micro-stereophotography play an important part.

In order to get a more or less accurate reproduction of an object on a negative using a single lens, besides the frankly technical matters (exposure, development and so on), one has to maintain the following conditions:

(1) The outlines of the subject must meet the requirements of full and detailed reproduction.

(2) The disposition of the dark and light patches by their relative brightness require carefully thought out and technically devised lighting.

(3) To avoid distortion of the linear perspective with a normal camera either a correct position has to be chosen for the camera or the object being photographed has to be moved.

(4) Reproduction of the visible perspective requires adjustment of the lens to a proper focal distance.

Even when all the above rules have been observed in taking the picture with a normal camera there are still limitations of reproduction in the result; to get a more accurate reproduction or bring out other details one has got to take several views at different angles.

The above requirements which apply to normal photographs lose much of their meaning in stereophotography.[2]

In the first place the clarity of the picture and its details are due to photographs on two planes, which on account of the exceptional sharpness of short-focus lenses used in stereoscopic apparatus give a mass of detail often not detectable by eye. Secondly the light patches of the picture and the illumination are on different planes, which emphasize the vividness and reality of the object. Thirdly the laborious correction of linear perspective by using single photographs taken with lens readjusted to the right focal interval each time, is automatic in stereoscopy, because looking at the image in the stereoscope with a focal distance equal to the focal distance of the camera lens the object in the picture appears just as it appeared to the observer in the original. Fourthly the artificial method of getting a visible perspective from separate pictures with uneven clarity on different planes is unnecessary. The stereoscope overcomes this by showing depths and the different parts on different planes creating a remarkable similitude of real perspective, in spite of uniform clarity of reproduction on all planes.

Moreover, we must bear in mind that in normal photography many subjects are difficult or impossible to reproduce. Such are subjects with different planes of perspective very near the front and with lines interlacing in different planes (foreshortening). To reproduce them would often require an artist who would show them by complicated conventions. In stereophotography such subjects present no difficulty. For example leaves and branches in a tree-top, a mass of machinery, or, what archaeologists come up against more often, the panorama of an excavation with objects resting on monoliths, bone heaps, collections of human skeletons in collective graves, the intricate perspective of structures being uncovered in earthworks—all these are reproduced in sharp contrasts on the stereo-print.[3]

As a distinct merit of stereophotography we may regard the natural reproduction of shine on objects, the transparency of water and glass, shadows, smoke and cloud, which greatly raises the value of this type of reproduction.

By its methods and techniques field research takes time to reach completion. The archaeologist is always confronted with the task of excavating the site with precision and maximum attention to detail, so that there should be no doubt about the completeness of his record and accuracy of his evidence. Therefore his field work, the quality and fullness of his observations, depends upon various factors. Amongst the chief of these is the shortness of the summer season, which threatens the archaeologist with insufficient time to complete examination of vital details and aspects of the site being studied. There are all the facts to be recorded in diaries, sketches, drawings and normal photography, which occupy his

[1] M. A. Volkov, *Photography in Invisible Bands of the Spectrum* (Moscow, 1935); A. I. and G. A. Didebulidze, *Photographic Reproduction of the Invisible* (Tblisi, 1946), p. 149.

[2] A. Donde, *Stereoscopic Photography, Its Theory and Practice* (Moscow, 1908); A. W. Judge, *Stereoscopic Photography* (London, 1926).

[3] A. K. Klementev, *Stereoscopy in Architecture and Building* (Moscow, 1952).

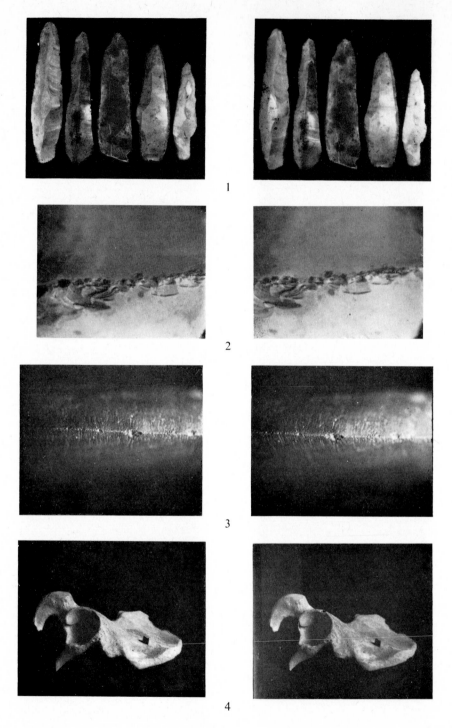

3 *Stereo-photographs of various objects: 1 upper palaeolithic flint blades; 2 method of blunting by retouch for handle on blade from Kostenki I; 3 traces of use on ground axe from Verkholensk; 4 human pelvic bone transfixed by flint head from Fofanov, L. Baikal area.*

attention and whose significance he assesses in the course of the excavation. Every student knows from experience that the longer something is the object of his interest the more the observations accumulate, which will not only bring corrections but commonly a radical alteration of deductions. Field research in practice has its own peculiarities which rarely allow the student to return to the site or the right part of it, so that work can be continued in the next season. The excavations finished and recordings completed, the finds are then removed and taken for ever from their original position and conditions of deposit. Verification of recorded data and the search for additional evidence are no longer possible.

So an archaeologist is extremely concerned that, together with his own documentation, facts and details that he himself took note of, he should have others which escaped his attention or to which he did not attach proper weight. This evidence, these details, can be noted and assessed by studying his photographic record. Stereophotography alone, especially in colour,[1] with its great power of making things stand out, can provide this kind of documentation, recording many facts and details from various views. Stereophotography has one more advantage. The print allows accurate estimate of the size and disposition of objects in cases where measurements were not made at the time of discovery.

We have in mind stereo-photogrammetry,[2] which forms an important branch of metro-photograhy and plays a large part in strict scientific methods of measurement, especially in geodesy and astronomy.*

From what has been said above it follows that stereoscopic photography is of great value whenever precise and full documentation of the objects being studied is required in their natural three-dimensional aspect. On stereoscopic prints of palaeolithic flint knives one can see not only the retouch but the whole bow-shape of the blade without a sectional drawing (fig. 3.1). The way a blade has been blunted by retouch, traces of wear on the blade of a neolithic axe or the position of the flint arrowhead that killed him in the pelvic bone of a man (fig. 3.2–4), are all reproduced by stereoscopic photography with many details. It will be fully appreciated that, pressed into service for recording and documenting of a different kind, on traces of work on ancient tools and objects which are three-dimensional, micro-stereophotography is of no small value.*

---

[1] S. P. Ivanov, *About Coloured Stereoscopic Photography* (Moscow, 1951).
[2] N. M. Tokarsky, *Educational Library of the State Academy for the History of Material Culture*, 3 (1931).

Section two | Stone

1. Basic minerals and rock types used in the Stone Age for the manufacture of tools

STONE, like wood, bone and antler, is one of those gifts of nature which man had at his disposal from the first stages of his existence. Stone, however, occupied a special position among these materials. Only by means of stone could man more or less extensively exploit wood, bone and antler for tools. However simple the methods of working these materials, however trifling the changes produced in the natural forms appear to be, without stone tools there was no possibility of development; the working of wood by bone, or the other way round, is a very difficult task indeed. Only in special geographical circumstances where technically suitable stone was absent, but, where instead there were such inadequate substitutes as shells, tortoise shells or fish jawbones, did man contrive to manage with very few stone tools, although needless to say at a lower technical and cultural level.

In considering the rocks which man had at his disposal for his needs we may look at the deciding factors in the choice of material. The important rocks suitable for the majority of tools belong to one mineral group, the quartz group of rocks, which have a single chemical constituent, SiO_2 (Si 46·7 per cent, O 53·3 per cent), and a number of important physical characteristics in common. Varieties within the group have important differences in colour, lustre, fracture-structure, specific gravity, external shape and size, origin, occurrence, impurities, transparency and other features. But these differences are overshadowed by a few qualities in common. Of these an important one is the extreme hardness, an average of 7 on the 10-degree scale of Mohs.[1] Only topaz (8), corundum (9) and diamond (10) are harder. An essential quality of many varieties of quartz, which determined its choice by man, was isotropism (glassy quality), that is completely uniform physical properties in all directions, as opposed to crystalline rocks.

Quartz (silica) is a very important element in the lithosphere, occupying 12 per cent of it, and occurs in a great variety of forms, being part of many rocks, forming complicated combinations, and also occurring in crystalline varieties. Quartz crystals are often encountered in the form of rock crystal. Its crystals, which may be large, are elongated hexagonal prisms terminating in hexagonal pyramids (hexagonal bipyramidism). It is characteristic of this that the individual crystals have isotropic structure and do not break down into new crystals or crystalline grains, as is the case with many other non-isotropic materials with completely ill-knit structure. This means that large crystals are very suitable material for tools. They are not often found on the ground surface and the deposits where they occur were not easy of access to prehistoric man.

Non-crystalline silica is known to us principally as flint, chalcedony, agate, jasper, Lydian stone (*lidit*), hornstone, quartzite, obsidian and other rocks with isotropic properties. Due to their isotropic structure and their consequent conchoidal fracture, when struck these rocks yield an uneven surface with receding concentric waves and very sharp cutting edges.

In the course of development of techniques in working stone prehistoric man attempted, so far as possible, to reduce the conchoidal swelling of fracture and the curvature of the flakes struck off, by a change from working by blows to working by pressing-off. By means of the latter he produced a comparatively slight concavity on the core and reduced the bulb of percussion on the flakes. This can be observed in the techniques of the upper palaeolithic, and especially in that of the neolithic, period. In addition prehistoric man found a method of altering the properties of the rock surface, which was employed in neolithic times. By grinding he could level off the rough surface of diorite, basalt and so on, rubbing away the irregularities left by primary work (flaking and retouch). Thanks to this higher level of technique man was able to make general use of minerals and rocks very dissimilar in their natural properties.

Minerals and rocks used in the Stone Age differ markedly in the micro-relief of their fracture surfaces.

---

[1] Talc is number 1 on the Mohs scale. If a rock will scratch another it is the harder of the two. T.

With some the surface is shiny and bright, others dull gleaming (waxen), others dull or mat, others rough, others with lumps and hollows, sharp edges and crevices and so on.

We can arrange in order of increasing roughness of the fracture the different rocks preferred by prehistoric man with details of their mineral characteristics in the following table:

1. ROCK CRYSTAL. Quartz group. Hardness 7. Specific gravity 2·5–2·8. Watery-transparent in colour. Glassy lustre. Fracture flat conchoidal. Ill-knit jointing. Crystalline form, hexagonal terminating in hexagonal pyramids. Large crystals occur in rock fissures or on the surface. Rarely used in palaeolithic times. Very simple objects of rock crystal found among the tools of *Pithecanthropus Pekinensis*.

2. OBSIDIAN (volcanic glass). Magmatic rock. Chemical composition variable. Contains 75 per cent quartz (SiO_2). Hardness 6. Specific gravity 2·35–2·5. Colour from black or dark grey to silvery, but there are other colours. Glassy lustre. Conchoidal fracture. Brittle. No jointing. Occurs in certain lavas and surface remains of volcanic origin. Used by palaeolithic man from the earliest times. Example: Chellean and Acheulian hand-axes from Armenia (Satani-Dar). Widely used in neolithic of southern Europe, America and other countries.

3. CHALCEDONY. Varieties: chrysoprase, carnelian, quartzine, sapphirine. Quartz group. Hardness 7. Specific gravity 2·65. Colour variable. Opaque. Dull sheen. Flat conchoidal fracture. Edge in fracture very sharp and thin. No jointing. Latent fibrous crystalline structure under the microscope. Occurs as crust in kidney-shaped lumps or spherolites forming in the voids of veins or fissures in magmatic rocks. Palaeolithic man rarely used chalcedony and only where there was no chalk flint. In the neolithic period it was widely used in many countries.

4. AGATE (onyx). Varieties: sardonyx, carneolonyx. Quartz group. Hardness 7. Specific gravity 2·5–2·7. Colour variable. Opaque. Dull sheen, or mat. Flat conchoidal fracture. Internal structure analogous to chalcedony. On a fractured or polished surface horizontal or concentric lines of different colours visible. Texture sometimes 'mossy' ('panoramic'). No jointing. Sharp, thin edges in fracture. Latent fibrous crystalline structure under microscope. Formed in many effusive rocks (lavas that have flowed). Occurs condensed in almond-shaped or larger forms (geodes). Like chalcedony widely used in neolithic times for the manufacture of small cutting tools and insertions in arrowheads.

5. FLINT. Quartz group. Hardness 7. Specific gravity 2·37–2·67. Besides SiO_2 (90–95 per cent) contains traces of sand, clay and other materials. Black, grey or pink colour. Opaque. Conchoidal fracture. Dull or greasy sheen in fracture. Flint can be subdivided into four types. Three of these were produced in chalk deposits: (*a*) opal-chalcedony (gezites), (*b*) chalcedony (silexes), (*c*) quartz-chalcedony flints (silexites). The fourth group, fresh-water flints, was produced in gypsums. The best qualities (by proportion of SiO_2 and flaking properties) are found in chalcedony flints.

Chalk flints had exceptionally wide use in the palaeolithic and neolithic periods in those countries where there are chalk deposits, that is strata of the Upper Cretaceous system.

6. JASPER. Quartz group. Hardness 7–6·5. Contains 70–73 per cent of pure quartz, the remainder being admixtures of clay and oxides of iron which gives jasper its varied colours (straw yellow, olive, green, cherry red, grey, raspberry). Sometimes one encounters banded or spotty jasper. The fracture is rough conchoidal, mat surface, almost rough. Flakes irregularly and technically therefore worse than flint. Occurs in rocks of palaeozoic origin. Does not contain organic remains. Used in the palaeolithic period in Asia and in neolithic times in several countries.

7. CHERT. Like jasper hardness 7–6 or less. Contains structural impurities. Usually dark grey or greenish in colour. Fracture rough conchoidal, rough surface. Flakes worse than flint and gives shorter, thicker flakes. Occurs in palaeozoic and less often mesozoic strata. Widely used in neolithic times when grinding had come into use. In Siberia and other Asian countries this material was used in palaeolithic times.

8. QUARTZITE. Silicified sandstone. Specific gravity 2·5–2·8. Colour light grey, almost white. Different impurities give this stone red, violet, cherry, greenish and other tints. Dull, glassy lustre. Rough conchoidal fracture. Fracture surface granular, slightly lumpy, rough to touch. In general use in palaeolothic times (from the oldest period) in countries where flint was scarce or absent, for example, in Asia, particularly in its southern half. Rarely used in neolithic times.

9. DIORITE (greenstone). Contains little quartz or none at all. Basic mineral constituent is felspar (75 per cent). Contains hornblende, augite and sometimes black mica (biotite). Hardness 6–5·5. Specific gravity 2·8–2·85. Grey, dark grey or greenish grey in colour. Feeble conchoidal fracture and rough surface with fine or small grains. Outcrops in northern Europe, and occurs as erratic boulders in the south, and is also known in Asia, Africa, Australia, and America. Used by palaeolithic man where other rocks absent, for example in the older palaeolithic of Central Asia (Aman-Kutan). In the neolithic period it was one of the principal materials for axes and adzes, due to its toughness. Some varieties approach nephrite in their toughness and stringy structure.

10. BASALT (trap). Young magmatic rock. Does not contain quartz. Basic constituents: felspar, pyroxene.

Hardness 6–6·5. Specific gravity 2·6–3·11. Black or dark grey in colour. Dull sheen. Rough, uneven fracture. Compact, fine-grained structure. Often occurs as hexagonal columns. Widespread in mountainous volcanic areas. Widely used in neolithic times in southern Europe, and in countries of south-eastern Asia and Oceania.

11. LIPARITE (rhyolite). Magmatic rock of tertiary or post-tertiary origin. It contains quartz, but its basic constituent is felspar. Hardness 6. Specific gravity 2·3–2·7. Colour, white to grey with yellow and red specks. Dull sheen. Rough, uneven fracture surface. Small-grained porphyritic structure. Like basalt, it occurs in volcanic areas. Starting with the mesolithic period it was used in south-east Asia and other countries.

12. NEPHRITE (actinolite). Hardness 6. Specific gravity 3·1–3·3. Colour, usually grass green, less commonly other colours and speckled. Latent crystalline, tough rock. Fibrous structure. Splintery fracture, sharp points, shimmery sheen, slightly laminated. Found in eastern Siberia (area of Lake Baikal), eastern China (Kwen-Lun), Central Asia (Pamir), New Zealand, Tasmania, New Caledonia, North America (New Jersey). Used in neolithic period as a result of the development of new methods of working stone, grinding and sawing.

The above list far from exhausts the whole range of minerals and rocks used by man in the Stone Age as material for stone tools. That would have to include varieties of shale, soft and hard, fossilized wood (varieties of opal), siliceous tufae (geyserite), granites, sandstones, ironstones and ochre. But these taken as a whole were not basic but auxiliary materials in the technology of prehistoric man. They were used as striker-stones, retouchers, rubbing stones, sharpeners for bone and stone tools, grinders for colouring matter, querns, and also as colouring matter. The short list of minerals and their properties illustrates how man only gradually took into his use stones which did not possess conchoidal fracture and great hardness, and which could not be quickly worked by the early methods of percussion, pressure and retouch.

2. Obtaining stone material in the palaeolithic and neolithic periods

THE kind of rocks used by man in the lower palaeolithic period shows that the material was selected on a basis of practical experience. In those countries (Europe, Africa) where there was flint it was chosen in preference to other rocks, because its physical properties were understood. When there was no chalk flint or flint of other formations (rarely found in open exposures), as in southern Asia, man used quartzite,[1] fossilized wood, flinty tufa,[2] rhyolite and other rocks, collecting them in the pebble beds of river banks. Many of the lower palaeolithic tools known to us retain a pebble crust on them. Lower palaeolithic finds made by S. N. Zamyatnin and M. Z. Panichkina in Armenia show that man of this time used obsidian extensively, collecting lumps of it at surface exposures.

In the upper palaeolithic period the range of material was somewhat increased. Besides those rocks (flint, quartzite and so on) out of which tools were made (knives, end-scrapers, burins, awls, etc.) other rocks (granite, sandstones, slate, calcites, ochre, ironstone) are found on the sites, out of which striker-stones, pestles, retouchers, colouring and ornaments were made.

It is difficult to grasp why even by this time with his more advanced technique man should not have obtained all these materials by very simple mining. Yet undoubtedly palaeolithic hunters searched for and collected the necessary raw material on the ground surface. When they did use flint from undisturbed strata, they dug it out of exposures in cliffs and river gorges, never making any significant excavation in these outcrops.

This is explained by the fact that in a hunting way of life collecting played an important part in the economy and did not allow settled life, and wandering did not encourage the development of techniques of extraction. In such an economy the quantity of stone in demand was still not very great.

There are no grounds for assuming the existence of trade in the upper palaeolithic period to which people could resort to get types of stone which were not found

[1] V. D. Krishnaswami and K. V. Soundararajan, *Ancient India*, 7 (1951), pp. 40–46.
[2] L. Movius, *Transactions of the American Philosophical Society* (Series 3), 33 (1943), pp. 348–50.

in their home areas. Sending specially equipped parties into the home areas of other friendly tribes is likely to have taken place, for we know of similar practices among the Australians. The diorite exposures at Mt William in Victoria and the MacDonell Mountains in Central Australia were visited by envoys of different tribes living several hundred kilometres away.[1]

In the neolithic period important changes in technique and economy took place. Hunter-fisher tribes in the northern and farmers in the southern areas of Europe and Asia began to lead a more settled life. The development of productive means and technical practices, wider economic demands and the manufacture of substantial ground tools (adze and axe) created the need for regular and permanent sources of stone. At this time most simple rock mining arose of quartzite, chert, diorite, basalt and even nephrite.

Neolithic stone mines have not yet been encountered within the Soviet Union, but workings of some kind evidently existed on the upper and middle Volga, in Karelia,[2] on the Dnestr, and in other areas where there is evidence of workshops. In Switzerland, Denmark, northern Germany, Belgium, France,[3] Sicily, and England workings were opened in the form of a shaft, hole or trench. The flint workings at Grand Préssigny, Mur-de-Barrez, and Champignolles are very widely known. In England flint was obtained from holes at Cissbury (Sussex)[4] and shafts at Grimes Graves (Suffolk) In Belgium chalk flint was worked at Spiennes (nr. Mons)[5] by shafts more than 15m deep joined by galleries, and also by holes at Strépy and Obourg. Amongst Egyptian flint mines the numerous well-shafts at Wadi-el-Sheik[6] are conspicuous examples, opened initially in Pre-dynastic times, but used as a source of raw materials in later times. S. Carr, who studied these ancient workings, observed well-like shafts and heaps of waste scattered about the desert sand. The flint was obtained here over a great area along the edges of old valleys, where rivers had flowed in pleistocene times and since dried up because of climatic changes.

Thus arose the rudiments of mining, albeit primitive, but still requiring specialized methods of work and special application of tools and devices: antler and stone picks, stone hammers, sledge-hammers, bone and wooden wedges, the simplest wooden clamps, and also forms of rock-splitting by fire. All this testifies to the new technical achievements of the period.

Commonly, in countries where during palaeolithic and mesolithic times man had had to make his tools out of poor-quality stone, in neolithic times tools appear of technically superior rocks, and also in greater quantity. An example is the area of L. Baikal where, besides the use of chert, we find axes, adzes and knives of nephrite in general use. The hard actinolithic rocks (nephrite, jadeite, serpentine) could not have been worked with palaeolithic techniques, flaking and retouch, because of their fibrous structure. The skills of sawing and grinding had had to be developed first. Nephrite is not found in Siberian palaeolithic sites even as an auxiliary material (striker-stones, retouchers, plaques), as the extraction of this rare material and its working is no easy matter. Yet Siberian nephrite is found as smooth rolled boulders at the base of the outcrop to the west of L. Baikal (Rivers Onot, Chika, Khorok, Zhara-Zhelga), where it occurs as actinolithic slate.[7] The use of nephrite of various colours for tools and ornament started in the neolithic period in China, where it was obtained from the Kwen-Lun Mountains and a variety of nephrite, jadeite, is found in Burma and in the Pamir area, probably the source for the eneolithic population of the Indus basin. In America nephrite was worked by the ancient Mexicans. In New Zealand the Maoris made nephrite axes, adzes and even clubs. Nephrite is found in the island of Tasmania, but the aborigines did not know how to use it for their tools. In Europe the neolithic population obtained nephrite (smaragdite) from outcrops in Silesia, Carynthia, and Styria, and also from the central Alps and southern Liguria.

The neolithic tools of south-east Asia are of especial interest. Upper palaeolithic sites are still unknown there. After the rough hand-axes of Java (Pajitanian), Malaya (Tampanian), Burma (Anyathian), Siam (Fingnoian), which are very inexpressive stone objects, found with remains of *Homo Soloensis* (at Ngandong), we meet nothing before the mesolithic hand tools of the Bak-Son type made of rhyolite. The presence of bamboo and shells in these countries, and the almost complete absence of flint, forced man to manage at an early date with very few stone tools or to use them only in extreme necessity. But in neolithic times, when man changed from hunting and collecting to agriculture, to the construction of pile-dwellings and the manufacture of dug-out canoes, stone axes appear in vast quantities; axes, adzes and chisels of beautiful workmanship made of coloured slates, jasper and agate. In Java slate workings and workshops occur near Punnung and Pajitan,

[1] B. Spencer and E. Gillen, *The Northern Tribes of Central Australia* (London, 1904), pp. 175–6.
[2] M. Foss and L. Elnitsky, *Materials and Researches on the Archaeology of the U.S.S.R.*, 2 (1941), pp. 182–91.
[3] M. Boule, *Materiaux pour l'Histoire de l'Homme*, I (1884), pp. 65–75; IV (1887), pp. 5–21.
[4] J. P. Harrison, *Journal of the Anthropological Institute of Gt. Britain*, 2–3 (1878), pp. 413–30.
[5] E. Munkk, *Comptes Rendus du Congrès International d'Anthroplogie et d'Archéologie Préhistorique* (Paris, 1891), pp. 569–615.
[6] J. de Morgan, *Prehistoric Man* (Moscow-Leningrad, 1926) p. 146.
[7] A. G. Betekhtin, *Mineralogy* (Moscow, 1950).

whence the stone objects were carried throughout the whole island and even beyond its shores.[1]

In southern India near Bellary (Kapgall) is a neolithic shaft explored by B. Foote. It cuts through a substantial hill which is made up of diorite of two sorts that was extensively used in the manufacture of chopping tools in antiquity. Large neolithic workings also occur on the diorite outcrop near Anantapur. Most of the rough-outs were worked by pecking, and flakes can still be found.

Evidence for neolithic trade cannot be regarded as accidental. Tools of Grand Pressigny flint recognizable by their yellow colour are distributed throughout the greater part of France. Very often nodules of flint, lumps of diorite, basalt, chert and jasper are found in neolithic settlements that are not close to natural occurrences of the rock. For example, on the site of neolithic settlements of central India large pebbles of agate (geodes), lumps of jasper and hornstone weighing several dozen kilograms are sometimes found mixed up with potsherds and other remains. In the opinion of one Indian scholar[2] this type of material could have reached the settlement only with the aid of some very simple means of transport (sleds) propelled by human strength.

Hornstone, and particularly agate, was obtained in such large quantities only in India and a few other countries. In India, however, the neolithic population rarely made axes and adzes out of this material, using it more often for small tools.

In making small unground tools (arrowheads, knife- and dagger-blade insertions, saws, scrapers, awls, burins sickles and so on) in India, as in the neolithic period in many other countries, semi-precious stones were widely used: chalcedony, agate, onyx, rock crystal, jasper, Lydian stone, garnet, bloodstone, hornstone. These occur as nodules, pebbles and even almond-shaped knobs. They are met comparatively frequently in nature but for the most part not as large objects; one can pick them up in river beds and gravels, which was what was done in antiquity. But usually they are filled with cracks and hollows due to their origin in veins, fissures and concretions of magmatic rocks. Mastery of minerals of this type is very difficult, and implies the rudiments of mineralogical technique in the neolithic period. The substantial quantity of objects of the above-named stones found in the New Stone Age allows us to appreciate the growth of technology in this period.

3. Significance of the properties of material in the technique of working stone

For a long time we have been aware of several essential differences observable in the external aspect of palaeolithic tools found in different countries over large areas of land. This difference has been especially confirmed by comparison of the stone tools of the countries of Europe and the Mediterranean area on the one hand and of Asia on the other. Although there are of course significant local peculiarities in palaeolithic tools in the Europe-Mediterranean area, there are several overall common characteristics: a substantial number of well-made Chellean and Acheulian hand-axes, highly finished forms of Mousterian points and scrapers. The tools of the upper palaeolithic sites of this area have very characteristic features.

We see quite a different picture in Asia. While in the Europe-Mediterranean area the upper palaeolithic tools as a rule were made on blades struck from cylindrical cores, and so had regular elongated shapes with thin

sections, in Asia, for instance Siberia, the tools differ in having less expressive external features. The blades there were shorter, less regular, more massive; the different types are less clearly distinguished one from another. On the whole the stone tools of Siberia are much less frequently made on blades struck from cylindrical cores. In the mass the Siberian palaeolithic tools have a more primitive character.

S. N. Zamyatnin devoted a special article to this problem, and wrote: '. . . in the technique of stone-working in the Siberian palaeolithic sites a feature most characteristic of this period is absent, which in Europe and Africa we find everywhere and which gives the tool series such a characteristic appearance. I am referring to the prismatic core, the development of which allowed the manufacture of a new type of implement, the long knife-like flake with parallel edges struck from it, which reached a high degree of regularity and thinness at the

[1] R. Heine-Geldern, *Anthropos*, 3–4 (1932), pp. 543–619.
[2] P. T. Srinivasa Ayyangar, *The Stone Age in India* (1926).

end of the palaeolithic period. Looking at a collection it strikes one at a glance that the use of this technique was very limited, if not quite absent, in the Siberian and Chinese areas'[1]

As examples of this Zamyatnin quotes the well-known Siberian sites (Malta, Buret, Afontova Mountain), sites on the Yenisei and in the Altai mountains discovered by G. P. Sosnovsky, A. P. Okladnikov's sites on the river Lena, the upper cave at Chou-Kou-Tien and sites in the Ordos area (Sho-Tong-Koy, Shara-Usu-Gol). In all these, besides the primitiveness mentioned, the insignificant number of burins of upper palaeolithic type is noticeable, as well as the absence of end-scrapers on blades. Instead of end-scrapers there are miniature round scrapers. Scrapers in several sites are of massive Mousterian type and often tools of hand-axe form are found.

While very properly criticising the tendency of some western archaeologists to regard these differences as a sign of the backwardness of the East compared to the West, Zamyatnin gave no definite cause to explain the peculiarities, although he draws attention to three factors: material, technology and economy. He denied the essential significance in quality of material as the explanation of the special features of the stone tools of Asia. Economy also failed to qualify as a fundamental cause, for in Europe and Asia alike the main means of subsistence in upper palaeolithic times was hunting mammoth and reindeer. Nor can the characteristic differences of the Asian tools be attributed to technology, since there can be greater variations in methods of work between local areas than between the large areas mentioned. When we are dealing with a matter of differences and peculiarities of most general traits observable over vast areas of ground, the cause of the differences cannot be sought in peculiarities of the manufacturing process. This view is confirmed for example by the absence of essential differences in the character of bone tools in Europe and Asia. The peculiarities in shape of the female statuettes of Siberia, that is artistic creations, to which Zamyatnin refers, cannot be put in the same rank as peculiarities in stone tools, as the latter developed in quite a different way.

Strictly speaking the purely formal division of geographical areas by techniques of working stone, a division for which there is no full causal explanation, can be made independently of any wish of the investigator to introduce the concept of race as a factor influencing technological development. Leaving this aside, study of the problems of sources and properties of the stone materials actually available to palaeolithic man in various countries might set us on the right road to an answer.

On what serious basis can the technology of the palaeolithic population of Europe and the Mediterranean area be arranged? The predominant material here was chalk flint. This occurs in the form of nodules of varying size, from small knobs and concretions about the size of a hen's egg up to lumps weighing several dozen kilograms. Each nodule is encased in a white opaque crust which is less hard and consists of hydrated silica. Rather less commonly chalk flint is bedded in veins or layers of variable thickness from thin irregular strata of 2–3 cm thick up to 15–20 cm and more. Its different colours and shades depend on the admixture of potassium, lime, alumina, ferric oxide, and other compounds.

It was the nodular flint that mainly caught the eye of palaeolithic man in Europe. Often occurring in fresh gravel and alluvial deposits it was relatively easy to obtain and work. The geo-chemical and mineralogical properties of chalk flint, its isotropism, conchoidal fracture (especially in a fresh state, when the nodule had only just left its parent bed) allowed him to make successfully tools of a very finished appearance.

The origin of this flint is closely bound up with the marine deposits of the Cretaceous period, that is clays, shales, sandstones and limestones, and chalk itself. The latter is a comparatively rare rock but was the essential medium in the formation of chalk flint.

In the Soviet Union flint-bearing chalk occurs only in the south European areas with its northern limits in the districts of Ulyanovsk, Voronezh and Bryansk. Flint found in northern areas occurs either in the lower strata of the Cretaceous system or in strata of previous formations, and besides having different qualities was less accessible to man of the Ice Age. In western Europe Upper Cretaceous strata with flint nodules or veins occur in England, northern France, the Netherlands, Denmark, Westphalia, and also in southern Mediterranean areas. Lower and Middle Cretaceous deposits are widespread in northern, eastern and southern Africa and Hither Asia. The flint occurring in the limestones of these deposits is different from the chalk flint of Europe. Over all the rest of the Asian continent Cretaceous formations are feebly represented and deposits of Upper Chalk almost entirely absent.

In the greater part of Asia palaeolithic man was compelled to use predominantly pebbles of chert, hornstone, jasper, quartz and rhyolite, all products of erosion and weathering of ancient sedimentary and metamorphic rocks. Such material could not yield fine cores and blades, with tools made on them like the tools of Europe and north Africa in the upper palaeolithic period.

---

[1] S. N. Zamyatnin, *Studies of the Ethnographical Institute*, 16 (1951), p. 13

The dependence of the morphological characteristics of stone tools on the quality and properties of the source material is insufficiently appreciated by scholars. The quality of the material formed part of the natural environment in which man lived; it showed its influence in the economic life and technology of society, impressing its mark on the types of tools, methods of work and manufacturing practices.

There is evidence of what part the character of the material plays in the choice of methods of work among backward tribes from the well-known study of Spencer and Gillen among the aborigines of Australia. They recorded that tribes of Central Australia simultaneously made and used roughly dressed tools, retouched tools of quartzite and ground axes of diorite, that is tools of both palaeolithic and neolithic form. Some quartzite knives were as rough as the Tasmanian ones, but with them were a series as fine as those from European upper palaeolithic sites. The type of tool depended on the quality of the material that the Australians had to hand.

King recorded beautiful retouched spearheads, leaf-shaped with denticulated edges, recalling Solutrean forms, made out of quartz and fine-grained milky quartzite, when such material was available. Where there was no such material the spearheads took on a more primitive aspect.[1]

Many workers, including Roth and Klaatsch, have confirmed the mixture of highly-developed types of stone tools with rough forms of eolithic appearance in Australia. In some places on the north coast and off-shore islands where there is no suitable material stone tools were entirely absent; instead the natives used shells or teeth of marine animals and kangaroos.[2] Spencer and Gillen wrote: 'If the Aranda or Varramunga should die out the future research-worker will be very confused by their stone industry with its intermixture of palaeolithic and neolithic types'.[3]

4. A study of the oldest methods of working stone

a. Percussion

PERCUSSION can be regarded as the oldest method of working stone. By this primeval striking method man changed the form of stone by deliberately breaking it into pieces with a few strong blows. In contemporary techniques of working stone this is called hewing or quartering when a lump of stone is roughly shaped. It is possible that in certain cases palaeolithic man had had to detach pieces of rock as flakes from an outcrop, for example in exposures of obsidian veins, diorites, rhyolites, quartzites, limestones and dolomites, using a heavy maul for this purpose. However, such activity, very familiar in neolithic times and representing an initial stage of mining, obviously was but rarely employed in early palaeolithic times.

Percussion techniques have interested many archaeologists and attempts have often been made to make very simple tools. Among Russian workers Gorodtsov carried out experiments on the banks of the river Istra, 40 km from Moscow, using the flint that occurs there. At the same time as his experimental work Gorodtsov made observations on the formation of natural eoliths in the cliffs of the valley, produced by temperature changes, falls of rock, water movements, and cracking by fire. He established that natural agencies very often produced traces closely similar to those left by human activity; eoliths may resemble flakes, even rough blades with signs of retouch. Similar results of the action of natural agents have been observed by Verworn, Arcelin and Breuil.

Among English archaeologists experimental work in making the simpler stone tools has been done by Reid-Moir who made hand-axes and tools of Levallois type.[5] Tools of Clactonian form have been made by Baden Powell,[6] experimenting in the field of primary palaeolithic technique. The French archaeologist, F. Bordes, studied percussion on glass, vitrified metallic slag, flint,

[1] P. King, *Narrative of a Survey of the Intertropic Coast of Australia* (London, 1827), II, p. 68.
[2] K. Klaatsch, *Zeitschrift für Ethnologie*, 11 (1908), p. 407.
[3] B. Spencer and E. Gillen, *The Northern Tribes of Central Australia* (London, 1904).
[4] V. A. Gorodtsov, *Soviet Ethnography*, 2 (1935), pp. 61–85.
[5] J. Reid-Moir, *Pre-Palaeolithic Man* (Ipswich), p. 67.
[6] D. E. Baden-Powell, *Proceedings of the Prehistoric Society*, 15 (1949), p. 38.

obsidian and other materials. The distinguished Chinese student of Pekin man, Pei Wen Chung, carried out prolonged researches on shatter and cracking in hard rocks under the action of natural agencies. He compared the products of natural alterations with the tools found at Chou-Kou-Tien.[1]

The results of all this experimental work and observations by archaeologists of different countries have still not been drawn together, but we can say at once that the deductions of the various writers do not fully coincide on the points that interest us.

From all the work it has emerged that the manufacture of bifacial hand-axes is well within the capabilities of modern man without any experience in hand craft. Our experiments testify to this, carried out near Tikhvin in 1935 in a limestone quarry where nodules of grey flint of tertiary origin occurred.

There can be no dispute, too, that the best results are obtained by working flint nodules taken at their point of natural deposition while they still contain moisture. Nodules that have lain on the surface and lost their moisture are appreciably more difficult to work, even if they have not become cracked. From dried-out flint the flakes come off shorter and more abruptly.

All workers are agreed that some stone 'artefacts' arise from natural causes and can be very difficult to distinguish from real tools made by early palaeolithic man, especially if they are not associated with his skeletal remains, or animal bones, or other undoubted traces of human activity.

Almost all experimenters recognize that the dressing of a tool like a hand-axe must have been done not against an unyielding body (anvil or rest), but in such a way that when the tool was being struck the man held it in his left hand raised to the level of his waist or chest.

Controversy arises over what material ancient man preferred for a striker; stone, bone, wood or what else? It was the mistaken opinion of Gorodtsov that the circular stones with traces of blows on their surface often found on palaeolithic sites were not strikers, but missiles or strikers used for flint working with an intermediary. He wrote: 'My prolonged experiments have shown that circular stones are quite unsuitable for dressing and especially for refined flaking technique. Their defectiveness is due to unsuitability for side blows, while in direct, less effective blows, the point at which the blow is directed is smothered. This is why I have reached the positive conclusion that for knapping and more elaborate flaking the striker must have been elongated in shape.'[2]

The view of Gorodtsov to some extent coincides with the opinion of Bordes, who also assumed elongated strikers, but with this difference, that he often worked not with stone strikers but with wooden ones. He believes that man made tools only of Chellean and Clactonian types with stone strikers. Tools of Acheulian type, in his opinion, were made with wooden strikers, and the part played by these grew as techniques of stone-working developed.[3]

Bordes based his view on his own experiments. Probably unstable materials (glass, slag) could be worked, albeit with difficulty, with a hard wooden striker of short length used like a stick. Some positive effect may be produced by striking with a wooden tool on a material such as metallic slag due to the physical law about the power of the force in movements of high speed. As regards flint its working undoubtedly required, not only great rapidity of movement in the blow, but also physical effects which a wooden striker cannot produce.

Baden-Powell supported this point of view, and after testing wooden strikers ('the stick technique') rejected them in favour of quartzite pebbles and rolled flints, believing the latter to have been the best tools for knapping. He selected egg-shaped pebbles 5 to 7·5 cm long for his tests.[4]

Gorodtsov did not test wooden strikers in his experiments. Our own trials with the 'stick technique' have also met with very ill success. Strikers of oak, birch, beech, and box quickly disintegrated into fibres from blows on flint, and no longer being serviceable had to be constantly replaced. Some effect was produced only by using them on the edge of a flint already dressed with a stone striker, which could be better called percussion retouch. Initial working in which the pebble or nodule has to be broken up into quarters, its cortex removed and substantial flakes struck off, was quite impractical with this implement. Wooden and even bone strikers were broken and splintered by strong blows on flint.

Dressing of flint nodules or any other rock was done from the beginning to the end of the Stone Age by means of striker-stones. These belong to that small category of tools which very often were not worked themselves, being simply ordinary river pebbles, elongated or flat in shape. The characteristic traces of wear for striker-stones, which distinguishes them from other tools, are signs of battering observable on their surface. The working part of the striker-pebble commonly has an uneven surface with deep scars and chipmarks. As an example of such a tool we may cite the striker-stone from the Mousterian site of Volgograd on

---

[1] Pei Wen Chung, *Revue de Géographie physique et de Géologie dynamique*, 9 (part 4), p. 54.
[2] V. A. Gorodtsov, *Soviet Ethnograpny*, 2 (1935), p. 73.
[3] F. Bordes, *L'Anthropologie*, 51 (1947), pp. 3, 28, 29.
[4] D. E. Baden-Powell, *Proceedings of the Prehistoric Society*, 15 (1949), p. 38.

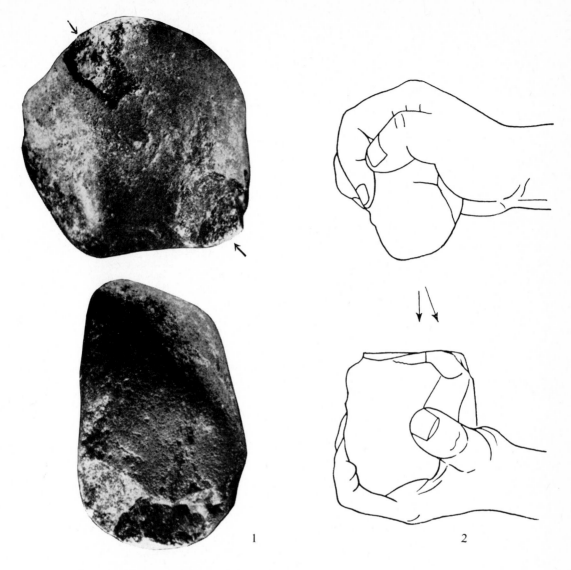

4 1 *Striker-stone from Volgograd with scars from use indicated by arrows; 2 method of use of a striker (reconstruction of flaking a core).*

the Volga, dug by Zamyatnin in 1952–4. This quartzite pebble of slightly flattened shape weighed about 400 hectograms. Its surface retained several scars produced by hard blows, and on parts traces of a large number of light blows (fig. 4).

River pebbles alone, of course, were not used as strikers. Beginning in the upper palaeolithic period, and possibly earlier, together with pebbles, worn cores were also widely used as strikers. These tools, whose surface is extensively starred, are well known in the upper palaeolithic, used not only as strikers but also as retouchers and pestles. They have a circular, often spherical, shape and commonly are smothered with traces of blows, pressure, friction and other kinds of activity. For precise definition of the function of each implement of this kind therefore, careful examination of the surface is necessary. So Gorodtsov's view that the spherical flints were used as missiles or strikers with an intermediary cannot possibly be sustained, because the objects in question bear traces of blows and pressure on hard material, which could only have been flint.

The manufacture of Chellean and Acheulian hand-axes has been fully carried out with a striker-stone. Experimental manufacture of the tool under laboratory conditions shows that the dressing can be done without any means of support (anvil). The nodule of flint, quartzite or obsidian was held in the left hand at waist- or chest-level. This was done to avoid a bounce blow from the side of the support producing a flake on the nodule in the wrong place. The left hand at the time of the blow 'gave like elastic', thanks to which the force of the blow nearly always was directed to the right spot. A modern mason or bricklayer goes about it in the same way when he has to dress a brick or cleave it at a required point. However, the danger of a bounce blow only arises if the object is on a stone rest. Bone, wood and especially earth were probably used by man for support during dressing. We have to remember that a more or less elastic and plastic support could only be used successfully when the stone tool was very light and could not be worked in the hand, or conversely if the nodule or rough-out was too heavy. The former would be required for Acheulian and Mousterian points, bifacially worked by percussion retouch on a bone anvil, and the second for 'gigantoliths' and some large tools probably worked on the ground.

Percussion as a method of work was widely used in the Stone Age. The breaking up or cleaving of stone into pieces can be regarded as its crudest form, just to get sharp lumps and flakes suitable for use as tools. From this arises striking or flaking off a part desired for use from a large nodule of flint or piece of obsidian. Connected with dressing is the removal of the cortex or pebble crust from the rock and cleaning it of patina and all other types of accretion and impurity. These methods of working stone by blows led to the Chelleo-Acheulian technique of making bifacially-worked hand-axes trimmed by rough retouch. Vayson attempted a rational classification of these tools based on the shape of their working part.[1]

There are two views on the problem of the origin of hand-axes. On one view the hand-axe arose to meet the need for a tool that would be suitable for various purposes (chopping, cutting, scraping, digging and so on). Such a tool could not be made in the first instance in any other way than by bifacial dressing if there had to be united in one tool the necessary weight for blows, a

point, two sharp edges and a thick butt. According to the second view the hand-axe is merely a touched-up core of the lower palaeolithic, arising from a developed technique of detaching rough flakes from a nodule (of flint, quartzite or obsidian).

In our view posing the problem of the origin of hand-axes without getting clear in our own minds what it is that we want to know about the oldest tools makes the matter too theoretical. Of course, almond-shaped hand-axes are not the products of some idea that suddenly struck Chellean man, for they must have arisen gradually from prolonged experience; the manufacture of hand-axes presupposes a fair degree of experience in knapping stone. These considerations, as well as the 'associated' tools,[2] consisting of rough flakes with scars and facets on the edge, indicate that hand-axes were by no means the only tools of the period.[3] The character of the tools of Pekin man testifies to this.

Mousterian methods of working constitute in essence a new achievement in knapping. The creation of these methods was a step forward in 'the economy of labour used and then economy in material'.[4] The laborious task of bifacial dressing was replaced by striking off a large prepared flake, which, it is true, then required retouch, but it was a completely different object with fine edge and point thanks to its narrow section. Bifacial dressing could produce one or two tools of hand-axe type from one flint nodule; the new technique allowed you to make as many points and scrapers, as flakes or leaf-shaped flakes you could strike off the nodule.

Baden-Powell, who carried out experiments over the course of several years on working stone, demonstrated some aspects of the technique of flaking which have been confirmed by our own work. In his tests he used pebbles 12–15 cm long. He clove the pebble into two halves, so that he got two cores, each with one side flat (the broken surface) and one with the bulge of the original pebble. The flat side formed the striking platform with flakes being struck off all round the edge. The first flake struck from the core had cortex over its back; the second flake had two surfaces divided by an arris, one being covered by cortex, the other part of the scar of the first flake. The third flake was struck off on the edge of the core between the scars from the first two flakes. It had two or even three scar arrises on it like a leaf-shaped blade, but no cortex.

Baden-Powell's blow on the very edge of the platform yielded a very thick flake. The angle of declension of the platform which was turned towards the operator was

[1] A. Vayson, *L'Anthropologie*, 30 (1920), pp. 441–90.
[2] V. Commont, *L'Anthropologie*, 19 (1908), pp. 527–72.
[3] M. Z. Panichkina, *Materials and Researches on the Archaeology of the U.S.S.R.*, 39 (1953), p. 31.
[4] G. A. Bonch-Osmolovsky, *Chelovek*, 2–4 (1928), p. 182. The same can hardly be said of contemporary Levallois technique which was very extravagant of material. T.

45° off horizontal. The angle of the blow varied from 80° to 140°. Before selecting a striking point the overhang on the core's edge and sharp angles formed by the previous blow had to be struck off. The flaking was done without resting the core on a hard support (anvil), just as in flaking hand-axes (fig. 4. 2).

Percussion dressing arising in its simplest form in pre-Chellean times played a basic part in lower palaeolithic times. Later it was used in the initial stage in preparing the cores from nodules in upper palaeolithic and mesolithic times, in making the rough-outs for axes in neolithic times, and also in a different kinds of touching-up, which required a technique of blows.

By way of example of the prolonged use of the most simple methods of working stone we may cite the settlement of the Tripolye culture excavated by T. S. Passek at Polivanov Yar. This illustrates how the development of technique enriched society with new methods of work in which old methods frequently were applied where necessary. The nearby exposures of flint gave rise to a workshop on the site for primary working, as well as for the manufacture of objects.

The inventory of half-finished and completed items found in the workshop area is rather large, and so we limit ourselves to basic objects:

(1) Nodules of grey flint 4–5 hg in weight, partly or quite freed from cortex.
(2) Cylindrical cores of various sizes with scars of blades removed.
(3) Unworked blades.
(4) Worked blades (end-scrapers, awls, reamers, reaping knives, blades of composite sickles, dart and arrowheads and so on).
(5) Striker-stone and pestles.
(6) Flint retouchers of various forms.
(7) Rough-outs for adzes and axes with or without grinding; fragments of rough-outs broken in dressing.
(8) Ground axes and adzes.
(9) Axe and adze sharpeners.
(10) Sharpener slabs for bone tools.
(11) Mortars for pounding hard materials, and so on.

Many of the tools mentioned showed signs of long use.

The flint nodules after extraction from their original deposit were subjected to preliminary flaking to remove the cortex, which has a spongy structure and contains crystalline impurities that sometimes penetrate the flint below. This was roughly flaked off by blows with a heavy striker-stone leaving as a nucleus the preliminary stage of a working core. After this the quality of the material and the possibility of further work could be assessed.

Rolled river pebbles of a different rock were not employed as striker-stones at this site, but instead, flint cores which had already been used for flaking. As

evidence of this were the traces of blows on the surface of cores, forming a starred pattern due to the intersection of numerous cracks. The cores used as striker-stones had differing shapes: oblong, circular and discoidal. The oblong ones were commonly used at both ends, the circular ones over all or most of the surface, whilst the discoidal ones remained unused on their edges where they had been held, and rubbed or polished by the fingers. Thus the cores from this site had been worked themselves by other cores. The patches of starring on some of the oblong cores were quite uneven, with projections and angles, crushed or even destroyed, which must be the result not of blows but of pushing or pressure. Such traces are very similar to those on the edges of the side pressure areas on cores from the upper palaeolithic site of Timonovka, regarded by us as retouchers (fig. 5.1–2).

Certain of the medium and larger strikers retained traces of another kind on their worn surfaces, where the rough starring characteristic of strikers had been rubbed and smoothed. So it may be assumed that these were pestles for grinding and pulverizing some kind of hard matter, possibly an additive in pot-making. Some of the larger examples had been used as crushers.

Consequently at Polivanov Yar we can regard it as established that cores were extensively used as manufacturing tools. Very similar facts were observed at Luka Vrublevetskaya.

Besides core retouchers, Polivanov gave us a large number of retouchers for use in fine pressure work on blades. These tools are large narrow flakes with sharp or blunt ends. Bifacially worked retouchers shaped like spearheads were also found, which possibly actually were broken spearheads re-used as retouchers.

The use of cores for pressure and strike retouch was evidently more or less characteristic of the whole Stone Age. In the northern forest zone of the Soviet Union, at points very isolated from the southern late neolithic Tripolye culture, one sees just such a simple technique of primary working of flint tools with its rather palaeolithic character.

Krizhevsky found evidence of a workshop at Gorodishchenskaya Mountain near Rzhev. Among his material we recognized cores with all the signs of use as retouchers (fig. 5.3, 4). They have inclined striking platforms on the rim of which is clearly visible a dull, rough-to-the-touch part produced by light blows and pressure on flint. On some cores this rim has a rough almost starry structure (fig. 5.4). In the use of these retouchers blows evidently preponderated over pressure. With these were found proper striker-stones, one of which is interesting in that traces of use show themselves in two ways (fig. 5.5). It is a massive flake of irregular shape with a patch of cortex on its surface. Its edge (AB) has been battered and blunted by blows. On the convex side and visible even to the naked eye is a second patch of scars from lighter sliding blows (C). These scars were caused as the striker-stone after each blow fell away, knocking its bulgy part against the object being worked. So before us was an interesting document revealing in great detail the technique of knapping stone, and confirming that a rough starred surface is the functional sign of a striker-stone.

b. Retouch by direct blows, with an intermediary, and counter retouch

The working of tools in flint and similar rocks passed through various stages of development. From an original shattering of a pebble or nodule with the object of getting fragments with sharp edges, gradually the objective altered to dressing the stone into the shape of a Chellean hand-axe. The number of necessary blows in making these increased. The transition to retouch meant essentially the creation of a new finer method of shaping tools, requiring many light and more frequent blows to remove small parts of the surface of the tool being made.

Consequently percussion retouch is one of the methods of secondary working of stone tools with a striker-stone, a more developed kind of dressing. Yet it is essentially different from pecking, which is an even more developed, finer form of dressing.

Flake retouch can be applied only in making tools of flinty rocks and then only on the edge, while pecking was employed predominantly for secondary work on granular rocks, and could be used at any point on the worked object's surface. The latter also differs in the direction of the blows which fall at right-angles to the worked surface. In flake retouch the striker-stone will fall at all angles from 0° to 90°, but always on the edge of the object worked.

Working by retouch arose very early, for obviously it was already in use in the lower palaeolithic period. At all events by Acheulian times retouch was already a mature method of stone-working. The hand-axes of Acheulian type found at Satani-Dar (Armenia) by Zamyatnin and Panichkina have retouched edges, and the tools of Pekin man bear numerous traces of retouch.

This method of completing work on stone tools was extensively used in the later phases of the Stone Age, as it was a simple way of touching-up a rough-out before grinding, or blunting a sharp edge, or in other operations.

In later times retouch was commonly done not with a single striker but with an intermediary, such as a stone or bone rod. Retouch with an intermediary has some advantage over simple retouch; a blow with a striker-stone on a flint does not always remove the precisely desired part of the struck surface, for the working part of this tool has a large surface. An intermediary with a narrow point made it possible to flake off a small part of the worked object at a more specific point.

We understand the use of an intermediary in stone-working only from ethnographic parallels, in particular from the evidence collected by Holmes in America and several other writers. The object has still not been identified in the archaeological material, although its existence in neolithic times is hardly open to doubt.

There is some reason to suppose that retouch with an intermediary was never widely employed in the Stone Age. Stone, wood or bone which could have been used as intermediaries were not sufficiently resilient. A wooden stick quickly splinters and becomes unserviceable. A stone intermediary also loses its shape at the end from the blows; moreover, it is very difficult to make and frequently breaks. A bone intermediary made from a long bone is the best of the three, but it is split by blows owing to its lamellar structure.

In counter retouch a wooden baton is used to strike the object being worked, which knocks its edge against a stone upon which it is resting, and so a tiny fragment of the object flies off. Counter retouch requires little physical force, as apposed to pressure work, and produces a steep retouch comparatively quickly on the edge of the blade or flake. It can be used to make a notch, or take off an angle or projection or a large part of the object being worked or trimmed.

We know about this method from ethnographic evidence. The effectiveness of counter retouch, as well as of retouch with an intermediary, has been proved by many archaeologists, including ourselves, but convincing traces on the so-called bone anvils, that really show use in counter retouch, are still not known to us. Bone anvils with traces of use usually were pressure retouchers or rests and supports in percussion retouch. Experiment has shown that successful counter retouch can be done with a stone anvil, such as a pebble.

Counter retouch had a snag in that it commonly gave rise to accidental, unforeseeable flaking, chipping and cracking. So it could not have been used in all forms of fine retouch, especially in the manufacture of shaped objects like barbed neolithic arrows or flint sculptures.

c. Flaking by pressure

Amongst methods of working stone the flaking of blades off prismatic cores can be regarded as the least studied. It has long been known to archaeologists that the flaking of prismatic blades was done not by blows but by pressure. However, the details have remained uncertain in spite of the fact that many students have been interested in blade-making.

The development of blade flaking constitutes a crucial point in the history of stone-working, for without it ancient technique would have been in a cul-de-sac. Its study is made difficult by the fact that blade flaking from

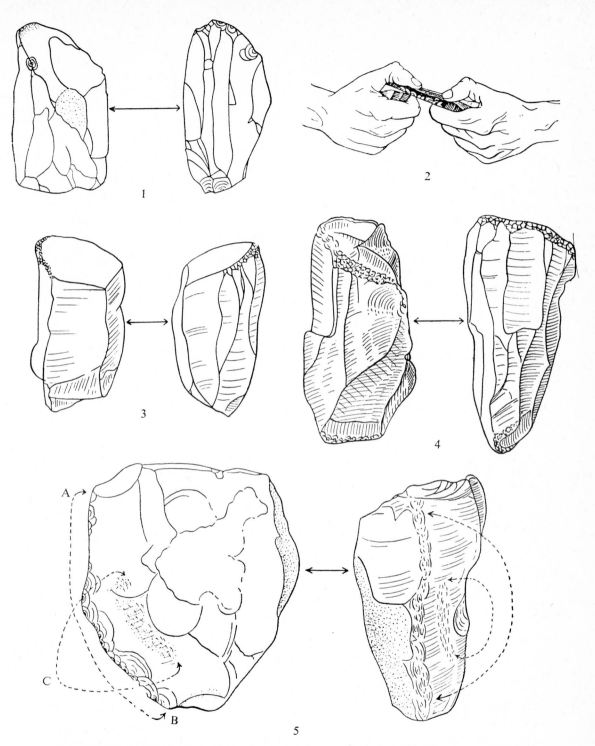

5 1 *upper palaeolithic core from Timonovka re-used as retoucher;* 2 *its method of use reconstructed;* 3 *and* 4 *neolithic cores re-used as retouchers from Gorodishchenskaya Mountain;* 5 *neolithic striker from the same site* (**AB**, *the keel of the stone used for striking;* C, *scratches and abrasions on convex side of stone due to glancing blows*).

cores in practice is no easy thing to do. Eloquent of this, at least, is that so far no archaeologist has been able to produce flint blades the practical way.

For this reason the theoretical side of the technique of pressure flaking lacks practical demonstration. Even now it is not fully understood how from an isotropic material with conchoidal fracture one could obtain prismatic blades of relatively regular shape, that is with comparatively slight curvature. Of course, such a flake has a roughly regular geometric form only in transverse section. Its long axis very often has a slight bend, giving it a bow-shape, particularly if it came off a large core, but it has a negligible bulb of percussion, while undulations are trifling or even absent. Sometimes the cores are almost regular, multi-scaled prisms.

The problem of the different methods of mechanical action in working stone has great interest at a theoretical level. We know from the law about the distribution of waves in isotropic bodies (taking fluids as an example) that the frequency of oscillation depends on the nature of the external impulse. A thrown stone falling into water produces numerous concentric waves and even turbulence on the surface, but a stone slowly immersed produces a smooth circular oscillation.

The example in a sense illustrates the contrast between percussion and pressure retouch. Both methods can be produced on glass. A blow on the edge of glass produces a deeply conchoidal scar and the thick flake breaking off will often have a sharp bulb. By pressing with a pressure tool on the edge the resulting scar is much less concave, and flatter, while the detached flake has a thin section. The experiment shows that in pressure the fracture line is comparatively straighter in an isotropic mass. The opposite is the case in a dynamic relationship. However, pressure requires incomparably greater force than percussion, because the power of the blow is magnified by the momentary conversion of potential into kinetic energy.

The technique of blade-making relies on the use of a brief push or impulse. It is quite obvious that blades could not have been obtained by direct blows with a striker-stone, as some students believe.[1] The striking platform on the end of such blades shows this; it is very small, sometimes barely discernible. Traces of blows can never be detected on the core's platform in optical examination of the surface, but careful preparation of this area before the detachment of each blade is at once recognizable. The preparation consisted mainly in removing the projections from its edge, the so-called 'platform fringe', left by the detachment of the previous blade. Preparation of the platform was a necessary

preliminary on the core to provide a resting point for the presser on its edge. The pressure point had to be as close as possible to the very edge and, when a platform for one reason or another did not offer serviceable support for the presser on its edge, it was improved by detaching a horizontal flake, that is partially removed. This was done mainly by pressure but also by percussion. Much depended on the core's condition. If its side was stepped by the fracture of unsuccessful (incomplete) blades, a large flake, thick in section, was struck off. Obviously this reduced the size of a core and the length of the blades. The pressure method of trimming the platform was designed to furnish the necessary angle on which to rest the presser.

The technique of preparing a core from a nodule or pebble, as well as the different methods of trimming it, have been more or less worked out by archaeologists. A fair amount of work has been done on blade-making, beginning with J. Evans and L. Capitan and going on up to recent times (F. Bordes, L. Coutier, A. Barnes and others).

It is, however, the ethnographic evidence that provides the most important and interesting material. Although it is true that the older ethnographers were little interested in problems of stone-working among backward tribes, yet whatever kind of evidence there is has been collected and extensively used by archaeologists.

Amongst the earliest information of this kind that we can use is the short description of making obsidian blades by pressure amongst the Mexican Indians left us by the Spanish Franciscan friar, Juan de Torquemada, in 1615.[2] This description was first translated from Spanish by Taylor, and, as later cited by Evans, has become very familiar to ethnographers and archaeologists.

According to Torquemada the Indians worked in a sitting position. The core was held between the feet, and a short pole with cross-piece at the top and pointed end at the bottom was rested on the edge of the core. By a quick push on the instrument with the chest and both hands the Indian detached a blade of the full height of the core. Torquemada wrote: 'As a result flakes fly off like two-edged knives and as regular in shape as if they had been cut off a turnip with a sharp knife or forged in cast-iron. . . . By this method the operator in a short space of time can make more than a score of knives'[3] (fig. 6.1).

Such a fleeting description left many important details unexplained which were not elucidated by a further description of similar work by Hernandez in 1651. He

---

[1] P. P. Efimenko in his *Prehistoric Society* (Kiev, 1935, p. 298) wrote that blades were detached 'by means of a hard blow with a hammerstone .
[2] J. de Torquemada, *Monarquía Indiana* (Seville, 1615).
[3] J. Evans, *The Ancient Stone Implements of Gt. Britain*, 2nd Edition (London, 1897) pp. 23–24. The last line is not quoted in Evans. T.

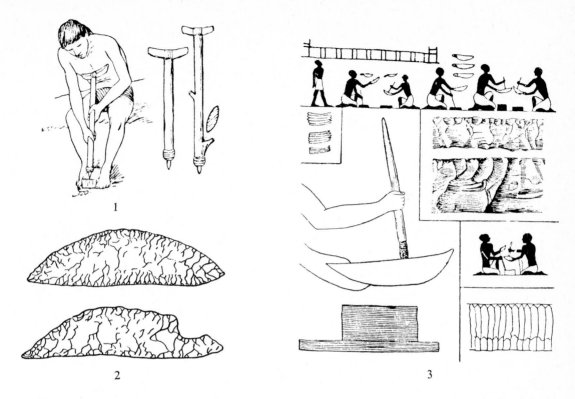

6 1 *Method of pressing-off blades used among the American Indians (after Holmes); 2 ancient Egyptian knives; 3 retouching of flint knives as illustrated in the tomb of Pharaoh Amen of the twelfth dynasty (after Barnes).*

made a valuable addition, which was that the Indians worked on the obsidian core with a hard semi-precious stone before they went to work with a wooden presser.[1] He himself thought that they used the hard stone to take the sharp angles off the platform and edge before exerting pressure. Coutier and Barnes considered that in addition the Indians scratched the platform with the stone to make its surface rough, so that the tip of the pressing implement should not slip and break away from the pressure point.[2]

This type of record and other facts have given rise to the view that it was necessary to give the core preparatory abrasion. Coutier carried out tests on blade-making from obsidian cores by percussion, using a short wooden intermediary and a wooden mallet made of hard wood. Barnes and other workers have made blades from glass using an intermediary and a wooden mallet,[3] but detailed accounts of this have not been published. There

are no documented accounts about tests on flint, which is appreciably harder to work than obsidian or glass.

A rough surface on the striking, or rather pressure platform, of a core was obtained in some places by retaining the cortex of the obsidian nodule, which is of granular texture. Such cores have been found not only in Mexico but in mesolithic and neolithic sites in the islands of Melos and Crete and elsewhere in the Mediterranean. Flint cores with cortex pressure areas also occur in this period in northern Europe, India and south Asia. Nevertheless cores with roughening by abrasion or 'crusty patches' of cortex are uncommon. The most widespread method of preventing the presser from slipping was to flake the platform, which made the edge slightly concave, due to the conchoidal fracture of flint, obsidian and similar rocks.

Rather fuller ethnographic information comes from the second half of the nineteenth century in a description

---

[1] A. Cabrol and L. Coutier, *Bulletin de la Société Préhistorique Francaise* (1932).
[2] A. Barnes, *Proceedings of the Prehistoric Society*, 13 (1947), 101.
[3] ibid., p. 104.

by G. Sellers, based on the observations of G. Catlin, the artist who lived several years with the North American Indians.[1]

He wrote: 'The instrument used for this is a kind of tube or rod 2–3 in in diameter and of varying length from 30 in to 4 ft depending on need. The stick was fitted with a bone or antler tip in its working end, lashed on with sinew or raw skin to prevent the stick from splitting.'

The core of obsidian or chert, according to Sellers, was set on hard ground and gripped between the operator's feet. If the work was done sitting the presser was short, if standing longer.

Sometimes the core was gripped between two strips of wood as in a vice. The ends of the wooden blocks were bound strongly together by rope or rawhide. The craftsman stood with both feet on the blocks, and pressed with his tool on the unyielding core in short powerful movements with the full weight of his body, the top of the tool held against his chest. The bone or antler point of the presser rested on the core's platform, which had previously been trimmed to a right angle so as to prevent the tool slipping. Usually at the pressure point the core's edge was slightly raised by percussion or pressure trimming of its platform, as has been described. As a point for the tool walrus tusk from the extreme north was especially valued.

Among the tribes whose life was described by Catlin there was a division of work in the manufacture of prismatic blades. One group of people specialized in obtaining the raw material, nodules of obsidian or chert; others prepared the cores by removing the cortex and making the pressure platforms; while some were engaged in flaking the blades. In ancient Mexico the preparation of different kinds of blade tools by retouch was sometimes done by different craftsmen. Sellers, again basing his information on Catlin, described another type of presser made from the stem of a young sapling. A tree with two low branches was selected, one near the root, the other higher up on the opposite side. The branches were chopped off to leave short stumps. To the upper one a heavy stone was attached to increase the force of the pressure. As for the second stump, the lower one, it was struck with a heavy club. The blow would be given by the craftsman's assistant, who stood opposite, if his own efforts had not successfully detached a blade, and the blow was accompanied by a short hard push on the presser. In this way by the action of two men blades 10–12 in long could be detached.

According to Marehead some Californian Indians made blades by blows of a mallet on a short presser, or, more strictly, an intermediary.[2]

Catlin described a similar method among the Apache Indians using the tooth of a sperm-whale and a mallet, the tooth acting as an intermediary. The whole operation was done in the hands without resting the core on a hard body; the operator held the core and intermediary in the left hand and the mallet in the right. Sometimes the work was done by two craftsmen; one held the core in his left hand and the intermediary in his right, while the second delivered the blows with the mallet. The work was carried out to the accompaniment of chanting.

We must leave the ethnographic evidence. The facts described form the basis of present views on the sort of practices employed in blade-making.

Sometimes in the western literature stone pressers have been recorded. For example Müller identified several late flint tools with traces of use as pressers or retouchers.[3] G. de Mortillet, referring to pressers, put them in the category of schist pebbles, which in reality can only be retouchers. Other examples could be given, but the facts adduced by the authors are casual ones without clear classification; commonly retouchers or strikers are confused with pressers.

Before turning to the results of our laboratory experiments we are bound to confess that the archaeological material does not wholly square with the impressions derived from ethnographic sources. Amongst innumerable bone objects of different types from the palaeolithic and neolithic periods we have not been able to identify any that could have served as pressers. Bone retouchers are found already in Mousterian levels, but pressers are virtually unknown to us.

On late neolithic sites archaeologists have found either the components of retouchers or complete ones. A bone tool from Brittany can be referred to this class of retouchers, found in the eneolithic site of Er-Yoh on the island of Houat, close to the megalithic area of Morbihan.[4] Its handle was made of a long bone of a large animal with the epiphysis cut away, and set into it was a thick bone plate (fig. 11.3). The overall length of the tool was about 28–30 cm. The authors record that the plate was damaged from pressure on hard objects with a sharp edge. The handle was polished from friction against soft matter, evidently the skin of the hand. Vayson de Pradenne and Breuil identified it as a retoucher for working stone arrowheads, comparing it with Eskimo retouchers.

Tools of deer antler found in later neolithic graves in

---

[1] G. E. Sellers, *Annual Report of the Smithsonian Institute*, 1 (1885), pp. 871–91.
[2] W. Marehead, *The Stone Age in North America* (London, 1911), I, p. 74.
[3] S. Müller, *Nouveaux types d'Objects de l'Age de Pierre* (Copenhagen, 1889), p. 158, fig. 70.
[4] M. and S. Péquart, *L'Anthropologie*, 45 (1935), pp. 362–73.

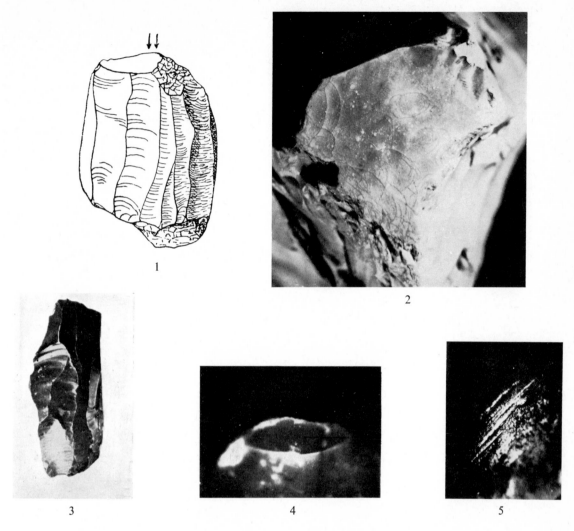

7 *1 and 2 Mesolithic core from Shan-Koba (1 general view; 2 pressure platform with cracks from exertions of the presser enlarged 3 ×); 3–5 upper palaeolithic core from Kostenki IV (3 general view); 4 and 5 enlargements of the edge crack and a hole and scratches on the platform.*

the Angar, Lena and Selenga areas, shaped like rods 9–12·5 cm long, should also be considered as retouchers for pressure retouch, but not as pressers for blade-making.[1]

Cores have been submitted to microscopic examination, mainly from Kostenki I and IV, Timonovka and Shan-Koba, which have shown interesting traces on their platforms. These consisted of holes, that is very small depressions or hollows, as well as cracks and scratches, always grouped around the edge of the platform and only in rare cases extending into the centre. It must be noted that holes were always combined in one area with cracks or scratches; single cracks and scratches without holes did not occur.

This indicated that the holes were traces of pressure on the platform left by the working end of the presser. The cracks were arc-shaped, semi-circular and sometimes closed up (irregular circles), if the point of pressure

---

[1] A. P. Okladnikov, *Materials and Researches on the Archaeology of the U.S.S.R.*, 43 (1955), pp. 16–17.

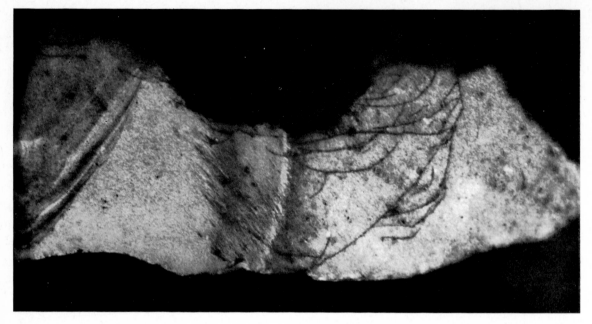

8 *Micro-photograph of the pressure area on an upper palaeolithic blade platform (cracks, holes and scratches) from Kostenki I.*

had been further back from the platform's edge. These cracks were produced if pressure was insufficient to consummate the act of flaking or if the pressure point had been badly chosen.

As for the scratches, sometimes single but usually in a group or whole batch, these were caused by the presser when its working tip tore off the pressure area and slipped off the platform. Not one but usually several scratches led away from a hole. This may be explained by the end of the flint presser crumbling when it was damaged by the sharp angles of the platform (fig. 7.5).

The platforms of several cores from Shan-Koba were exceptionally revealing in their combinations of holes and cracks. There was no trace of the action of fire over the whole area covered by cracks, which is recognizable by its net pattern. In this case all the cracks were disposed around the edge and were arc-shaped, open towards the edge. The lip was smothered by innumerable projecting splinters caused by repeated unsuccessful attempts with the presser. Splintering is a normal occurrence on almost all cores, but what is noteworthy is the persistence of the craftsman, who after one unsuccessful attempt to detach the flake, repeated it numerous times, still without result. When the edge was splintered and broken he moved the end of the presser back and exerted it several times in the centre, before he finally threw the core away. The pressure traces in the centre of the platform are not arc-shaped but irregular rings (fig. 7.1, 2).

During preliminary observations doubts arose as to whether these traces might be accidental, due to fire or some other factor, and even that all the holes, scratches and cracks were the result of roughening of the surface, as was sometimes done in Mexico. It was obvious that these marks owed their origin to human action carried out not with a bone, still less a wooden, presser, but with an instrument that could not have been less hard than the material itself, i.e. flint.

The 10-degree hardness scale of Mohs used in science is based on the principle of scratching, a harder mineral scratching a softer one. In practice, naturally, minerals of equal hardness will produce marks by scratching on each other, but this requires a good deal of force when hard bodies are involved. We have very often made a mark with flint on flint which was visible under a magnifying glass.

After establishing that the traces on the cores had been produced by a very hard presser we turned our attention to the study of the platforms on the blades themselves. For this a series of blades was selected from Kostenki I retaining their platforms just as they were after leaving the core. They had neither traces of retouch nor use on them, so the evidence of detachment was unaltered. With a binocular microscope observations were made at a magnification of $65 \times$, the pressure platforms being treated with a violet colorizer to bring out the traces and intensify contrasts in the marks observed.

Examination of the pressure platforms revealed four

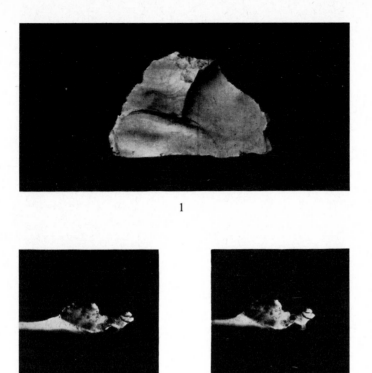

1

2

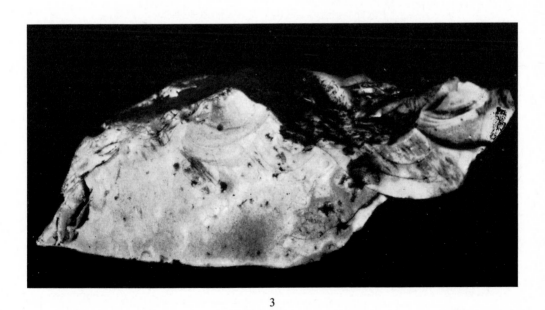

3

9 1 *Upper palaeolithic blade fragment from Kostenki I; 2 stereo-photographs of it; 3 micro-photograph of pressure platform (holes, scratches and cracks).*

51

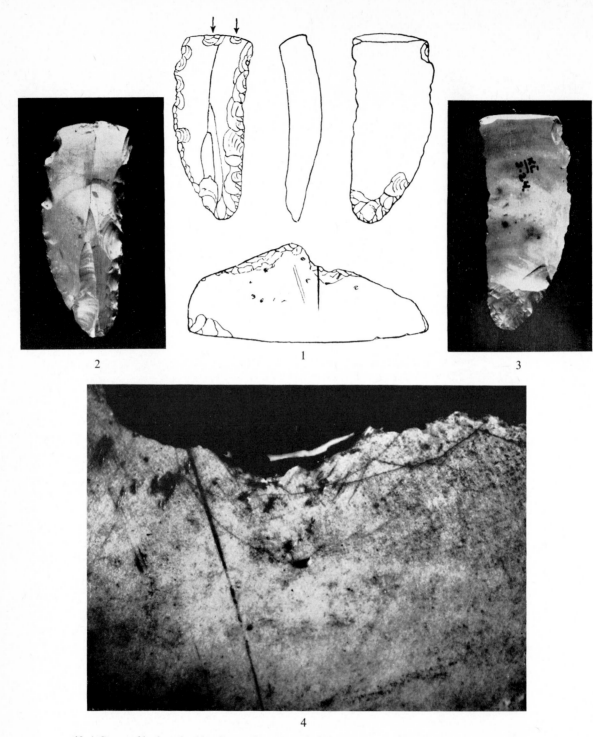

10 1 *Stump of broken shouldered point from Kostenki I showing attempts to use it as core; 2 and 3 both faces; 4 micro-photograph of part of the pressure platform with traces left by the presser (scratches, holes and cracks).*

kinds of trace: scratches, holes, cracks and crushing on the rim. The scratches crossed the narrow platform diagonally (from right to left), the blade held upright as it was in the moment of flaking, i.e. with dorsal side away from the operator. These scratches start wide and become narrow, indicating like an arrow the direction of the presser's movement in the hands of the operator. Their depth is evidence not only of the use of flint as a presser, but also of the great force applied; while their diagonal direction (right to left) shows that the man worked with one hand, the right one.

The holes and cracks around them indicated the number of exertions with the presser on the platform. In some cases the number of holes and cracks was large, up to several dozen, showing that the operator had had to expend no little effort before successfully detaching the blade. The crushing (splintering) on the outer edge of the platform (dorsal) confirmed this. There were no marks of retouch or use whatever on the blade, which was fresh flaked with sharp razor-like edges without a single scar, and yet the pressure platform was crumpled on one side, and covered with minute cracks and ridges. The presence of holes, scratches, cracks and crushing testifies to the fact that the operator using the core repeatedly exerted pressure before producing a successful detachment, in order to find a favourable spot to apply his strength. Only in rare instances did he detach a blade at the first exertion.

The four categories of traces enumerated occurred in various combinations. Sometimes scratches and cracks preponderated, sometimes holes and cracks; rarely was there only one type. Much depended on the shape of the platform and its angle of declension. Scratches were more numerous on platforms whose angle of declension did not allow use of the full force of the presser, because it broke away and slipped off. The platform of a blade from Kostenki I can serve as an example. Holes preponderated where the edge rises, so preventing the presser from breaking away or slipping. We can see such an example on a broad blade from Kostenki I (fig. 9.2, 3), recalling a Mousterian flake, but produced by pressure instead of percussion. Here there are deep holes with little cracks, or without them, but very slight trace of the presser breaking away.

One can illustrate the combination of the two types of platform on one blade (fig. 8). Here on one half we see scratches with slight, almost unnoticeable holes, and on the other more marked holes enclosed by cracks. On this large irregular blade, in the flaking of which a lot of time had been spent, we have, in fact, two platforms at different angles to each other. Blades are found on whose pressure areas there are neither scratches, holes nor even cracks, or albeit very few. Such blades were detached from the core by almost first or second exertion of the presser.

Cases may be noted where attempts were made to convert fragments of tools into cores. For example on a fragment of shouldered point from Kostenki I attempts had been made to detach blades, but the dried-out flint would not allow it (fig. 10.1–3). Traces of pressure from a flint presser (holes, scratches and cracks) are visible on the tang, as well as facets on the dorsal side.

How do we reconcile the results of microscopic analysis with the general view of pressure flaking as having been done with bone tools? Perhaps there were two basic operations in the production of blades: first work with a stone presser on the platform, and then the final detachment with a bone tool. But such a conclusion does not tally with the sum of the evidence.

At Kostenki I the primary working of the flint had not been carried out on the site. The flint was obtained outside in a deposit where the blade-making was done, and the blades were taken as rough-outs to the settlements. There the blades underwent secondary treatment according to need, that is they were shaped into tools by retouch. The absence from the site of cores (apart from certain uncharacteristic examples), strikers and flint retouchers shows this. For the latter were substituted slate and bone retouchers.

The rare examples of flint retouchers found on this site bore all the signs of use in working flint tools: large patches of starred surface and polished areas (from friction against the skin of the hand), numerous cracks and scratches, and traces of splintering from strong pressure. These retouchers were probably used to some extent as pressers. Thanks to their rough surface they would not have slipped in pressure on the core, but would have held firm on its edge. Their circular or oval shape lent itself to free pressure with the hand for the strong physical effort demanded in touching up platforms (fig. 11.1).

In blade flaking the core did not rest on a stone support, for the lower, and usually conical part, of cores does not show traces of crushing and splintering, nor signs of pressing on a very hard object. Support for the core was evidently supplied by wood or bone which would leave no trace.

An essential feature in blade flaking was the shape of the core's base. The direction of the force of the presser from above could not coincide with the resistance from the rest below. If the base was flat, like the platform, the flaking line (fracture line) would not follow the desired direction, and as a result the core could shatter or shed a short flake. When a core was originally cylindrical the craftsman deliberately made its base oblique, that is conical or chisel-shaped. The blade came off with its lower end slightly curved underneath, and in a good core the blade's central arris and its side edge met in one point at the base.

This description of the external aspect of the operation

cannot re-create the work as a whole. In blade flaking critical dynamic and kinematic factors arise, which could only be worked out by prolonged experiments, for they leave no evidence in the traces.

The shapes and dimensions of the pressers undoubtedly depended on the core size. Neolithic cores from Siberia, commonly of chalcedony or agate pebbles the size of a walnut, would require small pressers. There are grounds for supposing that pressers in blade flaking were composite tools consisting of a bone handle and stone point.

Microscopic study of pressure areas on cores and blades has introduced serious corrections into our picture of the technique of blade-making. However, the problems cannot be regarded as conclusively settled until prismatic flint blades have been actually made in tests in the laboratory.

Upper palaeolithic flint blades were only rough-outs from which end-scrapers, burins, whittling and meat knives, needles, drills, awls, lanceheads and other tools were made by pressure retouch. In mesolithic times they were divided into triangular or trapeze-shaped segments for insertion into composite knives, spears, harpoons and arrowheads, as we know from examples in southern Europe. Mesolithic hunters of the Swideriam culture of eastern Europe made small leaf-shaped arrowheads out of blades, but they also used them for other everyday purposes. Blades were rarely used in the Stone Age without retouch, but composite neolithic knives, daggers and spearheads are known whose edges were made from micro-blades struck from small cores and mounted unretouched. Characteristic examples of such are the insertions in the tools of the Lake Baikal area, and a dagger from Olen island (Lake Onega). The use of almost whole blades for insertion can be explained by the peculiarities of flaking micro-blades from miniature cores. On micro-blades the conchoidal fracture is barely detectable, as the blades came off as almost straight

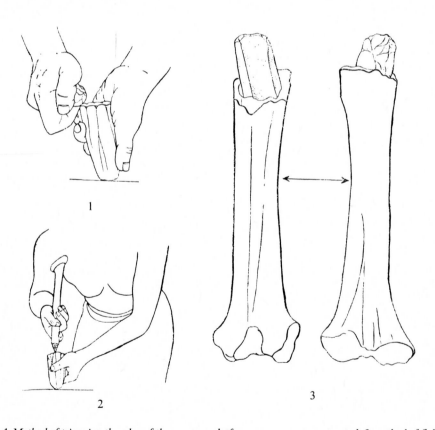

11 1 *Method of trimming the edge of the pressure platform on a core reconstructed; 2 method of flaking off prismatic blades from a core with a flint-tipped presser reconstructed; 3 retoucher with bone point from neolithic site at Er-Yoh (Brittany).*

geometrically regular prisms with thin razor-like edges which could be mounted in a groove in bone almost without trimming or retouch. In upper palaeolithic times such composite objects are rare, but we know of them from a find at Talitsky on the River Chusov and in Amvrosievka.

An intermediate position between percussion and pressure flaking in working flint is the method known as the burin blow. This name is applied to the method of making burins. It consists in flaking part off a blade edge vertically, commonly by a blow, as shown in medial burins and the steep scar on many angle-burins which are splinter-like, although many angle-burins were also made by means of pressure flaking.

However, a burin blow was not used only in making the tools whose name it bears, for it was very often employed instead of steep blunting retouch on blades of upper palaeolithic knives to provide a place to hold. In the same period this method of pressure flaking was used also as a means of obtaining micro-blades. The peculiarity of this method of work is that, instead of using a nodule or pebble as a core, a broad but short prismatic blade or a fragment of a large blade was split lengthways into two or three pieces. We can see this use of burin spalling to get micro-blades in the large series of cores, rough-outs and objects in the upper palaeolithic site of Kostenki IV,[1] where the micro-blades have a high back and are thick in section.

In Kostenki IV small sharp needles (awls) and tiny knives (lancets) were made from these micro-blades by fine pressure retouch to remove the sharp edge on one side, probably to provide a rest for the index finger. On some of the edges there were small notches. Other details of the secondary working of micro-blades were of interest.

In addition to the ordinary run of tools, the manufacture in Kostenki IV of these minute flint implements, which are counted by hundreds, indicates some tendency towards specialization whose character is still not understood.

d. Broad pressure retouch and the problem of the so-called Solutrean technique

The technique of pressure retouch, as is well known, arose in a rudimentary form in Mousterian times, shown by finely worked points, scrapers and other tools, as well as by bone retouchers with traces of pressure on their edges. Even among the flint tools from St Acheul of the Acheulian period some of the simplest specimens made on flakes show evidence of slight pressure retouch on their edge.[2]

In widening the scope of its application man did not confine the use of pressure to merely trimming and strengthening the fine delicate flint blades into the tools, which came into general use in upper palaeolithic times with the adoption of narrow blades for rough-outs. He went further and tried to use this technique for changing the form of flints to give the object an altered shape. In this way arose the so-called Solutrean retouch. The peculiarity of this is that it was a method of pressure on the edge of the flint rough-out, used by upper palaeolithic man, not just to remove tiny flakes and alter the angle of the point and shape of the blade, but also to take off large and relatively thin flakes from the surface of the rough-out. In other words it increased the plastic possibilities of stone working. By this means the irregular rough-out could be given a desired thickness at any point, made flatter, the end sharpened; the curve taken out of the top, edge or base; this or that kind of notch made; a handle, tang or shoulders formed, and so on. This was particularly important in making spear- or dart-heads, as well as double-edged knives. With all their advantages blades had one obvious snag; as a rule they were curved along their long section and so were more or less bow-shaped in profile (fig. 12.1–3). In order to get a straight tool the blade had to be basically transformed by removing a good part of it with flat pressure retouch.

To make a spearhead the blade had to be whittled down either at one or both ends from the ventral face, as this was the inner side of the chord made by the blade (fig. 12.4–6). On the top surface retouch was applied just to sharpen up the end.

Consequently from large and medium blades one could get straight tools only by shortening and retouch. Small blades detached from small cores and used in palaeolithic times for insertions in composite tools were an exception and very often had a straight axis. The object of bifacial work therefore was mainly to produce straight tools. Naturally this quality was particularly needed in projectile heads and certain types of knife. So we can understand why the extensive use of arrowheads and flint knives in neolithic times required the perfection of bifacial pressure retouch.

It was not just when projectile heads and knives had to be made from curved blades that bifacial pressure retouch was needed. Both in palaeolithic and neolithic times the character of the raw material might require its use. If tabular flint was employed, which prevented the use of a large core (because veins of flint are often very thin, uneven and twisted, with cretaceous or lime crust on both sides), no other course was possible except the use of bifacial retouch. The material from the lower

---

[1] A. N. Rogachev, *Materials and Researches on the Archaeology of the U.S.S.R.*, 43 (1955), p. 46.
[2] F. Bordes and P. Fitte, *L'Anthropologie*, 57 (1954), pp. 1–44, pl. v–xiii.

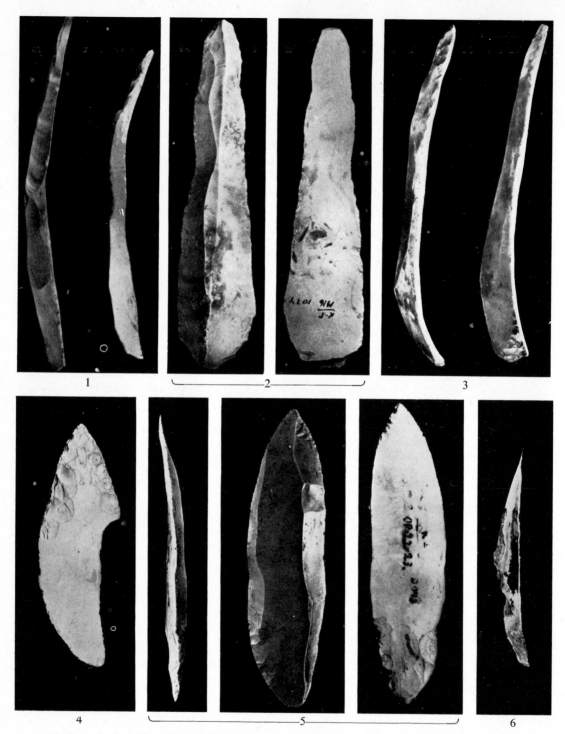

12 *Examples from Kostenki I that illustrate how the bow-shaped profile of prismatic blades gave rise to Solutrean retouch: 1–3 views of blades in profile and from front and back; 4–6 blades worked by Solutrean retouch either leaf-shaped (5) or shouldered (4 and 6) seen facially and in profile.*

layer of Kostenki I may serve as an example of the unavoidable use of this on nearly all the tools; the coloured tabular flint used at this time on the site was of local origin and had very cramping characteristics. Preparation of a knife from such flint could not be done without bifacial working, as the cortex had first to be removed from both faces of the block, which was done by pressure retouch. Due to the adoption of this technique and the quality of the material the best specimens of tools from the lower layer of Kostenki I rival neolithic ones, while at the same time the less successful examples are pretty rough, recalling archaic types of middle palaeolithic times made by bifacial percussion work.

In making the rare examples of Solutrean points of large size tabular flint was also used. One of these was the broken point found at Kostenki IV in 1937 by A. N. Rogachev, which was 20 cm long, 4–7 cm broad and 1·4 cm thick, carefully retouched so that no remains of cortex were detectable on it. Yet its straight profile and great width indicate that it was made not from a blade but from a piece of tabular flint, as was evidently the case with almost all the large laurel-leaf points of Solutrean type, as well as large neolithic points. Cortex can be seen on the surface of laurel-leaf points found by Okladnikov in the graves of the Serovsk cemetery (neolithic period in the L. Baikal area).

Once started in upper palaeolithic times the technique of broad, flat pressure retouch was not confined to making points and knives. Spearheads of Solutrean type, shouldered points (or knives) of the type of Kostenki I and Avdeevo, and leaf-shaped points of the Telmansk type are rare, but traces of pressure retouch in a less conspicuous form can be seen on flint tools from nearly all the sites. Different kinds of flat retouch trimming (inaccurately called 'snipping') may be seen very often on the back and front of blades, on core platforms and on the surface of blade rough-outs. It will be understood that by the term 'pressure retouch' we mean not only the flat retouch typified by that on Solutrean points, but retouch by pressure found on a variety of objects.

Pressing relatively large, but thin and fine, flakes off a flint surface is a technique that may depend as much on the physico-chemical properties of the material as on the method of work. Flint taken straight out of a chalk deposit contains 1·5 per cent moisture, and this is the most favourable condition for flaking and retouch. A boulder or river pebble that has been exposed to the sun does not respond so well in working. Such material yields short blades and flakes or shatters, and develops cracks that alter the direction in flaking and retouching. The scars on artefacts of dried-out flint have an angular splintery look. The lost plastic properties of dried-out flint can evidently never be fully recovered, but there is some ethnographic evidence that flint, chalcedony and agate pebbles and boulders of other rocks, after prolonged soaking in water or burying in damp earth, become more suitable for flaking and retouch, in contrast to similar pebbles and boulders that have not undergone this preparatory treatment.

Broad pressure retouch has been as little studied as the technique of blade-making. In the ethnographic literature the problem of pressure retouch is hardly mentioned, while researches by archaeologists in this field have been modest and controversial.

From what one learns about pressure retouch in the literature on the Eskimos one may conclude that retouching of stone tools was done with bone retouchers.[1] The latter sometimes had a wooden handle whose broad butt allowed the palm of the hand to exert considerable physical force. The working end of the retoucher was pointed, and sometimes a bear's canine was used as the tip, the point being lashed with thongs or sinews to a wooden handle. The retouching was done by pressing the end of the instrument on the edge of the object. In certain cases, when a much greater force was required than the hands could give, the Eskimo pressed on the butt with his shoulder. As a rule the object being worked stood on a wooden rest, or was held against it.

Of great interest is the wall painting on the tomb of the Pharaoh Amen of the Twelfth Dynasty at Beni Hasan, where the final stages of making flint knives are depicted.[2] In this picture (fig. 6.2, 3) a group of slaves is shown working under an overseer, each holding two objects in his hands and kneeling with the right knee drawn up to his waist, the left on the ground. In one hand he holds a crescentic object and in the other a stick about 50 cm long with a point, and in front of each slave is a kind of anvil. For a long time the picture on the tomb of the Pharaoh Amen was a puzzle, but it is now regarded as a representation of a workshop for flint knives.

The attitudes of the workers and the position of the objects is variable, but they show that the stick with its point on the edge of the worked object was held erect. In the opinion of Barnes the retouching was done not by pressure of the retoucher but by a slight blow or knock of the lower edge of the knife against the wooden anvil, while the bone or antler point of the retoucher was held against its top.[3]

[1] J. Murdoch, *Annual Reports of the Bureau of American Ethnology* (Washington, 1892), pp. 287–88.
[2] F. Griffith, *Beni Hasan* (London, 1896), pt. III, pp. 33–35, pl. vii–viii.
[3] A. Barnes, op. cit., pp. 111–12.

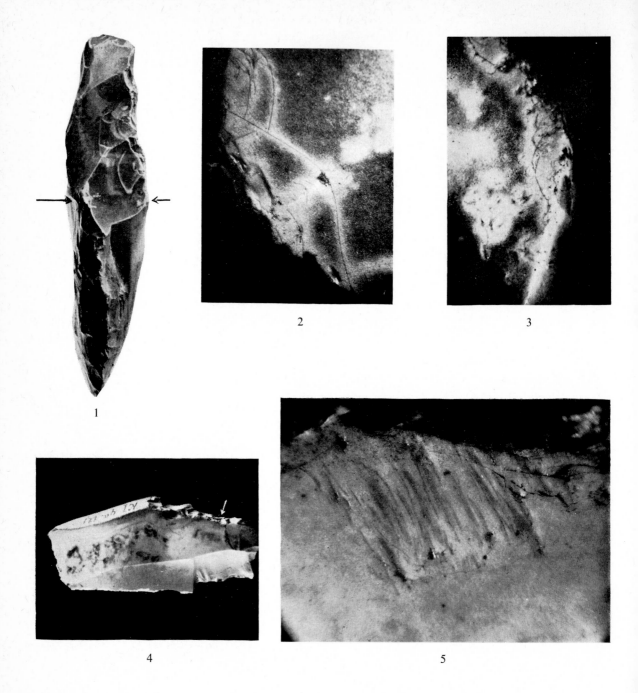

13 *1–3 Axe from Kostenki I (1 side view showing three large facets and, indicated by arrows, traces of work with a flint presser; 2 micro-photograph of left edge showing holes and cracks; 3 micro-photograph of right edge showing grooves and cracks, all intensely patinated); 4 and 5 flint knife from Kostenki I (4 butt end of knife worked by burin blow and steep pressure retouch, indicated by arrow; 5 enlargement of edge of knife showing traces of work by flint presser as holes, diagonal grooves caused by slipping and cracks).*

The inadequacy of our knowledge about the technical details of retouching, which for thousands of years played such an important part in the work of ancient man, is brought home to us by the above account. In fact, this would be counter retouch, but a wooden anvil against which the lower edge of the knife is struck would not detach a flake below, where the bounce effect would be softened. The flake would only come off at the upper edge under the action of the bone point of the retoucher. Wood was only an auxiliary agent in this operation. For one cannot agree with a number of western archaeologists, who seek to confer an important status on wooden tools in the technique of working stone.

For example, Bordes after carrying out a variety of tests in dressing, flaking and retouch, using strikers, retouchers and pressers of wood, concluded that wooden tools had played an important part in all processes of stone-working.[1] Even bearing in mind that he used such solid woods as acaccia, oak and box it is difficult to concede that hard materials, like flint or quartzite, could have been successfully worked with wood. Our own experiments in no way confirm this.

With a very quick and hard blow flint can be split with a wooden mallet, because in this case the effect is produced by the great rapidity of the blow. Even here a positive result is achieved only when a suitable point has been found for the blow. Ordinary slanting retouch can be produced by hard wood working a thin brittle blade edge. It is well known that wooden strikers can be successfully used on such materials as obsidian, glass and metallic slag, which Bordes used in his tests, but as regards blade-making by pressure or broad and steep pressure retouch, these operations cannot be executed on flint with wooden tools. Bordes himself felt obliged to recognize that the conclusions he reached could not have corresponded with historical reality.[2]

In laboratory examination of flint points, daggers and other tools with extensive pressure retouch traces of action by very hard pressers have been identified, which could not be detected elsewhere on the blade. These traces were often situated on the retouched surface and appeared as abrasions caused by the retoucher breaking away, slipping at right-angles to the blade edge and so knocking against the arrises of the facets. Sometimes the abrasions had the appearance of shiny stripes.

Where the actual traces of pressure were visible as dots and cracks (on large objects where the pressure platforms survived) all the marks of work with a flint presser were clearly visible (fig. 13.2, 3). The same may be said about some traces left from steep retouch. They consisted of abrasion or even scratches which

would only have been made by a stone retoucher (fig. 13.4, 5).

The instruments for pressure retouch must have been very varied both in material and shape. Broad or narrow retouchers of long bones, ivory or antler were used for light work, as well as slate and flint retouchers (figs. 14 and 15). Many types of flint retouchers were employed for penetrating retouch; notches, steep edge-facets and edge-toothing were made with these by working out the shape required.[3]

As is well known, west European archaeologists attach a special significance to the term 'Solutrean retouch', defining by this method of work a special division of the late palaeolithic period and even distinguishing tribes of 'Solutreans' who are credited with a definite place in history.

When G. de Mortillet originally employed the term he referred simply to a special technique, placed by him at the beginning of the development of the upper palaeolithic period. Laurel-leaf and shouldered points had been regarded as the basic, and probably only types of tool produced by the characteristic technique to which Mortillet added tanged points and thin flint awls. Subsequently 'blades with battered backs', a very inappropriate phrase, were referred to this culture, although these additions cannot be regarded as fundamental, for the objects referred to are found in sites of different periods.

Having conferred the title 'Solutré' on a cultural stage belonging to the beginning of late palaeolithic times Mortillet sought to find evidence of it in different areas of France and other countries. Only finds of bifacially worked points were used as evidence.

Subsequently H. Breuil created a new division, the Aurignacian, preceding the Solutrean which was now regarded as falling within the full flowering of the upper palaeolithic period. The Solutrean was followed by the Magdalenian stage when bonework preponderated.

Under the influence of Mortillet's views archaeologists began to seek out traces of Aurignacian, Solutrean and Magdalenian cultures in eastern Europe, Asia and Africa, assuming that human society in each part of the world must have passed through these stages of development.

However, later archaeological researches have revealed that, not only in the non-European countries, but even in Europe itself the matter was a good deal more complicated. It was found that in many cases the sequence of cultural deposits did not coincide with the accepted scheme: Aurignac, Solutré, Madeleine.* In Kostenki I bifacially worked tools occurred in the lowest

---

[1] F. Bordes, *L'Anthropologie*, 51 (1947), pp. 1–29.
[2] ibid., p. 2.
[3] S. A. Semenov, *Materials and Researches on the Archaeology of the U.S.S.R.*, 39 (1953), pp. 446–53.

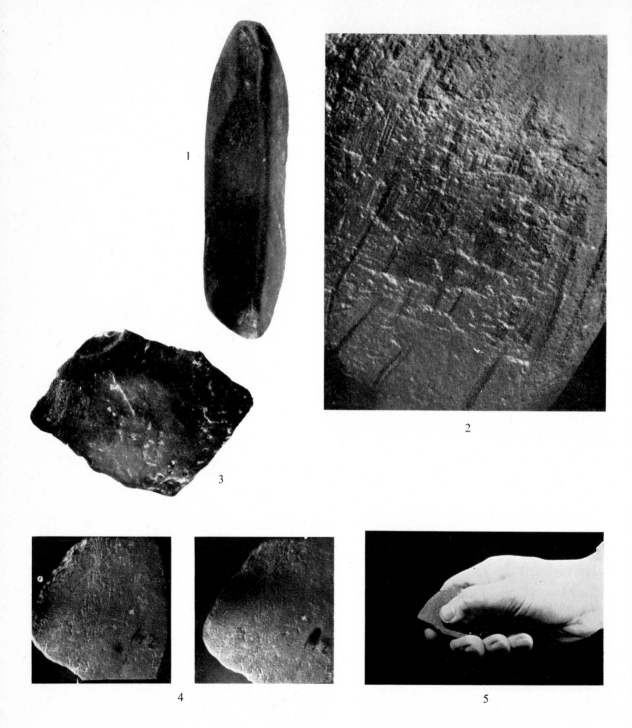

14 *Slate retouchers from Kostenki I: 1 slate pebble with traces of use as retoucher on its ends; 2 microphotograph of wear traces on its working part; 3 slate plaque with traces of use as retoucher; 4 stereophotographs of its working end; 5 the way it was held reconstructed.*

(sixth) layer, and in Telmansk tools of mature micro-lithic form underlay layers with tools, which in the opinion of Efimenko, had 'unusually archaic traits'.

Efimenko wrote: 'From the evidence given above it appears evident that the lower palaeolithic levels of Telmansk, of whose great antiquity there can be no kind of doubt both for stratigraphical reasons and on account of the archaic nature of the industry, have nothing in common with either Aurignacian, Solutrean nor Mousterian industries. An essential feature of those levels are the well made blades, testifying to fairly accomplished methods of flaking flint, and also numerous tools of microlithic form.'[1]

There are grounds for expecting that as the study of stratified sites advances the inconsistencies of the old system will grow even in France, in the very material on which the scheme was established.[2]

There can be no doubt that the separation of a Solutrean culture as a kind of independent phase of the upper palaeolithic period on the single basis of bifacially worked points was an error of G. de Mortillet, which has rendered more difficult the solution of a whole series of problems.

The theoretical difficulties in resolving these problems were still more increased when certain archaeologists, following H. Breuil, began to assign to the upper palaeolithic cultures (Aurignac, Solutré, Madeleine) ethnical significance, relating them to particular tribes, and explaining changes of cultures by victories of new invading tribes over the old ones.

Taking into account the numerous records of casual occurrences of points, both geographically and stratigraphically, some archaeologists have raised the matter of the debatable significance of the Solutrian leaf-shaped point as a chronological and historical factor. For example Wert was very sceptical about the chronological value of the Solutrean and Freund, who has written a large work on this subject, asked: 'Can we speak about the culture or cultures of leaf-shaped points, or ought we to think of a type of object arising for definite technical reasons in different cultures at various times and in various places? Notwithstanding its technical perfection and value as a weapon, for some reason or another it passed away, later to revive and flourish in neolithic times, and even today is in use among modern primitive peoples'.[3]

In constructing a scheme of development of material culture on the basis of the evolution of the working tools it is essential to explain properly what is meant by advanced and progressive, and what by backward and primitive, in relation to palaeolithic tools. Such an approach has not been worked out by western archaeologists, although, in so far as it is based on comparison, they have already used it in dividing the palaeolithic period into lower (Chelles-Acheul), middle (Moustier), and upper or late (Aurignac, Solutré, Madeleine). During these three periods the development of tools from simple to the more complicated form was clearly illustrated in some areas, like Europe or north Africa, by their more finished shapes, for they extended over a very great length of time. But once students attempted a finer subdivision, to split each of those periods into stages of development, they ran into difficulties. They have commonly seen decline and decay where there was undoubted progress. Thus Mortillet, for example, saw a decline and degeneration in Magdalenian from Solutrean tools which he regarded as the acme of palaeolithic work. This kind of evaluation of tools uses artistic, not technological standards. The bifacial work of flat points by pressure retouch created an impression of consummate skill, but technically this method of work merely arose from blade-making by pressure, a method which had been in reality the highest achievement of the upper palaeolithic period.

Pressure retouch in upper palaeolithic times can certainly be regarded as a higher level of bifacial work in comparison with the lower and middle palaeolithic work of this type, yet it was not this that made the period, so to speak, for it was merely one side of more important achievements of that time.

Bifacial pressure retouch on Solutrean points, as we have seen, was produced by two conditions: by a need for straight stone tools (points or knives), and by the character and quality of available flint material.

This retouch is not therefore any kind of criterion of an upper palaeolithic stage, as Mortillet believed, nor a tribal hallmark, as Breuil assumed, but merely a technical device, which man could have employed at any point of time in the upper palaeolithic period, if prompted by the needs of daily life or by the quality of the material available.

In the neolithic and early metallic periods this method

---

[1] P. P. Efimenko, *Prehistoric Society* (Kiev, 1953), p. 324.

[2] The author's views are a little unbalanced here. The main stratigraphical facts are known from scores of caves in France, Germany, and Spain; interpretations may change, but the evidence cannot. The sort of picture we have of the upper palaeolithic period today, which we derive from Miss D. A. E. Garrod, seems to be unfamiliar to Semenov. The Aurignacian (formerly Breuil's Middle Aurignacian) and the Gravettian (formerly Breuil's Upper Aurignacian) are known from western Europe to the Middle East. and probably constitute the earliest blade industries of these areas. The Solutrean, which has been described as a 'fashion' for surface pressure retouch, was perhaps experienced more intensely in France and. Spain, but known throughout eastern Europe. Finally there is the very circumscribed Magdalenian, known from France, Spain, and Germany. It seems very unlikely that the broad facts will require modification. T.

[3] G. Freund, *Quatär Bibliothek*, I (Bonn, 1952), p. 5.

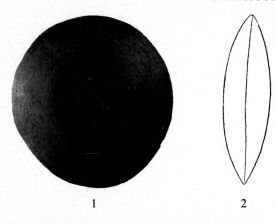

1   2

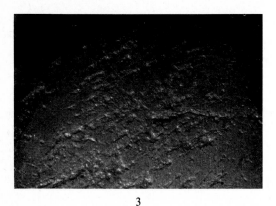

3

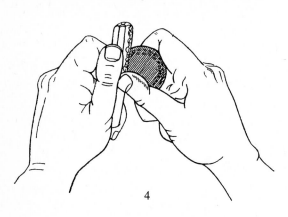

4

15 *Ground slate lense from Kostenki IV used as a retoucher; 1 general view; 2 profile; 3 micro-photograph of working edge; 4 method of use reconstructed.*

of working siliceous rocks was extensively employed and reached a high level of development. Arrow- and dart-heads, meat knives, sickles, daggers, large insertions for composite tools, drills and awls, side- and end-scrapers, rough-outs for ground tools (axes, adzes, whittling knives), sculptures of chalcedony, agate and hornstone (products of artistic activity)—this is a far from complete list of objects worked by this method. Numerous examples (daggers, arrowheads, lunate and toothed knives, sickles) show that the technique reached a consummate level of skill, especially bearing in mind the intractability of siliceous rocks under all other mechanical agencies apart from percussion and pressure at certain angles. At the new higher level of development retouchers were not the bone, slate or flint objects of accidental shape used by palaeolithic man. From mesolithic times onwards flint retouchers commonly have their own distinguishing marks; they are narrow tools made on large thick blades, one or both ends of which are severely worn, but whose side surfaces are polished by prolonged use in the hand. We have not yet studied neolithic bone retouchers. However if we may rely on ethnographic parallels (North American Indians, Eskimos) at the end of the Stone Age specialized instruments were developed consisting of a bone point set in a wooden handle, which increased mechanical pressure by allowing the use of the palm. For making small insertions for composite tools a vice was necessary, a bone or wooden object with a longitudinal groove into which the piece being retouched would be mounted, since microliths (triangles, trapezes or segments) would be difficult to make held between the fingers of the left hand.

Pressure techniques of working stone found expression in artistic creation at the end of the neolithic period. Having employed the plastic working of stone originally to satisfy his everyday needs, man gradually sought an outlet for his acquired experience in representational art. We are especially struck by the high technical level reached in the alterations of intractable material by human design. Sculptures of elk, reindeer, bears, beavers, swans, ducks, fish, lizards, snakes and even men are known amongst the finds of the late neolithic and early Bronze periods in the European part of the U.S.S.R. As Zamyatnin[1] demonstrated they occur in Siberia, Kamchatka, and other regions, where there was much experience of working flint, hornstone, agate, chalcedony and obsidian. Flint sculptures of Predynastic Egypt (antelopes, oxen, hawks, crocodiles, snakes), and the intricate symbolic carvings of obsidian in ancient Mexico and the Yucatan[2] show evidence of great skill in the field of silhouette reproductions by the use of deep notches in the material.

[1] S. N. Zamyatnin, *Soviet Archeology*, 10 (1948), pp. 85–112.
[2] T. Yoyse, *Journal of the Anthropological Institute of Gt. Britain*, 62 (1932).

e. Reverse retouch on the ends of flint tools

In descriptions of flint tools of upper palaeolithic times a technical term 'under-trimming' (*podteska*) is commonly used. Often there are references to: 'knives with under-trimming on the end', 'retouched blades with under-trimming on the end', 'under-trimming on the end' and so on. The reader's attention is drawn to the special character of this work on the end of the tool.

The term 'under-trimming' is not of course a simple one. In descriptions of material it usually has a formal connotation, not revealing the practical significance of this technique of stone-working for prehistoric man, which was to flatten the end of the blade. Sometimes one comes across a feeble attempt to explain the purpose of the peculiarities of this upper palaeolithic technique. The fluted appearance of reverse retouch has led some students to believe that this shape is the sign of a flint chisel or gouge, but this is an error.

This method of working was studied on the material of Kostenki, I where reverse retouch occurs very frequently; examples are counted by hundreds. Blade-tools with such trimming are fairly varied but for the most part of an everyday kind, used for cutting meat, cutting up skin and whittling wood. It very rarely occurs on end-scrapers.

Such work is not really 'under-trimming' since it was done by normal pressure retouch, that is by pressure with a retoucher. To judge by the facets it was done with a few exertions, from two to ten.

The intention of the work on an end of a blade tool was not just to bring this end into use in the work. It was one of the methods of straightening a blade out along its axis; in other words technically the objective was the same as in Solutrean retouch.

If all tools with reverse retouch are closely examined it will be found that the scars in every case (exceptions to the rule are very rare) lie not on the top but on the ventral face of the blade. Due to this, the 'under-trimming' cuts off part of the blade's bend (fig. 16.1). On the lower end of a blade, as it left the core, the curvature was commonly very sharp, towards 70°–90°. Palaeolithic man sometimes reconciled himself to this. In meat knives, for example, he might use the curved part as the handle and the butt-end with the pressure bulb as the working part, for this part may be comparatively straight. Very often, however, it would be necessary to get rid of the whole or part of the distal end of the blade by snapping or breaking it off, and then trimming up the blade with reverse pressure retouch. Even in making a short knife from part of a blade its ends would be worked by pressure retouch to remove the sharply projecting angle and give the blade a semi-circular end. A knife whose working end had not been treated in this way would meet greater resistance from the material

being cut than one which had. Thus 'under-trimming' on the end of a knife may be regarded as a purely technical device for enhancing the mechanical quality of a flint knife made on a prismatic blade.

f. Division of blades into segments and the retouching of microliths

At the close of the palaeolithic period prehistoric hunters and collectors, mainly in the steppe areas of Europe, Asia, and Africa, began to produce a new type of stone implement, the composite tool, used for knives, arrow- and spear-heads. Dividing a small prismatic blade into segments they worked each segment by fine retouch into the shape of a trapeze or triangle or lunate, and so on.

Each of these tiny flint artefacts had no meaning as an independent tool, but formed part of a composite implement, consisting of a collection of such flints inserted and fixed in a groove made in bone or wood.

Western archaeologists call the period to which these tools belong Azil-Tardenoisian, making it into a special stage in the development of the Stone Age. The period has been given two other names, 'mesolithic' and 'epipalaeolithic', however, which have a broader connotation covering all sides of life in the period.

Because microliths occur in a different kind of site of temporary character or even in caves, they were regarded even until recently by some archaeologists, as mentioned above, as an indication of the decay and degeneration of palaeolithic techniques. In reality the appearance of composite tools reflects a new step forward in the development of economic activity in ancient society. This technique allowed man to make straight points and knives to any length he required, so necessary in hunting, and also to reach a sharpness of blade to the very limit that the use of stone imposes.

The changed climatic conditions and the release of vast areas from ice gave ancient hunters greater opportunities for moving about in search of game, which at the same time became more varied but more difficult to hunt. Leaving the areas of deposits of chalk flint, many of which were destroyed by floods, the hunters often were obliged to utilize casual stone material for their tools (small pebbles of siliceous rocks from alluvial beds). Conditions of life confronted them with the necessity to make tools from any suitable material found by the way and to flake off blades from tiny cores.

Thus new techniques freed man from dependence on certain kinds of flint and by the same token extended his opportunities to become master in new fields. These important achievements were widely made use of in the subsequent neolithic period.

For manufacturing inserts, or microliths, fine narrow bladelets were flaked off small cores and then divided up

into parts. The latter stage consisted of a simple operation, which study of the body of the segment has shown
could be done in two ways. Very often the blade was
simply snapped in the hands. Such segments have no
bulb or facets found on struck segments. The fracture
line in this passes in an uninterrupted wave through the
flint body, sometimes making a zigzag at the end of the
fracture. Possibly the blade was not held in the bare
fingers but gripped in a deep groove in a piece of bone,
which would act as a conductor, allowing the blade to
break only into equal parts. Usually the blade being
broken was held with the dorsal face upwards.

A second method was to cleave the bladelet with a
blow, usually on its central arris. On the stump of a
blade so treated one can see the percussion bulb with
facet, or the negative impression. The blow obviously
must have been given not directly with a striker but with
a flint intermediary which could have been another
blade. Cleaving by means of an intermediary allowed
the point of the blow to be precisely fixed, and so made
it easier to divide the blade into equal parts.[1]

It must be noted that the first attempts to divide
prismatic blades into segments, so generally used in the
mesolithic period, have been observed in earlier times in
the upper palaeolithic period. Study of the flint material
from the top layer of Kostenki I has revealed that such
dividing was sometimes done there. Amongst the
material a small series of rectangular segments obtained
from large blades can be distinguished, which had been
very carefully retouched on the sharp edges. On the body
signs of cutting of the blade and traces of blows as
negative impressions of bulbs of percussion are visible.

On some segments the bulb is not in the middle of the
stump, as in most cases when the blow has fallen on the
central arris, but on its side. This indicates that they
sometimes clove the blade on one edge, the other edge
set on a rest which was evidently of bone.

The segmentation of blades presented no special
technical difficulties; palaeolithic man had commonly
resorted to it when he dressed or broke off surplus parts
of blades in making tools. He had to do this often with
bow-shaped blades whose distal ends were commonly
very curved on leaving the core.

However, the problem of how the segments obtained
from large flint blades of Kostenki I were used by the
inhabitants still remains an open one.

There are many technical difficulties that would arise
in the subsequent work on segments of small blades.
Trapeze, triangular and lunate shapes could only have
been obtained by fine pressure retouch, which required

the application of appreciable physical force, but segments of flint prisms often only 10×12 mm in size
could never have been held simply between the fingers.
In working them by pressure they must be steady and
immovable during the operation. The archaeological
material has yielded no evidence that in the mesolithic
period, when the technique of working microliths was
extensively developed, there were special holding
devices.

It is possible that such devices never existed and that
for fixing segments in an immovable position cuts or
grooves in a bone mount were made use of, into which
they would be inserted. A piece of animal rib with a long
groove would have been serviceable for this purpose
(fig. 16.2).

Segments were worked with a flint retoucher which
had a narrow working end that permitted exact movements on the edge of the prism, and the result produced
by each pressure of the hand to be visible.

g. Methods of blunting flint blades by retouch, burin blow and grinding

In the technical problems of making stone tools in the
palaeolithic period, apart from giving a tool the necessary shape to penetrate and alter another material,
provision had to be made for it to be grasped freely in
the hand. In early work (knapping, flaking) on siliceous
rocks with their conchoidal fracture the very simple
tools or rough-outs (flakes, blades) produced had sharp
edges, angles and projections, which could easily wound
the hand. To avoid this all the sharp parts of the tool
had to be blunted and deadened. The emergence of the
technique of flaking double-edged blades off a core in
upper palaeolithic times made such work even more
necessary.

For this purpose retouch was employed, pressure or
percussion, as a means of taking off unnecessary angles
and projections, as well as the thin, hard, razor-like tip
of the blade edge. Retouch produced a less sharp tool,
but tougher and less dangerous for the hand.

Examination of palaeolithic flint tools reveals that
man in the majority of cases confined himself to a
stiffening retouch, which only partially met the need for
safe-handling. Many knives were so minutely retouched
that they could never have been held in the hand without
a handle, although if necessity arose the retouched edge
was suitable for working. It will be appreciated that
stiffening retouch was intended to strengthen a knife
blade, and very often differed from proper blunting
retouch. The former was slighter and flatter and done

---

[1] This is reminiscent of the 'microburin technique', so widely known from the mesolithic period in western Europe and north Africa, which required two preliminary notches on the side of the blade. The top and bottom of the blade struck off at the notches were the waste products, the
'microburins'. T.

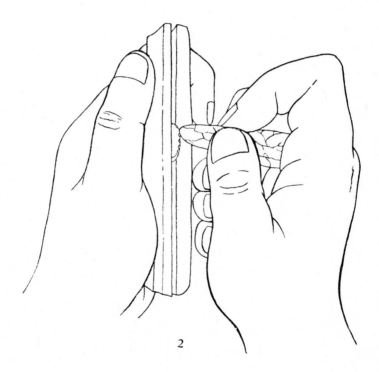

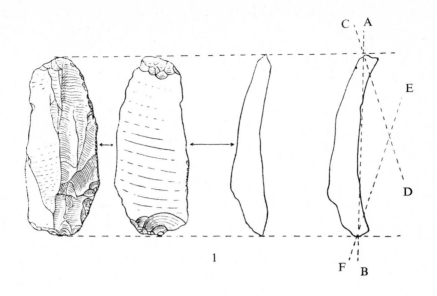

16 1 *Flint knife from Kostenki I with reverse retouch at the end (showing how the purpose of this was to straighten the blade); 2 method of retouching microliths reconstructed.*

with a bone retoucher; the latter was heavier and steeper, and done with a stone retoucher or by counter-blows (bounce-blows). This difference is especially noticeable on those flint knives which have an unmistakable part to hold, that is flint tools used without separate handles.

An especial difference of blunting retouch, which has emerged from careful study of the surface of palaeolithic flint tools, is the use of 'percussion trimming' (*podbivka*) or light percussion retouch. In contrast to lower palaeolithic percussion retouch, with which large bifacially-struck tools of Acheulian times were finished, this light retouch by blows was rarely used on working edges. It was employed for blunting tools and mainly for levelling off angles and projections on which it would have been difficult to apply pressure retouch.

As an example of light percussion retouch for blunting we may cite the handle-part of a knife from Kostenki I, whose crest had been treated by blows, which furnished a firm grasp for the fingers on the top when the tool was in use. A characteristic mark of percussion trimming is the presence of small flake facets as well as the battered condition of the central arris, which is crushed and scarred. Under a binocular lens the uneven lumpy surface with its multitude of cracks can be seen. Such a surface in some ways reminds us of the working surface of flint pressers and strikers with its rough pattern and high degree of cracking. Examination has shown that it was produced by light vertical blows with a flint striker.

Light percussion retouch in upper palaeolithic times, for blunting the non-working parts of flint tools, is interesting in that as secondary work it was the forerunner to the pecking technique, which was so extensively used in neolithic and later times.

Blunting the sharp edge of a flint blade by retouch did not always achieve the desired end. The retouched edge retained a certain sharpness and during use requiring great physical force could wound the hand. This was one of the main causes for the creation of handles in upper palaeolithic times.

For blunting the non-working parts of flint tools prehistoric man had two other recourses open to him: a burin blow and abrasion. A burin blow was given on the top edge of the blade held vertically either with a striker or presser, and the flake removed left a narrow scar on the edge.

The method of blunting a blade by an edge flake taken off was very widely used in making upper palaeolithic tools. It was more effective in blunting a cutting edge than retouch, but it had one essential disadvantage; the flake edge so worked was no longer serviceable as a cutting edge.

Various tools from Kostenki I and IV illustrate the use of this type of edge treatment. Generally the part to be grasped as a handle was subjected to the burin blow.

On many tools used as knives the part intended as the handle was treated by retouch on one side and a burin blow on the other. However, examples are found treated with a burin blow on both sides with parallel spall facets; such tools are commonly referred to the category of double-sided burins. In the material from Kostenki IV we have examined whittling knives whose handles recall medial burins; the spall facets on both sides meet at an angle. It is possible that such handles were inserted into a haft. Kostenki I and IV yielded not a few examples of single and double spall scars on the grasping part of end-scrapers and awls (fig. 17).

Often burin facets occur on the forward end of a knife, where they provided a rest for the finger (fig. 13.4). The flint material from Kostenki I has yielded several thousand examples of narrow blades with triangular transverse section. They are the product of this side flaking (burin spalling) and vary from about 10–15 mm up to 85–100 mm in length (fig. 17.5). Many of them have retouch on one of their three faces which indicates that the side-blow was applied to a finished tool. It could have been done to transform the tool for another purpose, or in other cases to enhance the blunting where retouch had been inadequate.

The occurrence of blunting of the non-working part of the tool by abrasion is a good deal rarer. In all probability this method was extensively used, but traces of slight rubbing can be detected only with great difficulty. Although it did not play an essential part in palaeolithic times, abrasion is interesting as an initial stage of grinding stone tools emerging already at this time. It was resorted to when the blunting of the edge of a flint blade, flake or bifacially worked tool by retouch was unsatisfactory. The object was rubbed against a stone, so that the denticulated edge of the retouch or projections of the facet arrises were smoothed off. Under the glass such brief rubbing gives the flint a mat, slightly rough surface with angles and projections removed.

h. Pecking

Neolithic objects are often found worked by a special method which has received the name of pecking. Usually traces of such treatment can be seen on rough-outs of axes and adzes, or on hollowed-out objects (mortars, cups, weights and so on). The surface of these objects has a hole-and-bump kind of appearance, very rough and recalling sponge or porous tufa. Examination reveals that in making such objects a relatively narrow range of materials was employed. Flint, chalcedony, agate, jasper, nephrite and obsidian are excluded, while quartzite and chert are rare. They are usually made of varieties of granite, sienite, diorite, gabbro (liparite, porphyry, andesite, diabase, diorite, basalt, etc.), that is granular rocks consisting of different mineral particles and with a high degree of jointing.

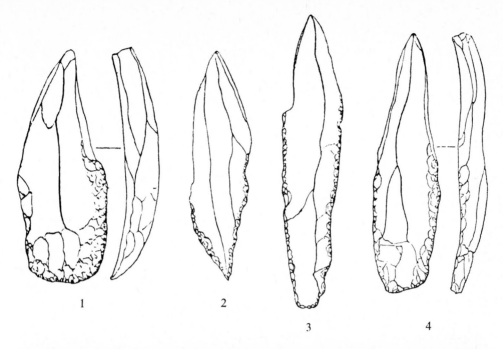

1   2   4

3

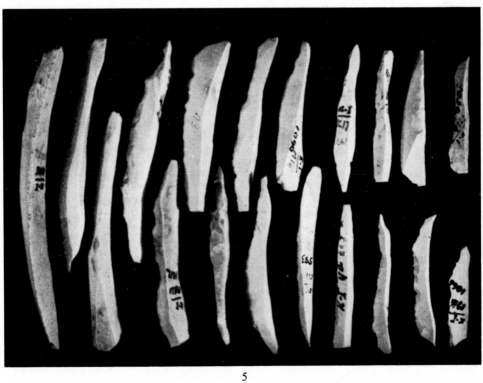

5

17 *Upper palaeolithic tools made by burin spalling from Kostenki I and IV: 1 end-scraper; 2 awl; 3 and 4 knives; 5 series of burin spalls removed from retouched blades at Kostenki I.*

Working by the pecking technique of a rock of uniform structure, like flint, which has a conchoidal fracture, is virtually impossible. Any blow, even a light one, on the surface of such minerals produces cracks, reduces the solidity of the object and can cause it to shatter, especially if the blow is delivered vertically on its flat face. Yet objects worked by the pecking technique all show that the blows were given at right-angles to the surface being worked. This is easily understood, as the object of the blows is not to flake off or 'trim off' but to remove an unrequired mass of material by particles, grains and bits, detaching them by light direct blows.

In contemporary techniques of working stone one operation stands close to the ancient method of pecking. After breaking-up the stone, shaping and dressing into blocks with a smooth or raised surface, 'shoeing' is carried out with a drag or claw chisel to obtain the required true face. The difference lies only in that the teeth are short and more numerous (on a claw five to seven, on a drag twenty-four to thirty-six), while Stone Age man in fact used only one tooth. In the pecking technique a narrow egg-shaped pebble was used or an angular lump of hard rock. Each blow left a small hole or hollow (peck-hole), just as arises in work with a contemporary steel punch designed for work on hard rocks, although a punch is only a pointed rod that acts as an intermediary to bear blows with a mallet.

Granular rocks were well suited for working by the pecking technique. The particles were crushed by blows and fell away, while projections and bulges broke up, even disintegrated into powder, and so by degrees surplus material was removed. Using this method, quite impressive plastic results can be achieved in certain materials: shaping the body of an axe for grinding, hollowing out a stone, or giving it any rough shape.

As an older analogy of this technique we may cite a method of working bone in upper palaeolithic times by which a mammoth tusk was severed transversely, bone mortars hollowed out and so on. Examples are known from palaeolithic times of working stone by hollowing it out. We are here referring to the lamps (for burning fat) and mortars found in the Magdalenian stage of the upper palaeolithic in western Europe.[1] In this area there was also a method of hewing out low-relief sculpture on rocks, although its details have not been studied. On limestone low-relief carving could be done by a combination of techniques: cutting and striking.[2]

The pecking technique developed in the neolithic period but, even with the appearance of metals, it continued to play an important part in architecture. In ancient countries, like Mexico, for example, where metals never played an essential part in technology, pecking was employed on a large scale in the construction of temples, for carving monumental sculptures and low-relief work. Naturally plastic working of stone with stone hammers and chisels (which frequently wore out and had to be changed) remained very inefficient, and required vast expenditure of time and labour that only the highly regulated early despotisms could provide by compulsion.

i. Grinding

In the Stone Age abrasive techniques developed extremely slowly. From lower palaeolithic times scarcely any traces of grinding have survived. As for the upper palaeolithic we have a few facts entitling us to speak about grinding and sharpening of bone objects (needles, awls, bone spearheads), and there are slight traces of grinding on some flint tools. Only Kostenki IV had a large series of ground objects of slate as evidence that abrasive work was not the exclusive property of the neolithic period. But inasmuch as we do not know any other analogous objects from upper palaeolithic times the unexpectedly early appearance of grinding in Kostenki IV must be regarded as 'invention before its time', when conditions were not yet ripe for its general introduction.

The systematic grinding of stone tools begins in early neolithic times. It was just then that wood-working began to assume major importance in prehistoric economy. Although man had been familiar with the useful properties of wood from the earliest times and knew how to use it over the whole palaeolithic period, he did not have at his disposal the means to employ this material on a large scale. Now came the cumulative effects of a more settled life (arising from the development of fishing, herding and agriculture) and the need for more permanently constructed living accommodation and a wide range of intricate structures and tools, and water transport (dug-outs, oars). All this contrived in a remarkable way to enhance the value of wood and consequently wood-dressing tools (axes, adzes, chisels). The technical qualities of the latter had to be perfected, and, more especially, the resistance of the face of flaked axe blades reduced by grinding.

The first steps in abrasive methods of working tools were very small. The grinding of hard stone is not just a fatiguing process that demands persistence, time and some working knowledge, but a method that gives very little external result in a given time. So in early neolithic times grinding was limited to part of the surface, the process being applied only to the blade of an axe or adze.

---

[1] J. G. Lalanne and A. Bouyssonie, *L'Anthropologie*, 50 (1947), pp. 121–2.
[2] ibid., pp. 128–31.

The tool itself was a rough-out worked by percussion and retouch, flaking or pecking, depending on the material.

Frequently to avoid additional labour a flattish oval pebble would be selected from gravel beds in a river. Sometimes this was done by necessity when the outcrop of desired rock was not in the same area as the settlement, and so a technically favourable rock was not at hand.

The earliest neolithic tools with ground blades have been found in Nøstvet (Scandinavia) in northern Europe and in Bak-Son (Indo-China) in southern Asia, where the axes resemble, by roughness of their appearance, the axes from Campigny or the Danish kitchen middens. They are of irregular shape, and the blade only was touched up by abrasion. Sharpening by grinding should not be confused with incomplete grinding that occurs on the large chopping tools that are found not only in the mature neolithic period but also later when metals had already come in. Incomplete grinding can be explained by the desire for economy of effort, but also, and it is especially important to emphasize this, by the requirement of the time to fix the tool to the handle by lashing. The butt-end, uneven as it was after dressing, possessed certain advantages for giving a purchase in contrast to the smoothly worked surface of a tool which had been ground all over.

Incomplete grinding can in some cases be explained by the fact that some hard rocks (flint, agate, chalcedony), even if available to neolithic man, were extraordinarily difficult to grind. Work for a given duration of time on grinding a flint axe was two to three times less effective than for the same work on a diorite axe. So in one and the same neolithic settlements flint axes will occur with only the blades ground, and axes of igneous rock that are ground all over. An example of this occurred at the neolithic settlement of Ronaldsway, Isle of Man, where both axes of flint and of other rocks were found.[1]

Methods of abrasive working were varied. Sometimes grinding was done by the friction of the rough-out against hard projections on siliceous tufa, gneiss, gabbro, granite, labradorite, and other magmatic rocks of porous or coarse-grained structure. Such traces occur on the cliffs of Scandinavia and southern India[2] in the form of grooves with a diameter similar to that of axes found in nearby neolithic settlements.

Ethnographic parallels are known for grinding axes against hard ground that contains silica sand. For example, the Australians, who use flat river pebbles for axe rough-outs, grind them by friction in the soil.

A more rational method, known from much archaeological evidence, is rubbing against special stone plaques, usually of sandstone or some coarse-grained crystalline rock. Sandstone blocks, regarded as the most valuable abrasive agent, consist basically of quartz grains bound together by clay, lime or quartz cementing matter. In addition to quartz, sandstones contain small crystals of felspar, particles of mica and trifling quantities of other materials. Friable varieties of sandstone, rock in which the grains are held together by a clay cement, allow grinding without the addition of sand, as these natural abrasives possess the property of 'self-sharpening',[3] and plaques of this rock need only have their surfaces soaked with water. Without this intervening (washing-off) agent the abrasive surface would quickly 'salt up', that is the sharp projections become blunted and their interstices choked up by the product of grinding, so that the abrasive soon becomes unserviceable.

Grinding was carried out on abrasive plaques, but the final touching-up of the blade, as we can see by faint traces of scratches on its surface, would be completed with a kind of hone or whetstone. Whetstones for sharpening (trueing) the blade were mainly made of fine-grained lime or clay sandstones of medium or even light compactness, friable and breaking easily with a blow, and quickly wearing in use. They are commonly shaped like small cakes of soap with a recessed (hollowed) area to fit the bulge of the axe or adze and bowed shape of its blade. For sharpening an adze on the facet side of the blade, or a gouge adze, the whetstone had a different shape, or a specially prepared surface was used on the whetstone. Traces of sharpening differ markedly from traces of grinding; the striations from sharpening with a whetstone are more numerous, smaller and shorter, while grinding leaves rougher scratches which are farther apart and fairly long.

Not just axes and adzes but knives also were ground, although it is true that ground knives are less commonly found on neolithic sites. The best known are the elbow-shaped knives of northern Europe and the half-moon-shaped (or close to that shape) knives of northern Asia. Now and again ground planes (Angar area), arrowheads, slate knives (like the knife from Olen Island, L. Onega) and other tools come to light. On their surface there are traces of the two operations of abrasive work; grinding and sharpening.

Examination of the surface of adzes from Verkholensk

---

[1] R. J. Bruce, E. M. and B. R. Megaw, *Proceedings of the Prehistoric Society* (1947), pp. 137, 139, pl. XVIII.

[2] B. Foote, *The Foote Collection of Indian Prehistoric and Protohistoric Antiquities* (Madras, 1916).

[3] By this word we mean that wear on the abrasive agent which destroys the links between its grains by the friction of the object against it, so that the blunted grains fall out only to be replaced by new sharp grains from the agent.

1

3

2

18 *Neolithic adze from Verkholensk: 1 general view; 2 enlargement 5 × of part A showing sharpening by fine-grained abrasive; 3 enlargement of B 5 × showing grinding by coarse-grained abrasive.*

confirms that grinding of the rough-out and the sharpening was done with different abrasives, one coarse-grained and the other fine-grained. Micro-photographs of the corresponding parts of an adze, which had not been used after sharpening, give some indication of this (fig. 18.2, 3).

With regard to ground tools it ought to be noted that the use of the term 'polished tools' as a synonym for 'ground tools' is quite improper from the point of view of technology. Although polishing falls into the category of abrasive work it differs significantly from grinding, for the two operations imply different objectives. While grinding completes a stage of the work on the object's shape during which quite an appreciable part of the material is commonly removed, polishing, or smoothing to a lustre, as the term is understood in contemporary technology, merely affects the surface. Polishing in the strict sense of the word was never used in the manufacture of stone tools. The gloss which is commonly seen on stone tools is either due to long use (friction against a soft material, such as skin of the hand, handle or lashing), or the result of the action of physico-chemical factors, that is conditions of deposition in the layer.

j. Sawing

Cutting up soft rocks into pieces was already known in palaeolithic times. For example, in Kostenki I lumps of slate survive with cuts on them from a burin showing lines where attempts had been made to cut through. Traces of sawn grooves made with a flint saw occur on soft stone. Amongst stone objects of the Crimean mesolithic site of Shan-Koba is a flint bladelet with traces of sawing stone on it. Its hard-worn blade is blunted and dulled while the linear traces or striations are strictly parallel to the blade edge on both sides and the microscopic evidence reveals two-way movement (backward and forward).

Systematic sawing of hard rocks only developed in neolithic times, although not to a uniform degree in different areas and countries. We can examine dozens of neolithic sites in the north and south of Europe where not a trace of sawing is discernible. Nevertheless the absence of direct evidence cannot be regarded as proof that sawing was not practised. Sawing is an auxiliary and intermediate stage of stone-working, and traces of it left on rough-outs can easily be completely obliterated on finished articles (axes, adzes, chisels) by grinding, sharpening, or just wear.

Sawing of stone has important advantages over percussion in dividing stone into pieces. These are: (1) the avoidance of cracking and splitting of crystals on the rough-out's surface which are difficult to avoid in percussion work; (2) greater precision in obtaining the right surface and freedom to divide the rock in any direction and to work on any type of rock. These advantages are exploited to the full in contemporary mechanical working of stone distinguished by its high productivity.

In neolithic times man had to rely on muscular force for sawing, whose efficiency is remarkably low. So full sawing (right through) of stone was extremely rare, used only in the cutting-up of precious rocks (nephrite, jasper, jade, serpentine), which can only be flaked with difficulty. Even in these materials the predominant method of work was flaking, and sawing was confined to making grooves. Sawing of hard and precious rocks was usually employed in the manufacture of personal adornments, such as rings and disks. The cutting out and boring of rings required blanks in the form of thin plates which could be obtained roughly by deep double saw-grooves to control a subsequent break. The blank could then be ground down.

Sawing of stone in neolithic times then played an auxiliary part in dividing up the material into rough-outs. This is in marked contrast to the contemporary usage of machines, where the entire cutting up of blocks from start to finish is done by sawing.

Stones of various kinds with traces of saw grooves have been found in the neolithic settlement at L. Ladoga,[1] in the Siberian sites in the L. Baikal area, in the pile-dwellings of western Europe and in many other places. Besides grooving, the stone saws themselves have sometimes been found, which for the most part consist of little sandstone or emery plaques with a sharply abrasive edge. These natural plaques have parallel lines of wear along their working edge, and similar striations can be detected in the sawn grooves on the stones themselves. There are no teeth on stone saws, for the action of sawing is due to abrasive grains which scratch the rock, and when blunted fall out, only to be replaced by the sharp particles behind them. Some emery saws, as shown by the shiny inclusions in them, contain small crystals of corundum whose hardness is 9, with which it was possible to saw even the hardest rocks. Nevertheless the process of sawing stone, even with the finest abrasives, could not be accomplished without water. The latter washes the saw groove free of worn particles, the stone dust, which quickly chokes the pores of the abrasive, and so by preventing the escape of blunted grains causes useless slipping by the saw.

When the abrasive grains were not hard enough to produce the required action clean silica sand mixed with water had to be poured into the groove. Washing the groove, it can be inferred both by ethnographic parallels and by analogy with contemporary usage in cutting stone with a frame-saw, had to be done systematically. Sawing with the addition of silica sand is commonly accomplished without a stone saw, but using instead bone, or even wood or rope. The Melanesians sometimes used rattan cord and North American Indians skin or textile string, but such sawing methods were never systematically used on stone. Bamboo splinters and flat halves of bivalve molluscs were used as saws by the people of south-eastern Asia and Oceania. Bamboo and shell saws were used like the link strips in a modern frame-saw; the angular particles of the abrasive mass cut along the strips and swept along by the saw movement the particles furrowed out the bottom of the groove.

Examination of neolithic material with traces of sawn grooves (nephrite, serpentine, and other rocks with signs of jointing) reveals that ancient man knew several rules about the orientation of sawing. The grooves often lie parallel to the fibrous lines of the rock, that is are oriented longitudinally.

The method of sawing stone with flint saws used by the neolithic population of the L. Baikal area is of considerable interest. To judge by the material from the graves prismatic blades with a retouched edge were used as saws. A relatively soft stone (steatite) with a greasy (soapy) surface was sawn up in order to make composite

[1] A. A. Inostrantsev, *Prehistoric Man of the Stone Age on the Shores of Lake Ladoga* (St Petersburg, 1882), p. 202.

19 *Neolithic period of L. Baikal area; 1 piece of sawn steatite with a flint saw; 2 piece of tabular flint used for sawing stone; 3 flint saw on blade; 4 microphotograph of traces left by sawing on the flint blade; 5 steatite weight of composite fish-hook.*

fish-hooks. From a small lump the craftsman sawed off a small piece not more than 3 cm long and 4 mm thick, which he then ground with an abrasive to produce the weight of a fish-hook with a triangle at one end and a lumpy swelling at the base for attachment. The rough-out was generally made by sawing the stone right through, for the craftsman did not care to risk spoiling the work by splitting. Traces of work on a flint saw which was found in position in a groove gave excellent opportunity to verify the characteristics of the microscopic marks of wear on a saw from use on stone (fig. 19.1, 4). In one assemblage of a flint saw, a stone with grooves and weights for fish-hooks, a saw of thin tabular flint with a convex working edge, retouched on both sides, was found. It was evidently the fragment of a flint knife re-used as a saw.

As a second example of the use of flint saws for minor work on hard material we may cite the objects from Jebel cave excavated by A. P. Okladnikov. This cave is in Turkmenistan, near the Caspian Sea. In all probability in early neolithic times a craftsman in jewellery had worked here, as is indicated by the different articles found here made from the sea shell *Didacna*, predominantly beads and pendants. Micro-analysis identified flint saws (fig. 20), drills (bow drills and reamers) for perforating beads, whittling knives, awls, scrapers, burins, strikers, grinding plaques and other tools. The inhabitants of the cave, in addition to the shells bearing traces of such work (fig. 21.1, 2), used other materials: amber, calcite, talc, quartz, tortoise bones, fish teeth and various fossils. The shells that were sawn up were evidently in a mineralized condition, as the traces of use, parallel striations, stand out sharply (fig. 21.3), which indicates that a hard resistant material had been worked. The used surface of the saws has a mat appearance.

On the problem of the existence of mechanical sawing in neolithic times there is still no definite contradictory evidence. R. Forrer made a reconstruction of a sawing machine making use of a pendulum,[1] which has found its way into many popular accounts of prehistoric culture and technology. It appears to be a witty attempt by the author to transfer into the distant past a model of the simplest machines upon which mechanical inventors were working only comparatively recently. The snag is that a pendulum swings through a chord and would saw a curved groove into the stone. No archaeological material known to us bears evidence of the use of such a method, nor is there any ethnographic analogy for such a machine among tribes at a neolithic level of culture, or even those with a higher level of technology.

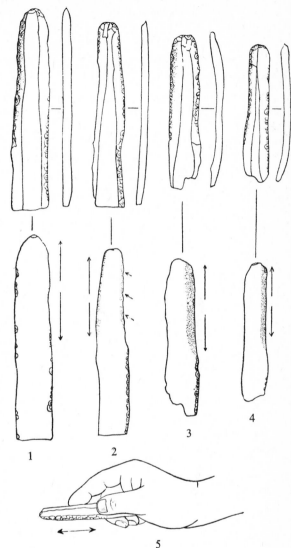

20 1–4 *Neolithic saws from Jebel cave with arrows indicating the direction of the striations (in one case, 2, the blade has been used also as a whittling knife); 5 method of holding the blade reconstructed.*

[1] R. Forrer, *Reallexikon der prähistorischen, klassischen und frühchristlichen Alterthümer* (Berlin, 1907), p. 780.

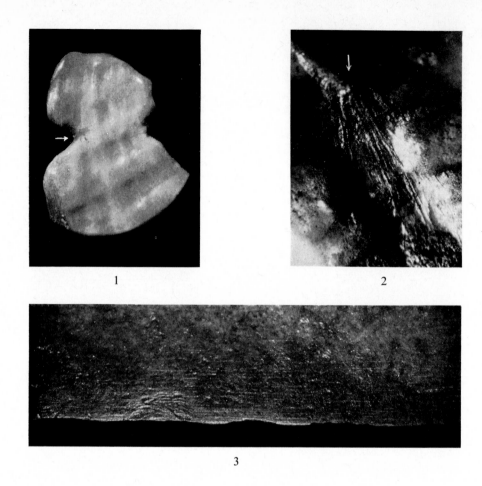

1   2

3

21 *Traces of sawing on shells from Jebel cave (neolithic period): 1 piece of shell sawn from both sides (3 ×); 2 traces of sawing on the shell enlarged 15× ; 3 traces on a flint saw enlarged 20 ×.*

k. Boring

Boring held a prominent place in Stone Age technology. This is because it was not an auxiliary or intermediate stage of working stone, like sawing, but constituted a quite independent technological process. In the operation of hole-making through a material boring is frequently the final stage of the work.

Boring started in palaeolithic times. Its origin is to be traced to the need for uniting two or more objects either as working tools or as adornments to be worn on the body. Boring of stones for adornment evidently precedes its use on tools as a means of work. Originally no doubt it was done partially by a circular movement of the hand and partially by even more rudimentary methods. The perforations in fossil spiral shells found at Sagvarjile, dug by N. Z. Kiladze in 1952, illustrate this (fig. 22.1). These perforated marine shells (*Turritella duplicata*, Zinne) were found in upper palaeolithic levels associated with other stone and bone tools. About a score of shells were found in all, perforated for suspension as adornments, and their compact deposition and arrangement in a closed circle show that they had been threaded as a necklace.

Laboratory examination has shown that the perforations in the shell walls were done in two ways, by scratching through and sawing through (fig. 22.2–7). The first method is crude work with a burin; the burin angle was pressed hard on the shell surface at the desired point. Each pressure with the flint burin left a small cut 1–3 mm long and 0·5 to 0·33 mm deep, which might be more accurately called a furrow. By numerous exertions of pressure with the burin angle on a small area the shell side was cut through, and then the hole was widened and made more regular. On the shell around the holes traces of work are visible, where not worn off during

74

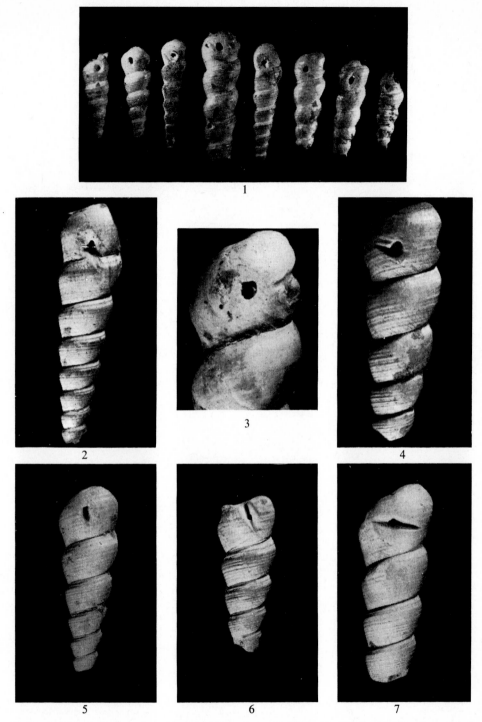

22 *Shells of Turritella from the palaeolithic site at Sagvarjile (Georgia): 1 collection of perforated shells forming part of a necklace; 2 and 3 perforation scratched through; 4 and 5 perforation scratched and sawn; 6 and 7 perforation sawn.*

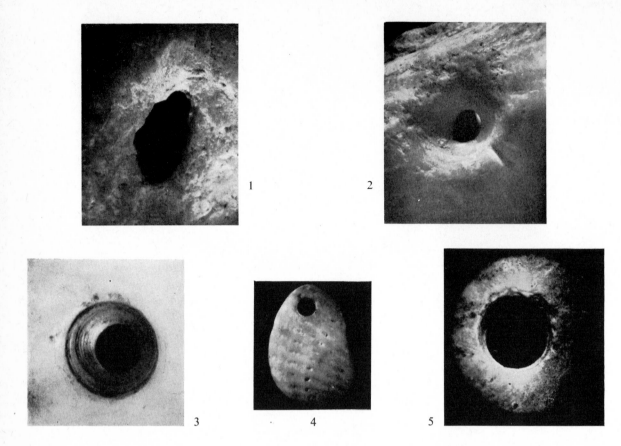

23 *1 and 2 Traces of work on shells of Turritella from Sagvarjile (palaeolithic period): 1 perforation scratched through (8 ×) and 2 perforation showing scratching sawing and hand drilling; 3 striations (3 ×) of a bow drill on a conical perforation in a shell of Didacna from Jebel cave (Turkmenistan); 4 and 5 cyclindrical bore with bow drill in a shell pendant (42 × and 58 ×).*

suspension on the human body as adornment (fig. 23.1). The traces have an uneven nibbled surface with irregular holes and crack lines.

The second method of perforating was analogous to that used in palaeolithic times for severing bone transversely by first sawing a groove across it with a flint blade. The groove was made with a small retouched toothed blade on the first twist in the shell either transversely or longitudinally. On certain shells the hole was obtained by a double saw groove, done evidently to enlarge the size of the hole. A combination of saw groove and a cross-scratch or cut can also be seen (fig. 22.4), where apparently it had been intended originally to use the first method to make the hole, but it was abandoned and the work completed by two parallel saw grooves.

The use of saw grooves for perforation had very limited possibilities: it was practicable only on hollow convex objects of cylindrical or conical shape (like long

bones, shells, bamboo and so on). In order to widen the holes produced by scratching or sawing man of the Sagvarjile cave sometimes used a flint reamer rotated as in drilling; the roughly conical form of the perforations indicates this (fig. 23.2).

The external surface of the spiral shells has not survived uniformly. The convex parts are strongly rubbed and even polished to a shine, while in the hollows of the shells the surface is mat or its degree of shine less. This difference proves that the perforated shells had been used, that is worn on the human body against which they had rubbed in movement. Further evidence of this is the polishing of the upper edge of the perforation evidently from friction by the thread on which the shell hung.

The question of whether the shells were already mineralized when they were worked, or not, still cannot be answered conclusively. However, it deserves mention that the hardness of the shells when mineralized is very

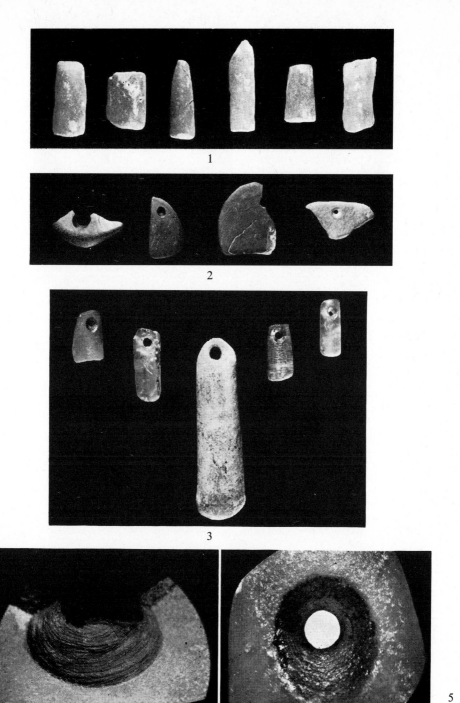

24 *Upper palaeolithic bored objects from Kostenki XVII: 1 rolled pieces of belemnites; 2 flat pebbles of slate and sandstone bored for suspension; 3 four belemnites and an elongated pebble bored for suspension; 4 and 5 micro-photographs of bores in slate (4) and belemnite (5) pendants.*

high, about 5 on the Mohs scale, and so to perforate this material with very simple techniques was a difficult matter. This fact offers some reason for supposing that the shells were worked before mineralization took place. Nevertheless this kind of work should be compared not to work on bone but to that on stone, whose physical properties are closer.

The stone pendants made of soft rock found in this cave had been perforated by scratching through and had all the marks characteristic of the perforated shells. On some palaeolithic stone objects hand rotation was the single method used to achieve perforations. Biconical perforations like this occur in the slate lenses from Kostenki IV. Pendants from Kostenki XVII have been drilled from both sides, and consist of slate pebbles (long and flat) and parts of belemnites, which look like semi-transparent golden amber (fig. 24.1, 3).

Pendants were bored, as the traces show, by a relatively swift rotation of the drill, evidently fixed to a rod which was operated between the palms of the hand (fig. 25.12).[1]

Thus even in palaeolithic times we already have two methods of perforating stone: (1) a combination of scratching and sawing through, and (2) rotary drilling. The more accomplished method of drilling was rotation of a wooden rod between the palms, but its use was confined to making small perforations, which did not require considerable force. The hill tribes of New Guinea use this method at the present day to drill wood and stone without a bow-drill, although the bow is known in this area. Like the Australians the tribes employ a stone drill fixed in a wooden rod which is rotated between the palms, the stone being lashed to the rod with vegetable fibres.[2]

In neolithic times the technique of boring came on to a new plane altogether, thanks to the adoption of the simplest mechanical devices in the bow and disk drills, and also the use of hollow drilling.

The range of neolithic and early Bronze Age objects that underwent drilling is fairly extensive. These were principally things worn on the body: pendants, beads, amulets, rings, disks, imitation tools and weapons with a symbolic or magical significance. The perforations may be peripheral (in lugs) or central, and small or large (as in bangles). Among perforated tools and weapons should be mentioned: stone spindle whorls, net-weights, hammers, maceheads and battle-axes.

Drilling small holes in objects of soft slaty rock, commonly used for adornment in neolithic times, was done with hand drills of flint or other minerals of the quartz family (chalcedony, agate, quartzite). Traces of

the work show that the drilling was done from both sides and in three ways. First they drilled a deep hole on one side in the desired point, and then they made a similar hole on the opposite side. Then a narrow drill (reamer) was used to perforate through, and the hole was now widened by one-way (not alternating) rotation. With alternating rotation the sharp edge of the 'reamer' would very soon have blunted. Moreover, with the hand it would have been more difficult to get a circular aperture with an alternating movement; the hand when it rotates to right and left does not make a full circle about its axis of rotation. In non-alternating and non-continuous rotation the movement of the hand would be smooth, carefully avoiding the risk of snapping or harming the side, if a hole near the edge was being drilled in a lug.

In studying the neolithic technique of drilling deviations from this arrangement will be found. Sometimes irregular perforations occur; an attempt may have been made to use a single drill, and so on. But generally the sequence set out here will occur, a sequence that was worked out in upper palaeolithic times, mainly on bone objects.

Drills for counter-drilling are not large, their short working part being conical with broad shoulders. They were made, like other drills, from flint blades or re-touched flakes and their dimensions varied only slightly. They were designed for making small perforations; as regards reamers the diameter of small examples averages 1·5–2 mm, large ones 20–30 mm. An example of the first is one from Khakhsyk (Yakutia) and of the second one from Voi-Navalok (Karelia). Large reamers were used for enlarging perforations made by different means, the initial hole into which they were inserted being made by the pecking technique, by numerous light blows with a sharp stone, as we can see on the weights from Voi-Navalok.

Cylindrical boring of small holes appears in mature neolithic times with flint drills shaped like narrow, strongly-retouched rods, and the work was done not by hand but with a bow drill. Drills of this type were found in the neolithic sites of Balakhna and in Jebel Cave (Turkmenistan). The working end was worn by rapid centralized rotation and the striations when magnified formed regular concentric circles with a projection (bulb) in the middle. With this kind of bow drill borings could be made right through from one side provided they did not have to go very deep. For deep perforations drilling was done, as with the hand method, from both sides, but without the need for counter-drills (fig. 25.7–10).

[1] S. A. Semenov, *Materials and Researches on the Archaeology of the U.S.S.R.*, 39 (1953), p. 455.
[2] H. Tischner, *Mitteilungen aus dem Museum für Völkerkunde in Hamburg*, 21 (1939), p. 47.

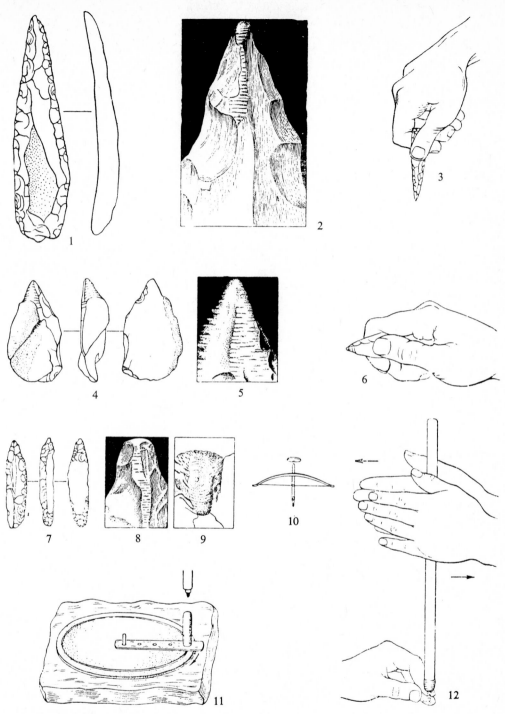

25 *Neolithic stone-drilling: 1 flint hand drill; 2 micro-drawing of its working end and wear on it (20 ×); 3 its method of use reconstructed; 4 flint hand drill; 5 micro-drawing of wear on its working end (7 ×); 6 method of holding drill; 7 flint bit for bow drill; 8 and 9 micro-drawing of working end with traces of wear (8 15 × and 9 40 ×); 10 reconstruction of bow drill; 11 reconstruction of device for drilling nephrite rings; 12 reconstruction of method of alternate rotation with drill between palm of the hands.*

It should be mentioned that cylindrical boring in neolithic times did not yet command the technical possibilities that arose later with the appearance of metals. The regularity of cylindrical bores depends on the form of the drill, and stone drills always showed some discrepancy from regular geometric shapes. Only with the adoption of hollow, or open-hollow, drilling in neolithic times was it possible to get a roughly regular cylindrical aperture. But this type of drilling both in neolithic times and later was done by hand, and regularity of the bore was only obtained at the cost of slow rotation. In this method the axis of the drill could be centralized more easily. Slow rotation was caused in its turn by the relatively large radii of material bored and the need to use great physical force.

The simplest features of neolithic cylindrical boring may be illustrated by the perforated shells from Jebel Cave. Study of the surface of the shell beads and pendants from this cave showed the majority were sea-worn when the boring was done. The edges of the pieces of shell folds that were chosen had been lost and the angles and projections worn off by the action of sand and water in surf movement. Only the circular beads (of varying diameter) had been ground into shape on stone, as could be seen by their regular shape and striations from being worked.

Some of the perforations on the shells are regular circles 2–4 mm in diameter, and examination under the binocular microscope revealed numerous parallel lines on their sides left by rapid turns of the drill (fig. 23.3). These two signs, a regular perforation and numerous parallel lines on its side, prove that the drilling was not done by hand, but probably with a bow drill, with an alternating continuous motion. The bow drill is an implement of the mature neolithic period, or at all events traces of earlier use have not so far been forthcoming from the archaeological material.

The drilling was done two ways: first the shell was bored right through from one side and then the aperture was made symmetrical by drilling from the opposite side. This explains the more or less biconical shape of many of the holes. Some pendants were bored from one side without the subsequent use of a reamer, so the hole is conical with a torn edge on the side opposite to that from which the drilling was done.

Experiments on the pendants from Jebel Cave to test the resistance of the shell to a modern steel drill showed that in its mineralized condition the shell had a hardness value of 4·5–5 on the Mohs scale. This means that it was harder than marble (3·5–4) and close to apatite (5). The drill (2 mm in diameter) was of tool steel with a hardness of 6 and the shell was made to yield to the drill only with great difficulty, but it was possible. If we bear in mind that neolithic flint drills had a hardness of 7, it will be seen that min-

eralized shell could have been bored with a bow drill.

Cylindrical drilling of large apertures would have been very difficult to do with a small bow drill. For this the bow drill would have had to be increased proportionally in size, requiring two or three men and not technically feasible without a rigid axis, which would entail an elaborate structure converting a hand into a mechanical drill. These technical factors explain why all the ethnographic evidence indicates that prehistoric bow drills never had large diameters.

For boring small holes a disk drill would be used, as was done by Oceanians and some North American Indians. Its construction makes use of the law of inertia in order to bring a wheel (wooden disk) into rotating motion, set on the vertical axis of the drill. At the lower end is a stone bit and at the top it is tied by a line to either end of a horizontal plank. Rhythmical pressure by hand on the plank sets the drill in motion about its own axis, first one way and then the other. As with the bow drill, the device is used not just for boring stone, shell, wood and bone, but also for making fire.

In order to obtain regular cylindrical apertures of some depth and diameter, like we meet in battle-axes of late neolithic and early Bronze Age times, there was another method. This was to use a bush (hollow) drill. Such drills were made of a long bone in the north and bamboo in southern areas, and consisted of a wooden hub and cross-piece. The work was done on the outside by pressing with the hand on the arm as it turned about the hub. Drilling was slow, but it was a very rational device for its time. What is particularly noteworthy is the economy of effort achieved on account of the reduction in area of friction relative to the large volume of material removed. The rotating edge of the bush worked with the aid of grains of silica sand systematically fed to it. A bush drill encounters resistance over and destroys only 0·3–0·4 of the whole area of the future aperture, while 0·7–0·6 of the area remains as an undisturbed cylinder in the middle.

The regularity of the aperture in this type of drilling is ensured by the cylindrical shape of the bush and its straight passage right through the material. Archaeological data illustrating the boring of stone with a hollow drill are numerous; many types of battle-axes of late neolithic and Bronze Age times were bored in this way. Some of them, Fatyanovo axes for example, are models of cylindrical boring. Ethnographic evidence for bush drilling is provided by the cutting out of shell rings with a bamboo drill among the Melanesians, particularly in New Guinea.

Archaeology has occasionally vouchsafed us examples of incomplete hollow-boring of an object whose hole is not regularly cylindrical An axe from Värmland (Sweden), briefly described by Montelius, had been drilled into from only one face and then thrown away.

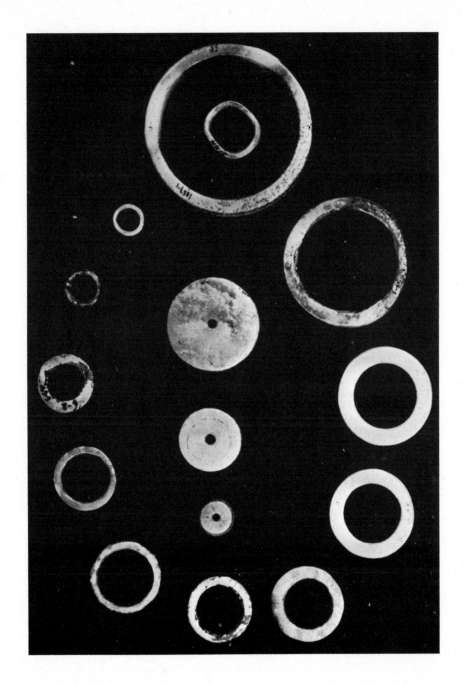

26 *Rings of white nephrite from the Irkutsk Regional Museum, 1/3 natural size.*

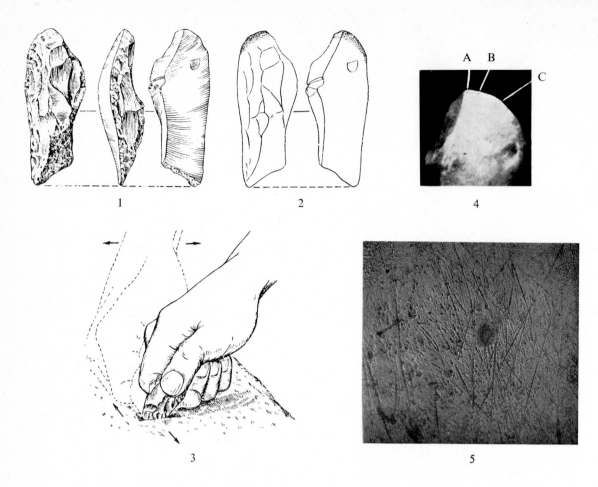

27 *A Mousterian side-scraper from Volgograd: 1 and 2 general views with areas of intense sheen indicated by stippling; 3 method of use reconstructed; 4 working end with parts enlarged indicated by letters; 5 micro-photograph of striations at* A.

Its hole with a bore in the centre was slightly conical in profile.[1] In practice such irregularity must often have arisen because a bone bush wore not just at the bottom of the groove but against the sides as well; ultimately the diameter of the bush was actually reduced in size. Such severe wear is avoided in modern boring by changing the bush, and so carrying the bore right through from one side to the other. It is difficult to say how craftsmen making Fatyanovo axes went about it, for these are distinguished by almost perfect cylindrical bores, but the possibility cannot be excluded that they were bored from both faces and then the central part worked out with abrasives.

All its imperfections allowed, hollow boring was a very considerable achievement for the Stone Age. The cutting out of small rings of nephrite and jadeite in parts of eastern Asia was probably done the same way. Hollow boring was extensively used later on in the technique of stone-working of the ancient Mediterranean states. In making the stone vessels in Egypt, which were in such great demand not just in the Nile valley but in other regions, a hollow bronze drill and an abrasive were used.

With regard to nephrite rings, which may be 10 cm or more in diameter, it is evident that they were made with a templet, as the inside could be cut out much more

---

[1] O. Montelius, *Kulturgeschichte Schwedens* (Leipzig, 1906), p. 37.

quickly this way than by drilling. Over a levelled-off and ground nephrite plaque one would put a stone or wooden circle, originally drawn out from a circle made with a cord. One would work round and round the circle with a flint or agate burin until there was a groove 0·5 mm deep, by which time the templet would no longer be necessary and work could continue with burin alone. With a little skill the burin could be made to continue in the same channel without deviating until the material had been cut right through.

Nevertheless rings could not have been made with a templet always. Regular and uninterrupted drill striations on many rings force one to conclude that very often a more accomplished method of work was practised. In all probability a circular device was employed (fig. 25.11). The presence of a perforation in the centre of the circular blanks which are often found with the rings suggests this, for they appear to be the remains of disks intended to assist in cutting out a series of rings. Such rings fit into one another concentrically (fig. 26).

5. Identification of functions of stone tools

a. Traces of use on a flint tool from the Mousterian site at Volgograd (Stalingrad)

FLINT tools of lower and middle palaeolithic times have not yet undergone systematic microscopic study in order to identify their functions. The greater part of the available material of this period is rolled, so that traces of use have been destroyed. Even material from cultural deposits in cave sites, like Kiik-Koba, present certain difficulties for study, as their surface has undergone partial alteration under the action, probably, of chemical agents.

Flint tools from the Mousterian site of Volgograd, where Zamyatnin began digging in 1952, proved of value in laboratory examination. Sealed in by a great thickness of later deposits, and cemented into the layer by continued accretions from the overhanging limestone, the tools survived in almost as good a condition as they had been left by man.

Study was mainly confined to one tool from Volgograd, whose worn appearance had already caught Zamyatnin's attention during the excavation. This was a small flint flake, short, wide and thick in section, retaining parts of the striking platform and bulb of percussion. Its surface retained yellow cortex in parts, but it was not patinated. The flint was greyish yellow in colour changing to black on the edge of the nodule. Retouch from underneath on to the dorsal side along the sharp edge had converted the object from a mere flake to a working tool (fig. 27.1, 2).

That the tool had been a long time in use was testified by the mirror-like sheen of the polishing on parts of the sharp edge (fig. 28.1, 2). A peculiarity of this polishing was that the working edge was covered by it on both faces (top and bottom) to more than 4 mm back from the edge. The polishing extended along almost half the length of the blade, gradually narrowing and finally disappearing. The remaining surface, especially on the bulb of percussion and the face immediately opposite, was lightly rubbed by friction of the hand. This rubbing varied in intensity; in the hollows which had hardly made contact with the skin it was very weak or virtually absent, but on projecting parts it was more marked.

Examining the traces of use with the naked eye one obtained the impression that we had here a cutting implement. Such an impression is created by the fact that the wear is on both sides, which would arise if the tool had penetrated into the material, and so had been affected on both faces.

However, microscopic examination of the surface showed that the retouch was not designed to create a cutting edge. The wear striations, as revealed by the microscope, were not parallel to the blade edge, but intersected one another at various angles (figs. 27.5, and 28.2).

Such a disposition of the striations is evidence that the tool was used as a scraper, but the working movement would not have been one-way, like that with an upper palaeolithic end-scraper. On the Volgograd tool the traces, as explained above, are not limited to one side, but extend to a depth of over 4 mm on both faces. Moreover, the edge had a rounded section. Such features indicate that the working movement of the hand was a two-way lateral one; the working movement of scraping started right to left and then altered left to right (fig. 27.3). A two-way movement is technically inefficient and primitive compared to a one-way movement, but it has the advantage that alternation avoids strain on the hand muscles and reduces fatigue. The intersection of the wear striations is interesting. This is due to the changing angle at which the tool was held, not only relative to the worked surface (leaning right or left), but also sagittally, that is it was not just the curved blade that made contact but also the end of the tool, which is equally blunted and polished. This kinematic variability of the working movement of a scraper is of great interest when compared with that of upper palaeolithic end-scrapers, as we shall see later.

The material which was worked with this tool could only have been skin. All other materials (wood, bone, stone) are excluded, because the texture of the wear traces arising on a flint tool by use on them is different. Only pliable skin yielding under pressure could have left the traces with the traits recognized on the tool from Volgograd. It may be assumed that this was not dried skin, with flesh removed, but fresh damp skin scraped on the flesh side to remove adhering fat and grease. Quartz grains that occur on dried skin produce a more marked scratching on the polished surface of the flint than was observed on the tool being studied; the mirror-like polishing on the surface would not have arisen by

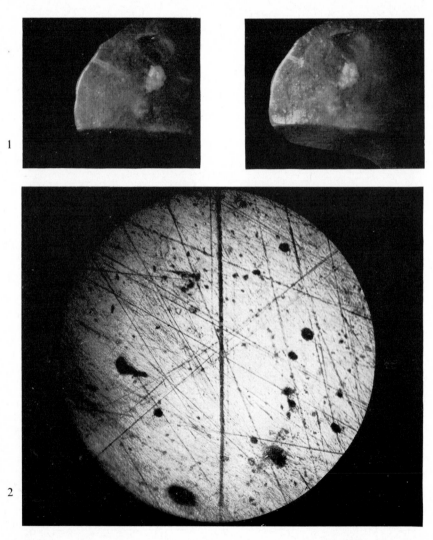

1

2

28 *A Mousterian side-scraper from Volgograd; 1 stereo-photographs of working end* (2 ×)*; 2 point* A *in fig.* 27 *under the microscope.*

scraping a dried pelt. Moreover, the working part of a scraper does not penetrate so deeply in working on a dried skin. The whole problem of the condition of skin when it was worked by prehistoric man is still ill understood. Proof of the existence of a very simple mechanical method of dressing skin in Mousterian times must be regarded as the most important result of our study of this tool.

b. Functions of end-scrapers and other scrapers established by traces of use

The end-scraper (*grattoir terminal*) is widely known from the beginning of the upper palaeolithic period. However, its purpose is a controversial issue; students have attributed different functions to this tool. Many workers have been misled by the very narrow width of the working part of the end-scraper. One from Timonovka has a working edge only 9 mm wide.

G. de Mortillet was not so imprudent as to give a functional definition to the end-scraper, but merely noticed the exceptional importance that these tools must have had in the Stone Age judged by their widespread occurrence.

He wrote: 'End-scrapers are tools whose general use it is difficult for us to understand, since we live in conditions that are so completely different from those of prehistoric times. Nevertheless their use was evidently a very important one, since from their first appearance in Solutrean times their numbers grew vastly, and they occur abundantly in Magdalenian and neolithic times alike. They are found in large quantities in the obsidian industries of Mexico and in the stone industries of Greenland, where they continue to the present day.'[1]

Early in this century Pfeiffer concluded that the end-scraper did not have a single function.[2] He considered its basic purpose was cutting. To cut skin into strips would require a round-ended tool, and he believed that its round end would also cut like a saw (*als Säge*) through hard material like wood and bone. In his view an end-scraper could also be used as a chisel, chopper or scraper (fig. 29).

Thus the end-scraper would be an all-purpose tool. Pfeiffer went further and contended that in all these cases it was rarely used without a handle, which formed an essential ancillary to it.

However, examination of the traces of wear on end-scrapers does not support Pfeiffer's views. A great number of these tools have been studied from materials of all periods, especially the upper palaeolithic. Let us begin with the first point that he put forward, that the end-scraper was a cutting tool. If an end-scraper was

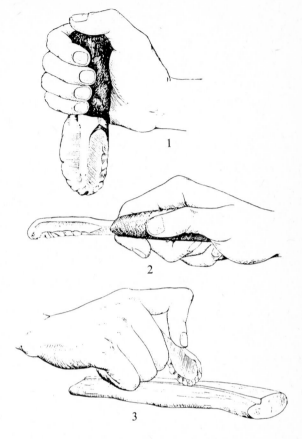

29 *Functions of an end-scraper according to L. Pfeiffer; 1 as a chisel; 2 as a knife; 3 as a burin.*

used for cutting up hide into thongs, for instance, then it should bear corresponding traces of wear. These traces should appear mainly on the under-surface of the tool as lustre, and as lines lying at 60°–90° to the axis of the tool. The width of polishing would depend on how deeply the blade penetrated into the material being cut; the same thing would be detectable either from cutting or sawing of hard materials.

Even more distinct traces should remain on the under-surface from use in chiselling or chopping, when the angle at which the tool is used causes especially severe friction between its ventral face and the worked material, but such traces do not occur on end-scrapers. The traces that exist occur on the working edge and extend only on

---

[1] G. and A. de Mortillet, *Prehistoric Life* (St Petersburg, 1903), p. 143.
[2] L. Pfeiffer, *Die steinzeitliche Technik und ihre Bezeihungen zur Gegenwart* (Jena, 1912), p. 132.

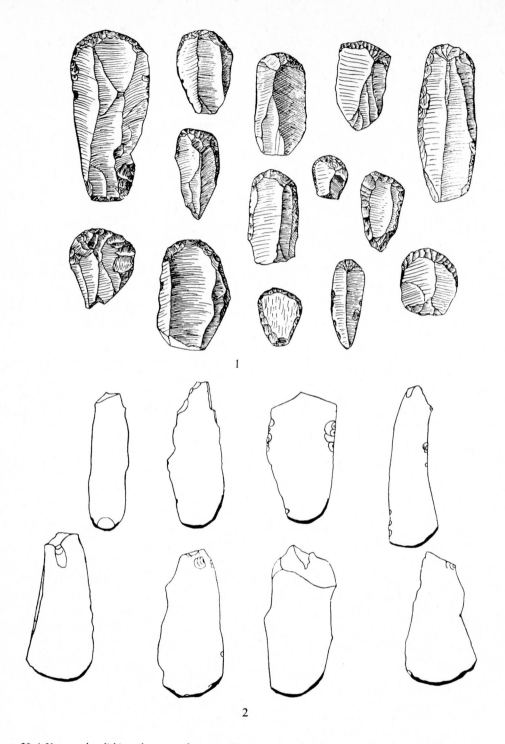

1

2

30 1 *Upper palaeolithic end-scrapers from west European sites; 2 end-scrapers from Timonovka (inverted).*

to its upper retouched surface. The thicker the end the wider is the area of polishing. A thick end is a frequent occurrence in end-scrapers due to repeated trimming to sharpen it, and this fact alone should be quite sufficient to dispose of any theory about their use for cutting.

How were these tools used? Traces of wear are completely absent on the ventral side, but are visible on the sharp edge itself and the lower part of the top, indicating that in use the tool moved frontally with the ventral face forward.

It is interesting that Herig also considered that the movement of the end-scraper was frontal. He came to this conclusion from studying a substantial number of broken end-scrapers from Petersfels.[1] Proceeding from this and bearing in mind the semi-circular form of the working end, Herig regarded these tools as gouges for making grooves in wood or bone, although he did not pose the question as to why prehistoric man should have been making grooves.

In reality an end-scraper was used for treating skin, for scraping and softening skins after they had been taken off the animal. This is a very important process in the manufacture of fur clothing, which cannot be made with hard and dried-out hide, as is used in a shield for instance. After scraping deer hide becomes pliable like a chamois leather; in contemporary furriery this process is called currying. The blade of the scraping tool needs to be sharp, but not so sharp that it cuts the pelt.

In all probability during upper palaeolithic times there were no special scrapers for cleaning the flesh side of the hide. Cleansing the skin of flesh, fat and muscle fibre which usually occur on freshly removed skin could have been done with end-scrapers with a wider and sharper working edge. The blunted ones were intended for rubbing the skin to make it soft, that is currying it.

The site at Timonovka was particularly rich in end-scrapers bearing traces of use, where strong wear was observed on eighty examples. Scrapers with faint wear traces were even more numerous. At Jebel cave traces of use occurred on all the 100 examples found in the site.

One sometimes finds mention of blunting and the occurrence of lustre on end-scrapers in reports by scholars, who have not made the logical inference from this. Traces of blunting were recorded by Renaud on quartzite scrapers in his study of American neolithic tools of the 'Fumaroles culture' of New Mexico. At the same time it must be remembered that he regarded end-scrapers as tools for cutting up animal skins.[2]

Were end-scrapers fixed in handles, as Pfeiffer contended? The available material yields evidence that the majority were used without them. The following facts testify to this. Firstly a substantial number of the tools are on elongated blades which would permit direct use. Secondly the wearing on the right side of these tools is more likely to have arisen if they were used without a handle. This fact is very important in the study of functions of end-scrapers. It indicates that they were held in the right hand, and also lends support to the conclusion, mentioned above, about the frontal use of the end-scraper.

About 80 per cent of end-scrapers are worn on the right side. Not only material from sites at home (Kostenki I, Timonovka, Mezin, Suponevo, Sakajia cave) but also published abroad (fig. 30) testify to this.

With what authority do we rely on material known to us only by published illustrations? Traces of wear are not indicated on them. On drawings of end-scrapers this type of mark is never shown. Nevertheless wear on one side is distinctly visible even in drawings of traditional type, provided they more or less correspond to the original.

This kind of wear was formed by secondary trimming of the scraper which sharpened its edge not all the way round the semi-circle but only that part blunted by use, that is the right-hand side. Thus the tool gradually became lop-sided, which is visible in the drawings.

Consequently the function of the end-scraper that has been described is confirmed by material from other countries. Let us turn to upper palaeolithic material from abroad, beginning with Capsian sites of the north Sahara described by Breuil and Clergeau.[3] The end and disk scrapers illustrated in this work from Wadi (dried-up river bed) Diffel are worn on the right side, while those from Wadi Mengoub are not all worn on the right side to judge by the figures. The greater part of the end-scrapers from Przedmost (Moravia) are worn on the right side. The same is the case on those from Magyar-bogy (Transylvania).[4]

Other sites that may be quoted are: Gorge d'Enfer, Font-Robert, El-Mekta (Tunis), Lespugue, Ercheu on the River Somme, Seriniá (Spain), and Campigny.[5] These and many other sites have yielded end-scrapers with signs of wear on the right-hand side.

[1] F. Herig, *Archiv für Anthropologie*, 22 (1932), p. 229.

[2] E. B. Renaud, *L'Anthropologie*, 40 (1930), p. 233.

[3] H. Breuil and D. Clergeau, *L'Anthropologie*, 41 (1931), pp. 57–58.

[4] H. Breuil, *L'Anthropologie*, 34 (1924), p. 536.

[5] *L'Anthropologie*, 42 (1932), p. 255; *Comptes Rendus du Congrès international d'Anthropologie et d'Archèologie préhistorique* (1906), p. 174; *L'Anthropologie*, 43 (1933), p. 465; ibid., 37 (1927), p. 253; *Congrès préhistorique d'Arras* (1911), p. 181; E. Cartailhac, *Les Ages préhistoriques de l'Espagne et du Portugal* (1886), p. 44; *Comptes Rendus du Congrès international d'Anthropologie et d'Archeologie préhistorique* (1900). pp. 208–9.

Fixing in a handle was necessary probably only for very small examples made on short blades. Such short end-scrapers are commonly met, and without a handle their use would have been difficult, although still possible. Broken examples found at some sites suggest the use of handles. In all probability changeable bone handles would have been used, in which the flint was easily mounted and removed when no longer serviceable. The existence of detachable bone and antler handles for burins and knives in upper palaeolithic times can be regarded as a strong probability.[1]

End-scrapers consitute a well-defined category of tools; confusion about their purpose is to be attributed to a too formalistic approach to the problem.

Analytical study of traces of use on end-scrapers has shown that they bear evidence of their employment in dressing skin. Especially significant are the peculiarities of shape of the working edge as revealed under the microscope. In the first place the working edge (the sharp part) is never straight; as a rule it is semi-circular or curved on an angle. This roundness and convexity was necessary in working on the under (flesh) side of the skin, which would yield under the pressure of a compara-

tively narrow implement like a scraper. Had it not been round but rectilinear it would have lacerated or even cut through the pelt at the angle. Secondly wear is confined to the edge of the flint which is blunted more or less uniformly by friction, because it was held with its axis at an angle of 75°–80° to the skin surface. Sometimes it was less, sometimes as much as 90°, depending on the thickness of the blade and the kind of retouch on its working edge. Thirdly the striations occur as minute grooves intersecting the blade-edge transversely. Careful study of the grooves shows that they are slightly broader on the ventral side and grow narrower towards the top retouched part of the tool. This again indicates that the tool was moved frontally with the ventral side forward (fig. 31.1–3). It can be seen best of all on flint, for on obsidian scrapers which wear more quickly and have sharp striations this peculiarity of the traces reveals itself less clearly. The formation of striations on end-scrapers, in the same way as on all other tools, is due to the hard mineral particles that found their way on to the skin: sand grains, loess particles and other scratching agents.

The identification of wear traces on end-scrapers as a

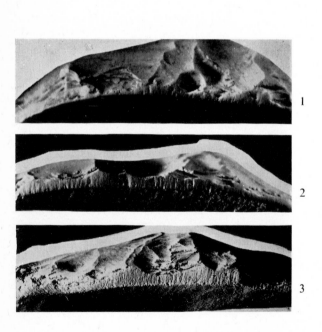

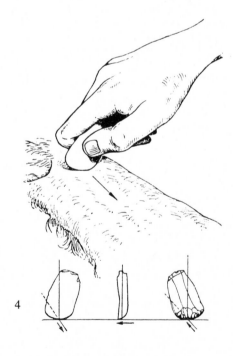

31 1–3 *enlargement (10 ×) of the working edge of upper palaeolithic end-scrapers from Timonovka;* 4 *reconstruction of the method of operation of an end-scraper.*

[1] S. A. Semenov, *Short Reports of the Institute for the History of Material Culture*, 35 (1950), pp. 132–7.

special functional criterion allows us to study these tools from sites of the different periods where they occur. Moreover, using our wear traces we can find tools with this function amongst stone objects of very different shapes, to which previously a different purpose had been attributed. In their study, as with other implements, everything confirms the view that tools can be very different in shape and yet have exactly the same function, and conversely identical shapes may have had quite different functions. The decisive factor therefore in the definition of function is traces of use.

Timonovka was a site which yielded a large number of end-scrapers, but also other tools which had not the remotest resemblance to them. These were massive irregular flakes, accidental products of flint-working (fig. 32). Retouch on them indicated use, but their shape could give no clue as to their purpose. By study of the traces alone the conclusion was reached that they had been used as scrapers in working on skin and hide. The traces were on the convex parts of the edge and had all the specific traits of scrapers. Some examples recall Mousterian scrapers.

The inhabitants of the Siberian palaeolithic site of Malta also resorted to flakes and chips for dressing skins (fig. 33.3). For this they employed short flakes one side of which was retouched and the angles rounded off to make the working edge convex (fig. 33.4). It is possible that this kind of scraper was mounted in a handle.

The use of flint cores at Malta as skin scrapers is of great interest. The broad convex striking platforms were trimmed to remove sharp angles and projections which would have spoilt the work (fig. 33.1, 2).

The scrapers from Afontova Mountain, which were made on flaked diorite pebbles, deserve special attention. Originally they were considered to be hand-axes (by N. K. Auerbakh) and subsequently were called disk-shaped chopping tools (by G. H. Sosnovsky) or axes (by A. P. Okladnikov). Examination of the traces of use on them has established that, in fact, what we have are scrapers for dressing skins (fig. 34.1). The kinematics they reveal are characteristic of palaeolithic and neolithic end-scrapers (fig. 34.2).

A different kind of flint for use on skins has been found in neolithic settlements. For example, in Luka-Vrublevetskaya besides ordinary end-scrapers we find tools on broad flakes recalling Mousterian examples. The working edge is not on the end but on the convex side of the blade (fig. 35.1).

There are some grounds for placing the neolithic scrapers with broad working edge in a special category. Generally the blade of such tools is less blunted and still has got its sharp edge, but linear traces are scarcely detectable on them. It is likely that they were used for primary dressing, for scraping off fat and grease, and so strictly they should not be called end-scrapers or

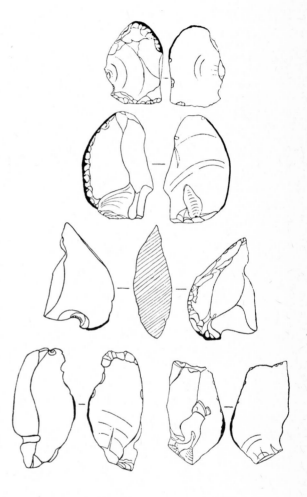

32 *Upper palaeolithic end-scrapers from Timonovka made on waste flakes, the wear on them being indicated by dark lines.*

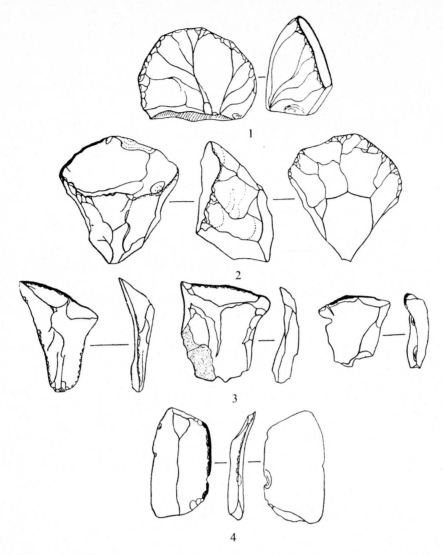

33 *Upper palaeolithic end-scrapers made on cores* (1 *and* 2), *waste flake* (3) *and blade* (4) *from Malta* (*Siberia*).

softeners. Possibly after blunting such broad scrapers were used for removing hair when the pelt was being made ready to be made up into skin articles. The removal of hair, of course, would have been done by crude soaking in lye. The Eskimos, for example, until very recently soaked skins in urine, which, as is well known, contains sodium chloride and lime.[1] But hair will not always come away easily from the skin surface and often it has to be scraped and struck off.[2] End-scrapers with narrow working edges would have been quite suitable for finishing the skin with softening by rubbing.

Cleaning and removing hair differ from softening; in the first the skin is spread over a stand, that is it is on a

---

[1] According to A. Middendorf (*Journey into North and East Siberia*, 1869, II, p. 641), in north Siberia for tanning reindeer liver, chewed and mixed with spit, reindeer brain and other organic material were employed.

[2] Neolithic scrapers are sometimes very large, as, for example, in the settlement at Yuryuzan (Bashkiria), dug in 1955 by Krizhevsky. These scrapers made of chert reach 8–20 cm in width, so they must have needed both hands in use. Tools of this type were previously regarded as knives.

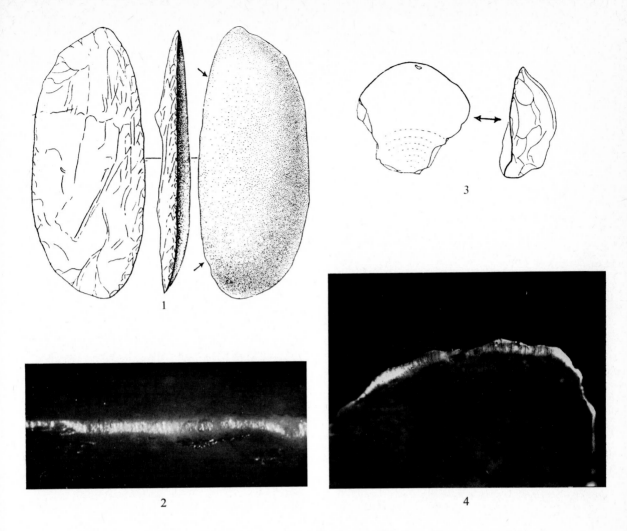

34 1 *Upper palaeolithic side-scraper on a flake off a diorite pebble from Afontova Mountain (arrows indicate working part); 2 micro-photograph of wear traces on 1; 3 end-scraper from Fofanov; 4 micro-photograph of working edge of 3.*

more or less hard support, while in softening it is stretched out, fur downwards, and worked unsupported.

It is not unworthy of notice that in contemporary skin clothing manufacture they still use a tool for softening which has a slight resemblance to a stone scraper, at all events in the shape of its working edge. This is a steel circle with a broad aperture in it for the hand of the operator, its edge lined with wood or skin to make it more comfortable to hold. The skin or leather being treated is held over special trestles, while the operator, supporting the edge of the skin with his left hand, holds the circle in his right hand and gradually pulls it over the whole skin. The tight bunches of fibres in the skin

are softened and freed so that the pelt and whole hide becomes soft without breaking. A contemporary chamois leather is produced by working on both sides, while kid, calf and other skins are treated only on the underside.

The flint end-scraper that appeared in upper palaeolithic times continued to be made of stone in later periods. The Eskimos and Tierra del Fuegans besides stone often used shell for scrapers. Stone end-scrapers only went out of use finally with the adoption of the use of metals in everyday life. Anthropologists have observed the use of bone scrapers among some American Indians, but in archaeological collections bone scrapers

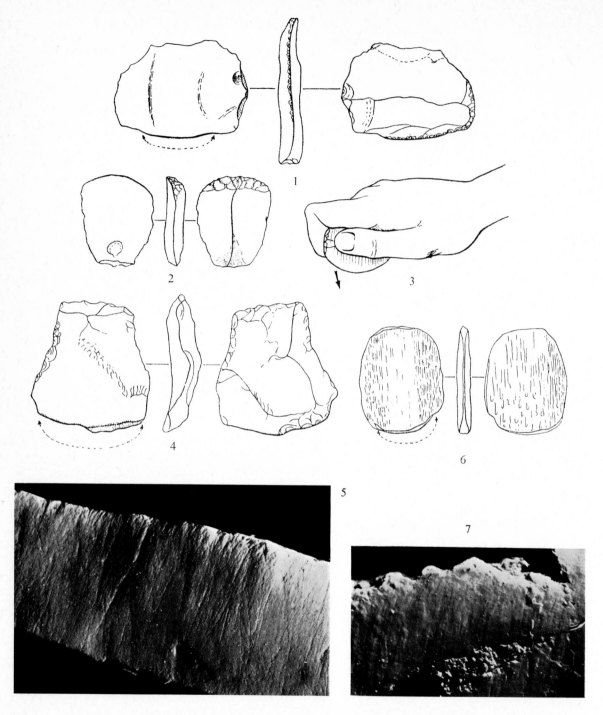

35 1–3 *Late neolithic end-scrapers from Luka-Vrublevetskaya (1, on waste flake; 2 thumb-nail scraper; 3 reconstruction of way 1 was held). 4 and 5 short end-scraper from ancient Eskimo settlement at Chukotka (after Rudenko) in general view (4) and micro-photograph of working part (5); 6 and 7 antler end-scraper of the Hellenistic period from Olbia seen in general view (6) and micro-photograph of working edge (7).*

are very rare. We may notice one curious example of a scraper of deer antler from Olbia (Scythian period) found in 1947 by S. I. Kaposhina. It will be noticed that it is shaped like an end-scraper (fig. 35.6, 7). The semi-circular working edge is also worn on one side and the striation traces of wear are analogous to those on an Eskimo scraper found in the Chukotsk Expedition of S. I. Rudenko (fig. 35.4, 5).

From neolithic times stone scrapers were used not only without handles or with one-handed grips but also with two-handed handles, like those we meet among northern peoples today. In such handles scrapers 5–7 cm broad on an average were mounted, where the increased force required to use them is considerable.

Finally it should be observed that examination of traces characteristic of different kinds of scrapers allows us to appreciate the purposes of a most varied range of stone tools. These traces can be discovered, for example, on old disused adzes and axes. Traces of such re-use are frequently found on the archaeological material from Siberia and Kamchatka.

As an ethnographic parallel for a similar use of adzes we may mention Wisler's description of life among North American Indians.[1] The facts mentioned by him leave no doubt that tools were used for dressing skin that consisted of slightly modified 'stone adzes'. This tool, a sort of adze, was mounted in a bent handle for dressing skin.

c. Shouldered points and their purpose

The lack of accord between the definition of a tool's function by the traces of use it bears on the one hand, and its apparent form on the other, has been most strikingly revealed by research on the shouldered points from Kostenki I. These objects were first identified as javelin heads, and the tang at their base was regarded as a device for mounting them in a shaft (fig. 36.1). These upper palaeolithic weapons would have been connected with reindeer hunting.

Shouldered points (*pointes à cran*) discovered at Willendorf (Austria) in an upper Aurignacian layer allowed Breuil[2] to identify them as characteristic of this period. They were known also from the caves at Grimaldi near Monaco,[3] at Sergeac[4] and at other sites. At home in the U.S.S.R., besides Kostenki I, they have been found at Avdeevo and in the site at Berdyga studied by Zamyatnin.[5]

Study of the shouldered points from Kostenki I has

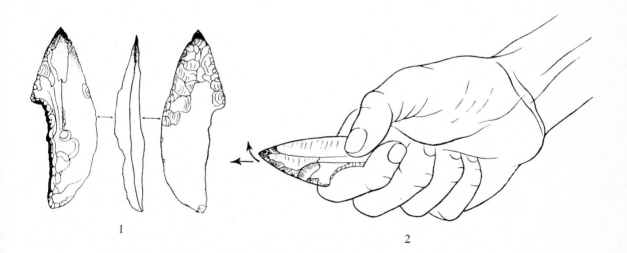

36 1 *An upper palaeolithic shouldered point from Kostenki I showing wear in the form of polishing on its tip and tang; 2 its method of use reconstructed.*

[1] C. Wisler, *American Museum of Natural History*, Handbook, Series 1 (New York, 1920), p. 57.
[2] H. Breuil, *L'Anthrolopogie*, 34 (1924), pp. 526–7.
[3] H. Breuil, *Comptes Rendus du Congrès International d'Anthropologie et d'Archéologie Préhistorique* (1913), p. 169.
[4] F. Delage, *L'Anthropologie*, 45 (1935), p. 235.
[5] S. N. Zamyatnin, *Reports of the Archaeological Commission of the Academy of Sciences of the B.S.S.R.*, (1930), p. 486.

introduced necessary corrections to the established view about their purpose. On the tips of the points polishing was in many cases observed, clear evidence of prolonged use, which extended over both faces. It encroaches over an appreciable part of the point; on the forward part of the blade at the opposite end to the tang it is more severe than on the tang itself. Moreover, it is a characteristic of this polishing that it occurs not only on the projections of the retouched surface, the scar arrises, but also in the hollows. An especially curious fact is the presence of polishing within the notch itself, where it is much less intensive but covers practically all the retouched surface.

The traces that have been studied reveal a new function for the tool, for it is impossible to believe that this kind of wear could have arisen merely by its use as a spearhead. A head would be polished by wear against the soft body of an animal only if it had transfixed the bodies of hundreds of animals. Such a contingency can be entirely excluded. A point often broke against an animal's bone, as the stumps of many points from Kostenki I show. Flint heads of ivy-leaf shape from Telmansk on the River Don well illustrate this, where both complete and broken specimens were found. There was a whole series of tangs which would appear to have been brought back to the hut on the end of the haft after the front part of the head had been lost in the hunt.

Very often these points would have been used as knives for dismembering game. Such a pointed tool would have been particularly suitable for disembowelling mammoths, whose skin would be quite impenetrable with a blunt-ended knife.

Grasped with the tang in the palm of the hand and pressed forward and up a point would make an excellent knife for ripping open a carcass (fig. 36.2). This would explain the polishing mentioned on the notch as due to pressure by the hand.

The functions of a point as a javelin or knife-dagger are in reality extraordinarily similar. Consequently the methods of manufacture of the two were similar, a circumstance which is even more clear in neolithic industries. We may cite as an example the material collected by T. Wilson.[1]

Wilson assembled under the title of stone knives (*couteaux en pierre*) a group of tools which from their method of manufacture appeared to be asymmetrical points for arrows or javelins. Functionally they were undoubtedly knives, although prepared in just the same way as points. The majority of these knife-points were mounted in a short handle for which there were two notches on either side of the base. Like a knife, the points were inserted into a split haft and lashed with sinews. 'Many tools which are regarded confidently by archaeologists as arrow- or javelin-heads in reality were used as knives', Wilson remarked.[2]

Thus a one-sided notch or shoulder on a point must be considered not only as a hafting device but also as one method of blunting a sharp edge so that it can be grasped by the hand without injury. A degree of polishing that hunting projectiles would not have experienced is not the only argument against an interpretation of these objects as just javelin-heads; another is their variable size. Besides specimens 85–90 mm long, small or even minature examples commonly occur not more than 40 mm long and 10 mm broad, which would be small even for arrow-heads, and it is very interesting that they bear traces of use as awls.

d. Palaeolithic burins

'In Aurignacian times there appeared a hitherto unknown implement, the burin. Excellently fitted to a new kind of work, cutting up bone, antler and ivory, which had then come into use, it was so remarkably suitable for this type of work that its origin would seem inexplicable. However, one need only examine large collections of Aurignacian cores in order to make an easy guess about this, for on them a sharp edge formed by two facets will often be found. This fact shows us the origin of the burin.'[3]

Such was the view of L. Capitan about burins. Without entering into polemics on this hypothesis about their origin we may observe that, in spite of their similarity to contemporary steel burins, their function had for long not been understood, and they had been given the conventional name of 'screwdrivers' (*tarauds*). However, by then the experiments of Leguay had demonstrated that this tool was used for working bone, and that it was done on the same kinematic principle as with a contemporary steel burin.

Thus the problem of the real use of the burin was settled, although the possibilities of further experimental work were not exhausted. It had come to be recognized that the basic morphological sign of a stone burin was the so-called burin facet. Using this, Bourlon worked out a classification of burins,[4] believing it would prove useful for assessing the characteristics of sites and dating them.

According to the position of the facet on the tool, Bourlon classified it as this or that type of burin: side, medial, angle, transverse and so on. If the burin scar was

---

[1] T. Wilson, *Comptes Rendus du Congrès International d'Anthropologie et d'Archéologie Préhistorique* (1902), pp. 298–324.
[2] ibid., p. 322.
[3] L. Capitan, *Comptes Rendus du Congrès International d'Anthropologie et d'Archéologie Préhistorique* (1913), p. 432.
[4] R. Bourlon, *Revue Anthropologique* (1911), pp. 267–78.

on a large flint it would be called core-shaped, multi-faceted or polyhedric. As the form of a burin arising by flaking and retouch is variable, the nomenclature grew apace, each student creating a new term as he wanted it. In order to put an end to this Gorodtsov proposed his own classification based on the material from Timonovka and Suponevo. He divided the types of burins found into thirteen groups, and these he further subdivided into seventy-five types.

Today Gorodtsov's classification of burins is not regarded as of much value. It only goes to show how far a student of systematics may stray from the basic duties

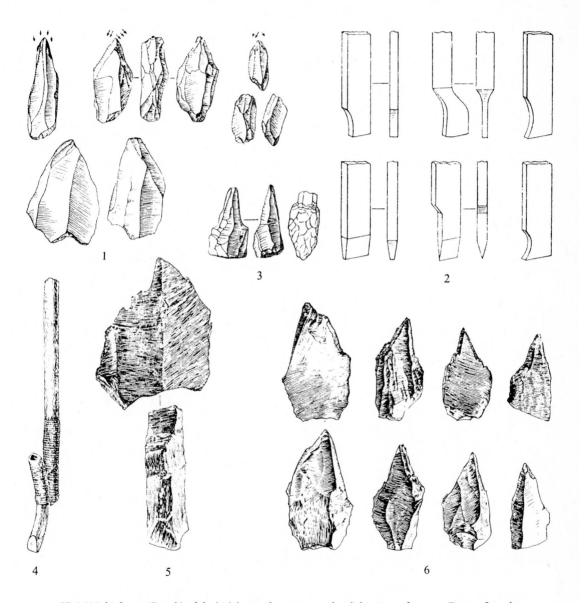

37 1 *'Multi-facetted' and 'polyhedric' burins from upper palaeolithic sites of eastern Europe; 2 modern steel burins; 3 neolithic burins from Khakhsyk (E. Siberia); 4 bone burin from Bororo tribe (S. America); 5 upper palaeolithic burin from Mezin (3 ×); 6 neolithic burins from L. Baikal area.*

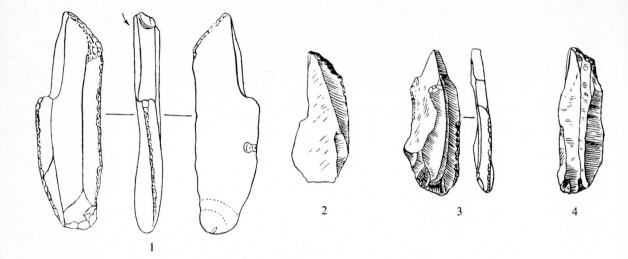

38 (AND OPPOSITE) 1 *burin from Mezin;* 2–4 *burins from Malta* (*Siberia*); 5 *method of use of a burin reconstructed;* 6–8 *enlargement of wear traces on burins from Timonovka, the arrows indicating the direction of movement. All upper palaeolithic.*

of science when he sets himself the task of only describing shapes and not seeking an explanation of their origin.[1]

The one-sided approach to the study of burins has been further extended by Terrade,[2] Peyrony, Garrod, Bouyssonie, Neuville,[3] Pradel and others.[4] Relying exclusively on the criterion of burin facets, or more exactly on the presence of a small flat edge produced by vertical flaking of a blade, they have begun to see burins even in Mousterian and Acheulian industries. However, there is no kind of evidence to support the real existence of the Mousterian burins that the authors have claimed. Such evidence would be provided by bone objects of the period bearing traces of work from burins, but, as is well known, such material proof is quite absent from Mousterian sites.

What are the so-called core-shaped or multi-faceted 'burins' with two, three and more burin scars (fig. 37.1)? Capitan considered them as the initial form of Aurignacian burins. Are we, in fact, dealing with burins at all? Could one conceivably cut bone or even wood with such a tool whose working part has several facets? It is well known that the most important structural trait of any burin, starting with undoubted ethnographic

specimens (for example, Eskimo ones), whether stone or metal, and finishing with modern steel ones, is the presence of only one facet or side on the working edge. A good specimen of a flint burin, for example from Mezin (fig. 37.5), is very close in shape to the simplest form of contemporary burin (fig. 37.2). It has one cutting face and one cutting angle only. This rule holds good for all burins.

We may add that the bone burins of the Bororo tribes made of an animal tooth (incisor) similarly have one working facet (fig. 37.4). It is very probable that some neolithic tools from Siberia, recalling small cores by their shape, were actually burins. Their side surfaces are multi-faceted (fig. 37.6), but on these the conical side lies almost at right-angles to the facet, which makes them more suitable for cutting. The traces of use on these burins, a few of which have just reached our laboratory from the Irkutsk Museum, have not yet been studied. Nevertheless they are quite different structually from the flint objects from Siberia known as 'neolithic burins' (fig. 37.3).

Traces of use have been identified on single-faceted burins; they consisted of groups of fine parallel lines on the side faces. On a burin from Mezin these striations

[1] V. A. Gorodtsov, *Proceedings of the Archaeological Section of the Russian Association of Scientific Institutes of Social Sciences*, 5 (Moscow, 1930).
[2] A. Terrade, *Mémoires de la Société Préhistorique Francaise* (1912), pp. 185–95.
[3] R. Neuville, *L'Anthropologie*, 41 (1931), pp. 13–51, 249–53.
[4] L. Pradel, *L'Anthropologie*, 52 (1948), pp. 220–8.

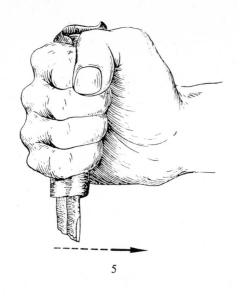

5

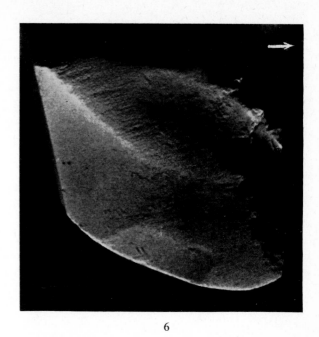

6

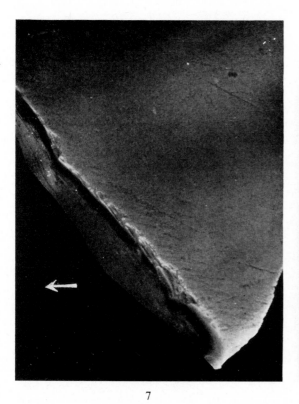

7

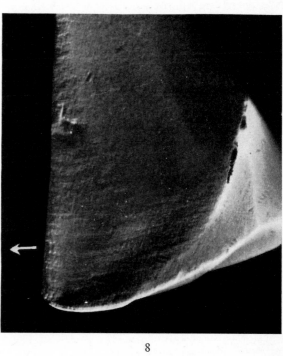

8

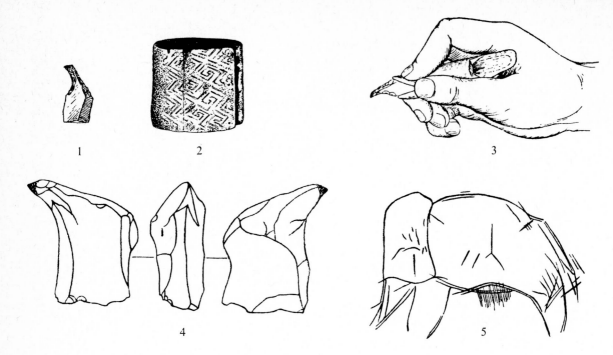

39 (AND OPPOSITE) 1 *Flint beak-shaped burin from Mezin; 2 upper palaeolithic engraved bracelet of mammoth ivory from Mezin; 3 reconstruction of beak-shaped burin in its handle in use; 4 beak-shaped burin from Malta (Siberia); 5 drawing of a mammoth on bone from Malta; 6 ancient Eskimo flint burin from Chukotka; 7 neolithic burin from Khakhsyk (E. Siberia) of tabular flint; 8 ancient Eskimo burin of obsidian from Chukotka; 9 micro-photograph of working part of obsidian burin, arrows on the right edge indicating the traces.*

lay not on the front but on the back, for the burin was wider here and so suffered the initial wear. The lines are at right-angles to the axis of the burin and parallel to the surface being cut. During work a burin evidently was fitted into a handle and held in a vertical position (fig. 38.5).

Observations by V. T. Ivanova in 1954 on burins from Timonovka made with a binocular lens are of considerable interest. These revealed severe wear on the burins whose traces showed that they had been used in a quite unusual way. The working edge on one (a medial burin) was not the burin angle produced by the facets but the ventral surface of the blade. So during use the under-face (flake surface) was in a frontal not a sagittal plane. The side facets were worn by use and so had lost their lustre and become mat. The linear marks of movement were very distinct (fig. 38.6).

Another burin (of normal type) with working edge produced by a burin blow had traces demonstrating its use not only as a burin but also as a chisel. This secondary function could be produced by altering the position of the hand so that the axis of the tool changed from a vertical to a horizontal position.

The presence of a burin facet, which is regarded as the morphological trait of burins, is not a criterion of function in all cases.

Kostenki IV has yielded material illustrating this point. It produced typical medial burins on long retouched blades; two opposed burin facets on one end should, it would be assumed, leave no doubt that these were burins. Archaeologists to whom these tools were shown unanimously agreed that this was so, and yet micro-analysis of the surface proved it to be otherwise. The use traces were found not on the burin facets but on the back of the blade. They took the form of striations running half-way across the back from one edge, and on this basis the tools were identified as whittling knives, or one-handed planes for use on bone and wood, with functional analogues in other sites (Kostenki I), where, however, they were made in a different way.

The burin facets at Kostenki IV must be regarded merely as a device to form a part either to be grasped in the hand or mounted in a handle. The use of the burin technique in the manufacture of other tools cannot be a matter for reasonable doubt. By striking off a single flake vertically with one blow the sharp blade-edge was

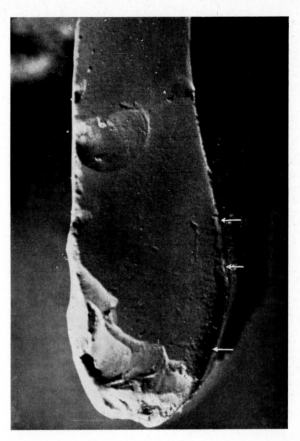

9

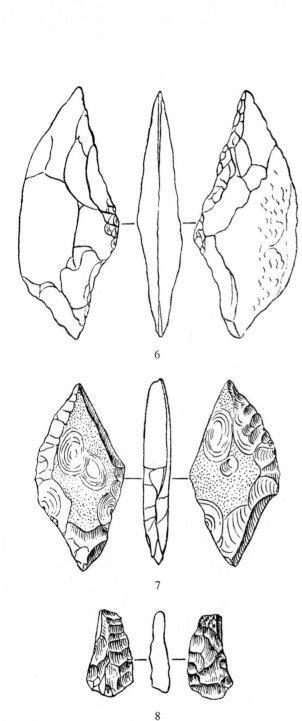

6

7

8

removed instead of resorting to more laborious blunting by pressure retouch.

In the material from Kostenki I and other sites there were tools with traces of use for cutting meat, and, as already mentioned, the traces take the form of a fairly wide area of polishing on both faces of the blade. The opposite angle of the blade has been taken off by a burin blow in order to provide a rest for the index finger.

The use of a burin blow to blunt a blade-edge, in the parts where its sharpness would have impeded its use when held between the fingers, can be observed on many tools used without handles. Sakajia cave yielded specimens of concave scrapers for use on wood and bone, made on massive flint flakes. The sharp edges of the flake had been removed on both sides by burin blows which would have allowed it to be held between the index finger and thumb.

It is very instructive to consider the use of the burin blow in the manufacture of flint drills in some neolithic sites. Such evidence has just been found in material from a site discovered by Okladnikov at Khakhsyk in Yakutia. Small tools made by flat pressure retouch from this site had pointed ends re-sharpened by taking off burin spalls from one or both sides.[1] Originally the tools were awls, but micro-analysis revealed clear traces of their re-use as drills, in the form of transverse striations across the burin facets. The facet arrises had acted as the cutting edges during boring.

New evidence that a burin scar is not an undoubted indication of use of the tool as a burin is provided by certain burins prepared without such blows. At Mezin, Eliseevich, Malta and other upper palaeolithic sites a series of small flint tools of beak-shaped form have been found. Research has shown that they were used as a special kind of burin. In some examples, as at Mezin, these burins were made by retouching irregular flint blades selected from the mass of waste flint (fig. 39.1, 4).

For what purposes were such tools used? The beak-shaped form with drooping conical point and the character of the lustre indicate that only slight physical force was needed. They were not therefore suitable for cutting bone transversely or longitudinally, for this requires great physical force and a solid cutting angle which is not present in beak-shaped burins. The sum of indications suggests that they were engraving instruments, tools for artistic sculpture of bone, especially for engravings of animals and ornament (fig. 39.2, 5).

In Mezin, Malta, Eliseevich, and Kostenki I, where the burins just mentioned have been found, engravings on bone are well known. In Mezin, moreover, a bone handle was found specially prepared for engraving on bone. It is probable that the burins from the Grotte d'Ammonites (France), known under the name of 'beak with notch' (*bec à encoche*), and regarded as engraving instruments, had an analogous purpose.

In conclusion it is necessary to turn our attention to one or two types of burin found in the neolithic site of Khakhsyk in Yakutia, and amongst the ancient Eskimo material found by S. I. Rudenko in the Chukotsk area. These extremely individual types are still not very numerous. For the Bering Sea Eskimos, who were already familiar with iron and iron burins, stone burins were an exceptional survival. They were made of coloured flint, chert and obsidian, and were either semi-circular or rhomboidal in shape. They were made not on blades but on either flakes or tabular flint (as at Khakhsyk) and retouched. These burins were commonly two-sided and intended to be mounted in a handle (fig. 39.6, 7). The cutting edge in some cases had been made by a burin blow and in others by fine trimming. Micro-analysis revealed the striations characteristic of all burins on their lateral faces. On the obsidian burins the striations were weak; the traces of wear took the form of rough patches without lustre along the side of the cutting edge (fig. 39.8, 9).

Thus the study of burins by traces of use has brought real revisions to the previous typological view of these tools.

e. Flint awls of upper palaeolithic times

The discovery of bone needles with eyes, and awls, in upper palaeolithic sites has caused the investigator to raise the question as to the existence of sewn skin clothing in this period. Although the majority of students at the present time do not doubt that hunters of the upper palaeolithic period protected themselves from the cold with skin clothing and knew how to sew, there are still some who continue to contest this view. They contend that the existence of needles and awls in such a remote period does not constitute sufficient proof of the existance of sewn clothing. In support of this they cite the Australians, who had no sewn clothing, but who used bone needles in sewing small skin articles.

Without dwelling on the fact that the tropical or sub-tropical climate of the areas where the Australians live is irrelevant to the conditions of Ice-Age Europe and Asia, we will confine ourselves to those tools which are closely connected with the working of skin and fur. Firstly there are the characteristic upper palaeolithic end-scrapers used for cleaning and softening the underside of the fur. Secondly in the same period there were bone burnishers used on the outer face of the skin. Thirdly there existed bone needles and awls. Fourthly at this period mineral colouring was widely employed, as revealed by the presence of stone and bone mortars, pestles and ochre of various shades on the sites. It is difficult to concede that all these were used for small skin objects (like bags, screens and so on) of secondary importance in the life of prehistoric man. The remaining category of tools, closely connected with the sewing of clothing, were a variety of flint awls. The existence of these tools has been established on many sites, sometimes in great numbers. There are some grounds for supposing that only thin skins, taken off small animals, could be pierced with a bone needle, and even in this case it would have been necessary to broaden the hole with a bone awl, so that the needle could pass freely through with a thread of sinew. Thus the skin would be pierced preparatorily, then the hole widened with a bone point, so that finally the needle and thread themselves could go through.

Flint awls would have been preferable for initial piercing. Using a flint awl it would have been possible to sew together skins and make composite articles without a needle by passing a pliable sinew directly through the pierced hole. On many palaeolithic sites needles have not been found and it is quite possible that in a number

---

[1] S. A. Semenov, *Materials and Researches on the Archaeology of the U.S.S.R.*, 39 (1955), pp. 455–8.

of cases sewing was done without them. Flint awls had a very sharp tip broadening out towards the base, which made them suitable for piercing a hole in the skin for the passage of the thread. However, work with an awl had its snags. A broad awl might not only pierce but also with the pressure cut the skin, while the projecting point was liable to break in use on thick skin, if there was a careless sideways movement of the hand. So to widen the hole to the necessary diameter a bone awl was required. The flint awl merely began the hole; a bone point of circular section opened it and stretched the elastic fibres of the skin, so that after the passage of the thread (with or without needle), the hole closed up and gripped it. Such would be the process of work with a piercer awl, bone point and needle in sewing skin and fur clothing in upper palaeolithic times.

We have studied flint awls from different palaeolithic sites. In Kostenki I, as remarked above, awls were made after the fashion of shouldered points. Small flint blades were subjected to steep retouch at the base where the notch was made, and then the tip was sharpened by fine retouch, whose facets can only be examined with a magnifying glass (fig. 40.1–5). Sometimes the sharp edge of the awl was retouched to blunt it or make it narrower. At Kostenki I in certain cases small elongated flakes with narrow sharp ends were used as awls. They were employed without trimming and their purpose can only be recognized by the traces of use on them.

Examples of the use of flakes or irregular blades as awls have been recognized on material from the Siberian site of Malta. The flakes varied in form; sometimes the tip was trimmed with fine retouch, sometimes not.

The awls from Kostenki IV are of great interest in research. At this site in the complex of a long house a large quantity of flint objects of microlithic appearance were discovered. Small fine bladelets, struck off with burin blows from larger blades, had been carefully treated with fine retouch on one or both edges, and a substantial number of them had a sharp tip bearing traces of use in piercing. Probably such awls were used for sewing together the skins of small animals without a bone needle. This supposition is based on the presence in the site of a large number of hare bones, about 100 individuals. Besides awls little blades were found whose ends did not come to a straight tip, but were bent over at angle of 120°–30° to their axes. In one instance the blade was blunted by retouch, and study of the end of the point showed that it had been used for cutting. In all probability the initial cutting of the hare skins (removal of paws and straightening the edge) was done with these tools before sewing them together. This suggestion will require further study for verification.

Study of flint awls under the binocular microscope has led to the identification of traces of wear of two types.

(1) Striations in the form of fine lines always on the very tip and parallel to the axis of the awl, that is along the line of the working movement. Sometimes they take the form of sharp lines produced by hard sand grains that had found their way into the pores of the skin, but this is a rare, not a characteristic trait.

(2) Polishing of the tip is often detectable with the unaided eye. Under the microscope the unevenness of the polishing can be seen covering the whole tip surface with an irregular lustre. The strongest lustre is on the projecting parts which during use encountered the greatest resistance from the material being pierced (fig. 40.2). This occurs above all on the facet arrises facing forwards, structural lumps in the flint or projecting pieces of impurities in it. On the reverse side the projections often have no polishing on them.

In rare cases attempts to sharpen the point by grinding can be recognized. An example of this is an awl from Kostenki I with a notch at its base (fig. 40.4). On both retouched edges on its underside there are definite traces of grinding the edges of the tip.

In Kostenki I besides normal awls on blades and flakes a completely individual type was identified. This was a beak-shaped tool made on a retouched flake. 'The beak' or chisel-shaped tool bore traces of strong polishing and striations indicating that it had been driven into some material, which might well have been skin (fig. 40.6, 7).

f. Upper palaeolithic meat knives

One of the most important functions of stone tools in palaeolithic times was skinning and cutting up the carcasses of game, and also cutting meat during eating. Animal skin, muscular fibre and tendons are very tough material and strongly resistant to cutting. Human teeth and fingernails, in contrast to predatory animals, are not at all suited to even rough and ready dismemberment of large game. A flint blade or flake with sharp edges would be an essential tool therefore in the hands of a palaeolithic hunter.

Since the division of a carcass and the cutting up of meat is not a formal creative act, like making a stone, bone or wooden object, it might appear at first sight that the mere division of a whole body into parts could be done with any kind of flint flake or blade that was to hand. So it might be concluded that to identify any specially prepared knife designed for cutting meat would be impossible. In point of fact this is not so.

It has already been shown that some shouldered points bore traces of use for ripping, disembowelling and cutting up game, which are specifically characteristic of this. Such traces could not be formed by any other kind of use. However, on many other sites in the Soviet Union shouldered points have not been found, although the dismemberment of game was undoubtedly done

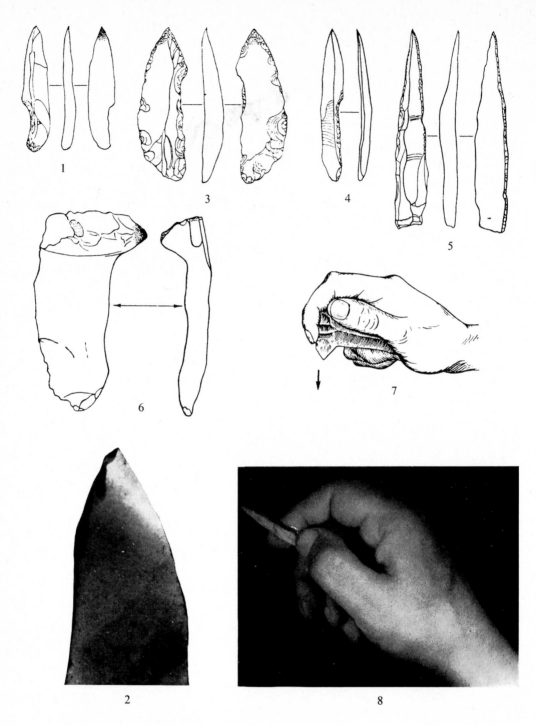

40 1, 3 and 4 Shouldered points from Kostenki I; 2 traces of use as an awl on one (1); 5 awl from Kostenki IV; 6 beak-shaped flake from Kostenki I used as a perforator; 7 its method of use reconstructed; 8 'shouldered point' (4) held with the index finger resting in the notch.

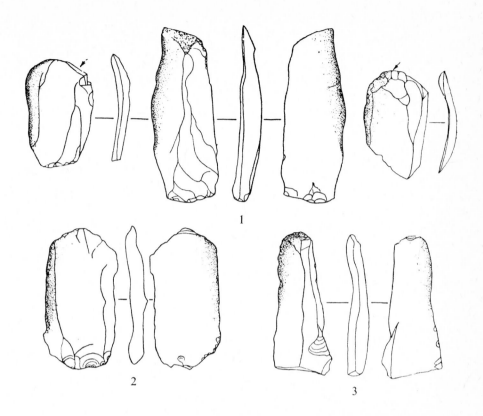

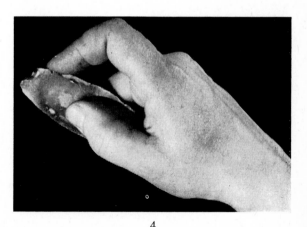

everywhere. Evidently therefore for this purpose there existed implements of another form.

Amongst the material from Malta were a series of short blades, barely retouched except for some relatively insignificant trimming. The largest were up to 80 mm long, the smallest up to 50 mm, and their width varied from 20 to 35 mm. On each of them one sharp edge was polished. The other edge either was not polished or it was too thick to be used for cutting. The polishing extended on to both faces of the blade, ventral and dorsal, which showed that its function had been to cut into a soft material into which it had sunk, probably meat. The polishing, however, did not cover the whole edge. The thick end had remained unpolished as opposed to the thin end (fig. 41.1–3).

Relying on the signs of wear, it can be inferred that the meat knives from Malta were used without separate handles, being held between the thumb, index and second fingers. The thumb and second finger held the sides (ventral and dorsal faces of the blade), while the index finger pressed from on top at the forward end of the blade, where an area had been blunted by retouch (fig. 41.4).

In palaeolithic times meat was the basic kind of

41 *Upper palaeolithic meat knives from Malta (Siberia): 1–3 one-sided knives on short blades; 4 how such a knife was held.*

103

food and was eaten either badly roasted, cured or raw. Generally pastoral or hunting people (like the nomads of Mongolia, Tibet, Abysinnia and other countries) eat such meat with a knife in one hand. Meat is normally cut into strips, and baked or cured in this form. Then each person takes a piece and, holding one end in his teeth, cuts it free with a quick movement of the knife at his mouth, repeating the operation until the whole strip has been consumed. The cutting is done upwards from

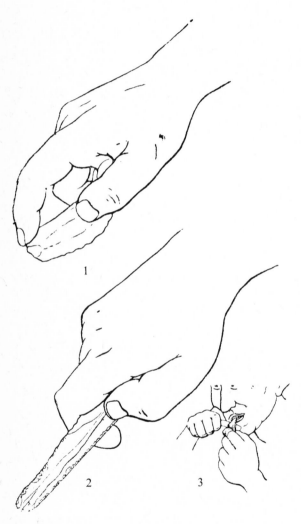

42 *Two types of upper palaeolithic meat knife in the material at Malta and Kostenki I: short knife (1) and long knife (2) as held in the hand. 3 cutting raw meat at the mouth while eating (a reconstruction).*

below. We have seen this done among Nenetz reindeer herdsmen in the Kanin peninsula in 1928. With raw reindeer meat and fat this method is uniformly practised among practically all northerners. It is due not to custom or habit but to primitive conditions of life, where it appears the most rational method.

In Kostenki I besides shouldered points a special type of knife had been used, the blunt-ended knife (fig. 43.1, 2). It consisted of a flint blade up to 150 mm long, neither side retouched, if we leave out of account the retouch on the very end. At the lower end, which was held in the hand, both edges were blunted by retouch.

A peculiarity of this knife was its method of use as indicating by polishing. This covered the working end of the knife on all sides almost at all points of its surface, and then spread from the edge almost to the middle of the blade, where it gradually weakened. On the working edge the shine was mirror-like. From this it is evident that the knife had had long use and was employed without a handle (fig. 43.2).

That this knife was employed in the treatment of carcasses cannot be doubted. The polishing covered all the hollows of the facets, and could have been formed only if the working part of the tool had encountered resistance from a pliable but elastic mass which made contact at all points on its surface. Such material could only have been the muscles, adhesive tissues and internal organs of an animal's body. Probably the knife was used for skinning. If a skin was to be taken off in one piece a knife would be necessary to cut it free at the head, neck, tail and legs of the animal. In taking the skin off fat animals a layer of fat is also peeled off stuck to the pelt, and commonly with the fat are tendons of meat. The skin therefore would have to be cut free underneath to release it from the animal's body, and a blunt-ended knife would be safer to prevent damage to the skin, which is easily pierced or cut through during this operation.

A blunt-ended knife would be unsuitable for ripping open a carcass when the skin has got to be severed, but cutting can be substituted for piercing by pressing the blade down hard on the animal's skin with the fingers of the left hand. Moreover, a palaeolithic hunter was supplied with sharp-ended knives (fig. 43.3, 4) and other suitable tools. There are some grounds for believing that when skinning he made use not only of stone knives but bone ones also, which have not yet been studied.

Microscopic study of the surface of a whole series of blunt-ended knives from Kostenki I has shown that these specimens, which had a specially long duration of use, have not only marks of polishing but also a close web of linear marks in the form of scratches and lines. The latter were not oriented in one direction, and on the working end, which was the most intensively polished,

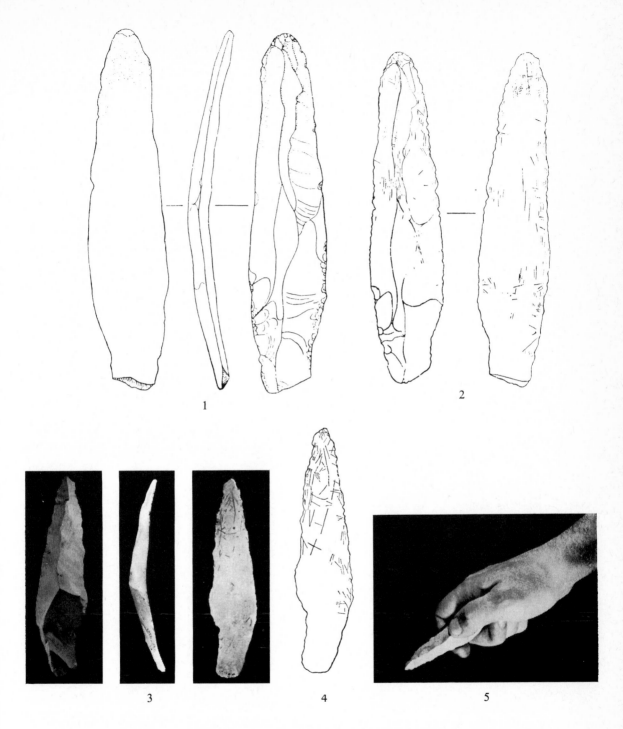

43 *Upper palaeolithic meat knives from Kostenki I: 1 and 2 blunt-ended (1 polishing on surface at working end on both faces; 2 striations showing direction of movement); 3 and 4 pointed knife (4 striations on ventral face); 5 working position of pointed knife reconstructed.*

they intersected at various angles. This kind of web of lines (fig. 46.1) indicates that during use the knife did not have one definite cutting plane, nor a constant angle at which it was held; the working position of the knife varied as one or the other edge was used on the material being cut. The hand could have such freedom of movement only in cutting muscular and other fibrous body parts.

As regards the striations on the blades themselves, they usually run almost parallel to the blade edge or slightly inclined to it, and occur on both faces almost over the whole surface (fig. 43.2, 4). This indicates that the knife was deeply embedded in the material being worked, and operated with a one-way or two-way 'sawing' movement necessary for the cross-cutting of muscular fibre, tendons and sinews.

g. Mesolithic flint knives from Crimean caves

Study of flint knives made on blades reveals the very varied uses to which they were put in daily life in the Stone Age. Those dug up by Bonch-Osmolovsky and Bibikov in the Crimean caves of Kara-Kush-Koba,

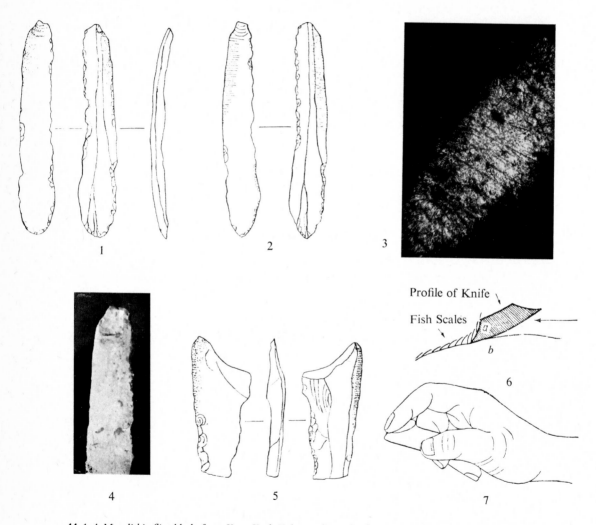

44 *1–4 Mesolithic flint blade from Kara-Kush-Koba used as a knife: 1 general view showing wear on both faces on one edge; 2 general view showing striations from wear; 3 striations on ventral face enlarged 50 × ; 4 working part of knife with left edge blunted and right edge toothed; 5 mesolithic flint knife from Fatma-Koba with wear traces on both faces; 6 method of work reconstructed (ab suffers friction); 7 method of holding the tool.*

Fatma-Koba, Shan-Koba, and Murzak-Koba must be put into a special categeory.

The first specimen came to light in Vekilova's excavation in Kara-Kush-Koba in 1949. It is a small flint blade (75 mm long, 10–12 mm broad) toothed along one edge and with intense wear on its surface (fig. 44.1), showing itself as gloss on top and bottom faces of the blade. In addition the arrises and the working edge are strongly blunted from the loss of large particles in the material itself. Such wear could only have arisen as the result of very prolonged use. It must be emphasized that taking all the facts into consideration (size of the blade, its section, the disposition and micro-structure of the traces) the evidence points to the use of the flint upon a resistant material with the elastic toughness of animal matter. We can quite exclude therefore stone, bone and wood.

The striations occur as very fine lines on the ventral face and on both facets of the dorsal face of the blade, and lie at right-angles to its working edge (fig. 44.2). The micro-photograph shows that they deviate markedly from a true right-angle and intersect with each other, indicating merely the variable position of the axis of the instrument, which is a common occurrence in work with the hand (fig. 44.3). In every case the texture of these traces differs from those on meat knives. Moreover, such strong blunting of the edge could not take place on meat knives (fig. 44.4).

Further examination of other material from Fatma-Koba, Murzak-Koba, and Shan-Koba revealed that blades with analogous traces occurred there (fig. 44.5). These blades differed in shape, size and section, but the marks of wear were identical. In all cases the polishing occurred on both faces of the blade, upper and lower, while there was a variable degree of blunting on the edge. In each case the striations were at right-angles to the working edge (fig. 44.5).

The decipherment of these traces gave rise to great difficulties. It was quite obvious that they were not used for cutting, but for some kind of scraping, and yet the material worked had affected both faces of the blade. It was also clear that the tool's movement was 'on himself' and the tool was undoubtedly used without a handle, as indicated by the weak polishing on the surface of the non-working parts. All that was known about methods of working on stone, bone, wood, skin, or cutting meat, or sawing different hard materials, had no relevance to the wear traces on the mesolithic blades from the Crimea.

The only possible use at that period which could have been responsible for such traces would be the scaling of fish.

In this operation a sliding movement is used with the blade held at a slight angle to the surface being cleansed. The blade edge encounters resistance on both faces; below it is in contact with the skin of the fish, while above friction arises between knife and scales, as the former sinks beneath them, tearing them off the skin (fig. 44.6).

Did the mesolithic inhabitants of the Crimean caves clean the fish for eating? Remains of fish bones have been found in the caves. Climatic conditions of the period gave rise to a primitive fishing economy accompanied by collecting. The fish were probably eaten both cooked and raw; they could be baked on a fire without removing the scales, but scaling was necessary if the fish were eaten raw, as is commonly done by northern fishermen, Oceanians, natives of the Australian coast and other peoples.

h. Whittling knives of palaeolithic and neolithic times

In the existing terminology applied to palaeolithic and neolithic tools a whole series of names are used for knives: 'knife-shaped blades', 'blunted-back points', 'points in the shape of a penknife blade', 'semi-lunate knives', 'elbow-shaped knives', and so on. Such names tell us nothing about the real purpose of the tool. Commonly every conceivable kind of cutting of different materials is attributed to the 'knives' without any explanation of the character and peculiarities of the work done by them.

In the Stone Age it was actually possible for tools to fulfil two or more functions, but divisions of functions between tools arose at an early stage. This division of functions between tools in the Stone Age invites comparison with the position in the early metallic period. Stone tools on account of their brittleness could not be used for different kinds of work requiring different degrees of force or angles of pressure on the edge or point in the same way as metal tools could. For example, a 'point with blunted back' but retouched working edge is very thin in section, and such a blade-edge could not whittle wood or bone although it might cut meat or skin.

For whittling wood and bone a new implement was introduced in upper palaeolithic times, the whittling knife, which we have identified in the material from Kostenki I and IV.

The whittling knife from Kostenki I consisted of a flint blade 120 mm long and 30 mm broad (fig. 45.1), which, as with the majority of prismatic blades, was bow-shaped in section. Both edges were worked by fine retouch. The left side is slightly blunted by retouch in the lower grasping part; the right side bears a slight notch made by pressure retouch at its forward end to accommodate the index finger (A).

The tool bore traces of prolonged use and the grasping part had been slightly polished by the hand. On the ventral face there is an area of intense polishing on the right-hand side, growing stronger as the edge is approached. On the upper surface of the tool there is no

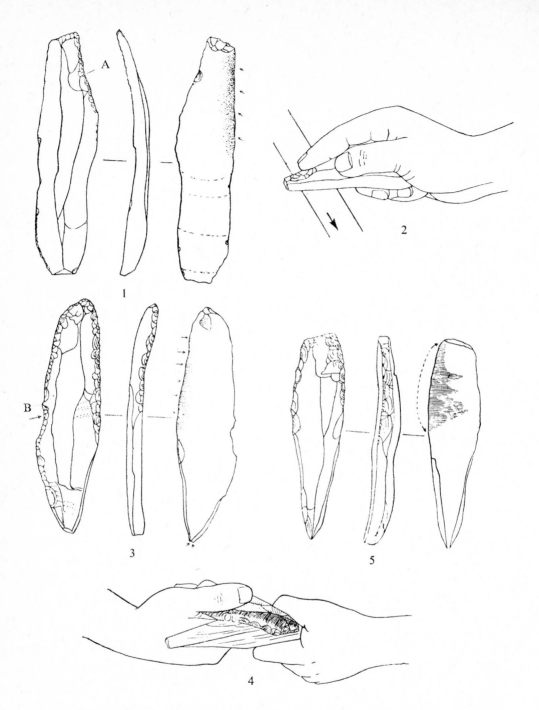

45 1 *Whittling knife from Kostenki I with notch* (**A**) *for index finger (area of polishing on underface stippled and general direction of striations indicated by arrows); 2 reconstruction of how the knife was held; 3 whittling knife from Kostenki IV with two burin facets at base and notch* (**B**) *for middle finger (direction of striations indicated by arrows); 4 reconstruction of method of working the knife ('from himself'); 5 whittling knife from Kostenki IV with broken end, the base worked by burin blows for mounting in handle (polished area shaded).*

intense polishing, but a weak gloss all over the tool caused by the friction of the human hand.

Careful examination of the whole tool showed that the lustre on the grasping part was transected by very fine short lines, running in different directions. This type of wear arose from sand grains in the pores of the skin which from the pressure and sliding of the hand left irregular traces on the flint surface.

The striations on the polished part of the tool were of quite a different kind. Here appreciable scratches and lines were found running at right-angles, diagonally or occasionally parallel to the edge (fig. 47). The blade edge was not only polished but to some extent jagged with tiny scars, mainly on the under-face, which had caused the tool to become unserviceable and be abandoned. During whittling particles of flint had been torn off the edge under the pressure of the hand, which probably also scratched the working surface of the blade. Extraneous abrasive elements might also have fallen on to the blade.[1]

The dorsal surface of the blade was not worn. We have already explained why the upper surface of a whittling knife is hardly ever worn. When we whittle wood with a thin metal knife the blade, as it sinks into the wood, suffers uneven pressure and friction, but even the side facing the paring will bear traces of wear. A flint whittling knife is a good deal thicker with a steeper edge angle, because a thin flint blade would crumble at the first movement. A thick blade produces a thin paring which curls up into a circle and so hardly ever causes friction on the upper side of the blade. This applies particularly to bone from which only a very thin paring can be removed. There are some grounds for supposing that the whittling knife being discussed was used to best advantage on bone; traces of whittling on bone objects from Kostenki I are numerous.

In Kostenki IV whittling knives of another type were employed (fig. 45.3–5). They were made on blades, but have retouch on both edges except at the grasping end, where both sides have been removed by two strong burin blows, giving the butt the form of a medial burin. It is customary to call such tools burins, but in fact, in spite of the traces of prolonged use found on them, there are no traces of their use as burins. The wear traces on the underneath were not on the right side as at Kostenki I but on the left which is their especial peculiarity. On the micro-photographs the traces emerge as scratches either at right-angles or slightly inclined to the edge (fig. 46.2). There are no notches for the index finger on the knives from Kostenki IV, but on one (fig. 45.3) there is a notch in the middle of the left-hand side (A). In holding it the second finger of the right hand would rest

comfortably in this notch. Its presence and the position of the wear traces on the left side are evidence for reconstructing the process of whittling differently from that with the Kostenki I knife. Here the whittling was effected by a movement 'away from himself' (fig. 45.4). This method allowed the application of much greater force by making full use of the shoulder muscles. Even the left hand, which in the 'on-himself' movement merely grasped the object being worked, in the 'from-himself' movement played a full part by exerting pressure in a contrary direction to the right hand.

The whittling knives from Kostenki IV evidently had prolonged use. The intensive polishing, particularly on one of them, the indications of repeated trimming of the blade with secondary retouch, as well as a fair degree of gloss caused by the hand over the whole surface, all testify to this. The possibility cannot be excluded that the opposite side of the blade (right on the underneath) was sometimes used in work, but striations there were scarcely detectable.

A third kind of whittling knife has been identified from the Timonovka material (fig. 48.1). This is a short knife, sometimes trapeze-shaped. The palaeolithic craftsmen whittled with this knife, holding it between the thumb and two fingers, or possibly inserted it in a haft.

Thus the whittling knives which we have identified in upper palaeolithic industries, allowing for their differences and individual peculiarities, are distinguished by the following characteristics:

(1) They are made on blades.
(2) They can be trimmed or even formed by retouch and burin blows, but sometimes they are not shaped and have no retouch.
(3) The most important criteria for functional identification are two types of wear; polishing and striations.
(4) The main wear is, as a rule, confined to one side of the tool, and on the other side the traces are less distinctive.
(5) The worn side must be the ventral side of the blade, as the smooth side always faced the material.
(6) The polishing is along the edge of the tool and gradually weakens away from the edge.
(7) The striations indicating the direction of the hand movement appear as microscopic scratches or lines lying at right-angles to the edge or slightly inclined from this.

The marks just enumerated of palaeolithic whittling knives are general traits for stone whittling knives of all periods. This is confirmed by study of ground neolithic

---

[1] The micro-photograph of the worn surface (fig. 47) shows a rather intricate picture of striations on a 'ribby' fracture surface.

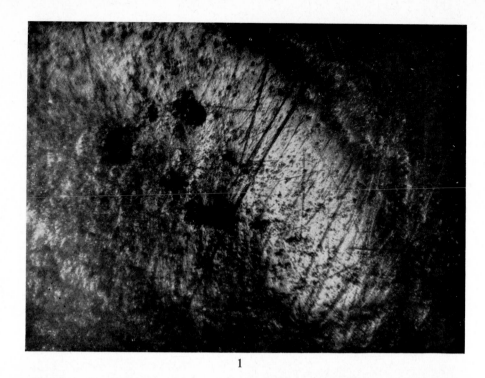

1

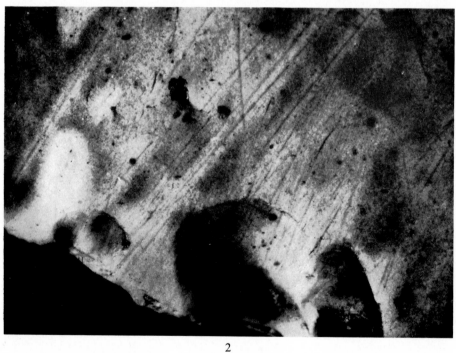

2

46 1 *Wear on meat knife from Kostenki I in fig. 43.1 magnified 75 × 2 striations on whittling knife from Kostenki IV in fig. 45.5 magnified 30 ×.*

110

47 *Wear on a whittling knife from Kostenki I in fig. 45.1 magnified 300 ×.*

knives from the L. Baikal area made on nephrite blades. Generally these knives are semi-circular in shape with either a concave or straight blade. They have had the name 'knife' conferred on them, quite accurately, but without giving any clue to their specific function. In fact, ground nephrite knives were not all-purpose tools for various methods of cutting. For example, in disembowelling game, cutting meat or skin these semi-circular knives would have been quite impractical, because this type of work requires the blade to be either thin edged or denticulated by retouch. In these knives the blade generally has a long narrow facet on one side and no sign of toothing. This facet has been made by grinding to strengthen the cutting angle in an analogous way to the fine retouch on palaeolithic tools. The flat surface would cut the wood away, giving a small thin paring. So these knives must be regarded as cutting tools preferably for wood, but also suitable for bone. Their use on wood is testified by the position of the polishing, which occurs not only on the under-face but also on opposed parts of

the facet where it has been caused by the paring. The cutting edge of the blade of these knives is 45°–50°. With such an angle the paring would be thin, but because of its softness thicker with wood than bone.

Neolithic whittling knives from Siberia are of varying size. One from Khakhsyk of miniature size, 30 mm long and 10 mm broad, is made of a cherty rock and has a concave blade (fig. 48.2). Knives from Verkholensk have straight or slightly concave blades (fig. 48.3–6) and distinct wear striations (fig. 49.1, 2), which run as straight lines from the side of the blade inclined towards the butt, and sometimes intersect. These intersections are due to the sharp curve of the axis of the knife in relation to the worked surface (inclination of the tip or butt), which might arise during whittling.

Some nephrite knives have a double facet on the blade (fig. 48.4). One facet is narrow and steep, the other broad and sloping gently. The latter faced the worked material and so suffered severer wear.

Study of the knives from Verkholensk shows that in

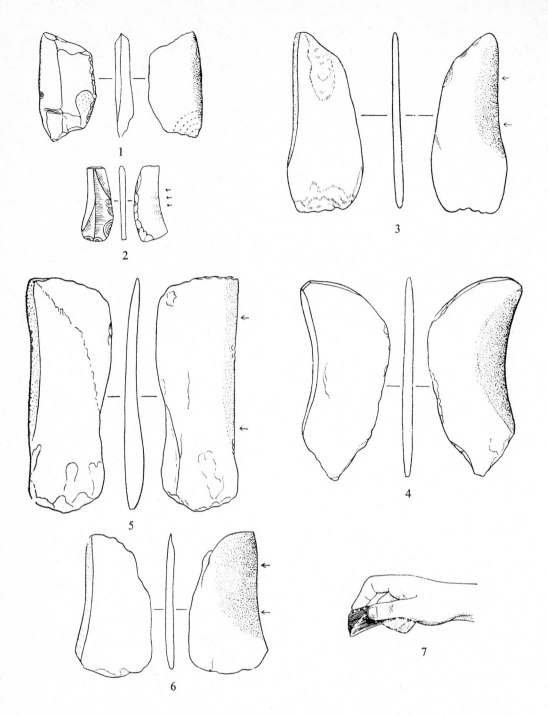

48 1 *Short upper palaeolithic flint whittling knife from Timonovka used without handle; 2 neolithic ground chert whittling knife from Khakhsyk (Siberia); 3–6 neolithic nephrite whittling knives from burials at Verkholensk on R. Angar (facet ground on one edge only except 4 which has two facets, broad and narrow, the former facing the material); 7 method of holding knife reconstructed.*

neolithic, as in upper palaeolithic, times two methods of work were employed: 'on himself' and 'from himself'. On one specimen the wear traces are not on the right-hand side (looking from the butt end) but on the left, while the facet had been ground down on the right (fig. 50.1). Knives of this type could only have been used 'from himself' with the application of great physical force by being mounted in a handle (fig. 50.2, 3).

Ground whittling knives played an important part in working bone. There were numerous traces of whittling on the bone and antler objects from the Verkholensk graves, besides evidence for the use of burin and chisel. Some objects could not have been made without whittling knives (fig. 50.4, 5). This was particularly so in the important job of cutting out the barbs on antler and bone harpoons. On their surface, in spite of the grinding down in the final stage of manufacture, traces of cuts made with whittling knives are visible. The removal of the material between the barb and the stem of the harpoon, to judge by the traces of work and form of the cuts, was made in the way indicated in the attached reconstruction (fig. 50.6).

Semi-lunate neolithic knives with concave blades were used for whittling spear and arrow shafts, axe and adze handles, and objects of slight diameter made from saplings, such as poles, stakes, palings and so on. A concave blade was well suited to this. However, for treating broad expanses of wood in large objects it was no use, and for this a two-handed plane would be necessary. That such existed in neolithic times is shown by the two-handed stone plane found on a site in Kamen Island in the River Angar (fig. 51). It was made on a flake or blade of a light-coloured cherty rock, and was 160 mm long and 50 mm broad. It had been ground on both faces, but the working side was flat and the other convex. The working edge was convex, and there were notches at either end for the fixing of handles. The strongly polished part near the edge bore striations, which, as the micro-photograph reveals (fig. 51.2), ran at right-angles to the cutting edge.[1]

1

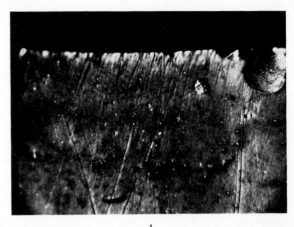

2

49 *Micro-photographs of wear striations on ground whittling knives from Verkholensk (the almost horizontal lines in 2 are from grinding and are overlain by the clearer vertical striations from whittling).*

i. Sickles

Research on stone reaping knives arose through Bibikov's excavations in 1947 at the early agricultural settlement of Luka-Vrublevetskaya on the River Dnestr. In the stone industry from this site a large number of prismatic blades of grey flint were found with traces of severe wear in certain places on their surface, which took the form of a mirror-like lustre on one edge of the flint, the other side being mat. The polishing covered a broad area at one end, dying out towards the middle of the flint to form a triangular shape (fig. 52.1), and it occurred

on both faces of the flint. On the ventral face it died away from the right edge inwards, and on the dorsal face from the left edge, but, if this side had two facets, it did not pass on to the right one. Where the dorsal face had three facets the polishing might lightly extend into the middle one, but the central arris of the blade acted as a barrier to its further extension.

There was very little retouch on the blades and an attempt to denticulate the edge was never observed. The working edge appeared not only to be polished but in many cases blunted by prolonged uniform use involving

---

[1] S. A. Semenov, *Materials and Researches on the Archaeology of the U.S.S.R.*, 2 (1941), p. 209.

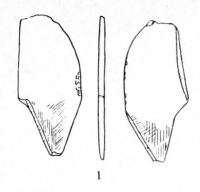

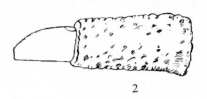

1

2

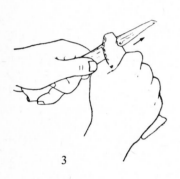

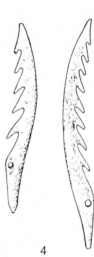

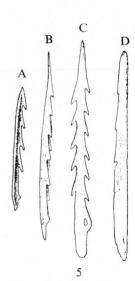

A B C D

3

4

5

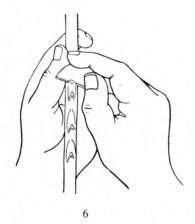

6

50 *Neolithic objects from Verkholensk in the L. Baikal area: 1 ground whittling knife with facet on right and dulling of surface on tang indicating insertion into handle; 2 the knife reconstructed in an antler handle; 3 method of whittling with knife ('from himself'); 4 curved harpoons; 5 straight harpoons (barbs one side (A), on one side but in two planes (B), on both sides alternating (C), early stage of manufacture (D)); 6 cutting out of barbs with a stone knife reconstructed.*

considerable physical force. Some blades had been broken during use.

It was quite obvious that these tools had been fixed in a handle, as the application of considerable force with short blades less than 60 mm long would be impossible if they were grasped in the fingers, especially when not blunted by retouch. Proof of the use of bone or wooden handles can be seen in the sharp demarcation between the polished and mat surfaces.

The essential clue revealing the character of the material worked by these tools was the even wear on both faces. Such a disposition of the polishing could only have arisen if the blade penetrated the worked material at right-angles and did so rapidly. It follows that it could not have been a hard material like stone, bone or wood. Yet intense and sharply demarcated polishing leads one to suppose that this material was not plastic, like skin or meat, for the latter would never leave such traces on a flint knife.

Examination of the polished area gave the accompanying micro-picture of the wear (fig. 52.2). The polished area appeared to be covered by tiny streaky scratches running parallel to the working edge of the tool. Only in a few cases did they intersect. Besides this on the paths of these streaks were holes of irregular shape and variable size, evidently surviving remains of the uneven flint fracture surface.

Analysis of these holes revealed another important detail which solved the puzzle of the function of these knife-like flint blades. The holes, as a rule, were higher on the right side than the left; the left edge was appreciably more worn than the right. Consequently in the course of a long period of time the wear of the worked material had produced one-sided attrition on the holes. With the Opak lamp in an oblique position it could be seen that the holes have a comet shape, the tail pointing towards the working end of the blade, the head towards the handle. This fact is proof of the one-way movement of the knife during use, more specifically a movement 'to himself'. The linear traces (streaks parallel to the blade edge) which cover the polished area indicate that the movement 'on himself' was a rapid one, for had the blade been slowly imbedded in the material the striations would have run obliquely to the blade edge.

Of all possible types of work in a primitive economy which involved a sharp blade in a quick movement 'to himself' the only conceivable use is as a sickle blade.

All that has been said about the traces of work on the flint blades from Luka-Vrublevetskaya (disposition and degree of polishing on the surfaces, character of the wear and direction of the streaks), relative to the kinetic peculiarities of the work and the comparative toughness of the material, therefore brings us to the conclusion that these tools were used for reaping. Other inferences cannot be reconciled with the accumulated evidence of the

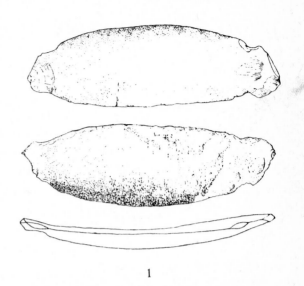

1

2

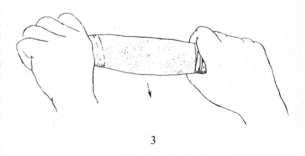

3

51 *Neolithic two-handed plane from the L. Baikal area; 1 general view; 2 microscopic use traces on the edge; 3 suggested method of use.*

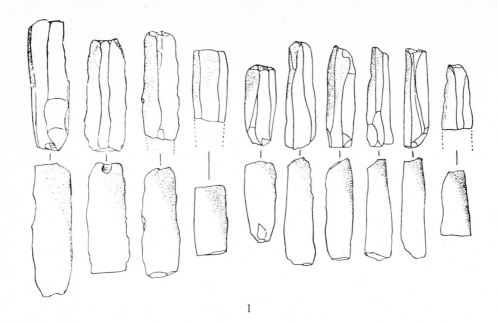

1

2

52 1 *Late neolithic flint sickles from Luka-Vrublevetskaya;* 2 *wear on working edge of first flint on left magnified 120 ×.*

traces. So on the evidence we have before us a very ancient type of stone sickle used in an early agricultural economy.

We announced the results of these researches and conclusions about the purpose of the flint blades with traces of polishing at the 1947 session of the Palaeolithic and Neolithic Section of the Institute of the History of Material Culture of the Academy of Sciences of the U.S.S.R., and they were published in 1949.[1] Soon afterwards direct evidence emerged of the existence of agriculture among the inhabitants of Luka-Vrublevetskaya; on the clay female statuettes Bibikov identified impressions of millet grains which for ritual reasons had been mixed into the clay paste.

A reconstruction of the sickle (fig. 53.1) that we originally put forward, directly hafted into the end of a wooden handle, is not the only possibility. Since the traces of wear on the blades from this site occupied a larger area at their end, it can be assumed that the end of the blade encountered a greater resistance from the material. This circumstance indicates that the blade was at an angle to the axis of the handle. Such a position of the blade was possible if it was set sideways in a slot at the front end of the handle (fig. 53.3), a reconstruction which is supported by finds near Lucerne, Switzerland, of neolithic sickles fixed in comparatively long wooden handles (fig. 53.4–6). The handles projected forward with pointed ends which acted as a trap for numerous stalks of the cereal being reaped, gathering them into a bunch, as the sickle moved forward, which could be held with the left hand.[2]

The second reconstruction corresponds better to the kind of wear found on the majority of flints at Luka-Vrublevetskaya, although the first cannot be entirely rejected. By this simple method of insertion it is likely that flints were originally used for reaping. Support for this view is provided by the existence at this site of reaping knives of peculiar construction, which, although they look more advanced, only differ slightly from those fixed directly in the body of the haft.

Amongst the flint blades bearing traces of gloss there are two specimens of somewhat individual character. Like the others they are worn on both faces, but in their case the polishing extends almost the whole length of the blade. If they had been fixed in a slot at an angle to the handle, as shown in the second reconstruction, there would not have been traces of work along their whole length, as half the blade would be in the slot. It is obvious that the blade here could not have been mounted at an angle to the handle, but must have been

parallel to it in a longitudinal groove cut in the forward part of the haft (fig. 53.2).

Such a method of hafting had certain advantages by comparison with seating the flint in the wood, although it would be less efficient in use. Firstly, a blade mounted for almost the whole of its length would not break during use, and secondly, it would be easy to use the blade twice in the same handle by taking it out and turning it round, so the blunted edge was in the handle.

One condition had to be observed, however, in re-using a blade. Flint blades have a slight curve, concave below and convex above, so naturally the grooves in the handle would have to be made to allow for this. To use the other blade edge the flint would have to be reversed in the handle from back to front. That this was done is confirmed by traces of use on both edges of these sickle blades.

Luka-Vrublevetskaya evidently marked a very early stage in the development of agriculture in south-eastern Europe. In the Tripolye settlements we would be unlikely to find such a simple technique of reaping.

The stone industry from Miss Passek's excavations at Polivanov Yar revealed a high level of technique. The flint blades used for reaping had retouched edges, often jagged or even with proper teeth. Cases were found where a blade had been originally used without retouch, but after it had become blunted in use it had been retouched and given a toothed edge. Double-sided use of the blades was not exceptional, and the wear traces proved both longitudinal and diagonal hafting of the blades. In addition the site yielded authentic inserts of a composite stone sickle, consisting of retouched bladelets or segments with wear traces on one or both sides.

Material from different parts of the Soviet Union (Central Asia, Caucasus, Crimea) and from different periods of ancient agricultural societies has been examined, with the object of making a full study of the microscopic differences between stone sickles and other stone tools.

A group of sickles bearing the labels 'unworked arrowheads' or 'end-scrapers' has been identified among the small collection of stone tools from the lower layers of Anau (fig. 54.1–4) preserved in the Archaeological Section of the Museum of Ethnology of the Academy of Sciences. In Pumpelly's main publication these flint blades were called 'flint knives' or 'flint saws'.[3]

The associated finds from the lower layers of the north tell at Anau testified to an agricultural economy; Pumpelly found stone querns, rubber stones, barley and millet grains, as well as evidence of deliberate irrigation.

---

[1] S. A. Semenov, *Soviet Archeology*, 11 (1949), pp. 131–54.
[2] K. Keller-Tarnusser, *Jahrbuch der Schweizerischen Gesellschaft für Urgeschichte*, 42 (1952), pp. 38–42.
[3] R. Pumpelly, *Explorations in Turkestan* (Washington, 1908), p. 164, pl. 42–44.

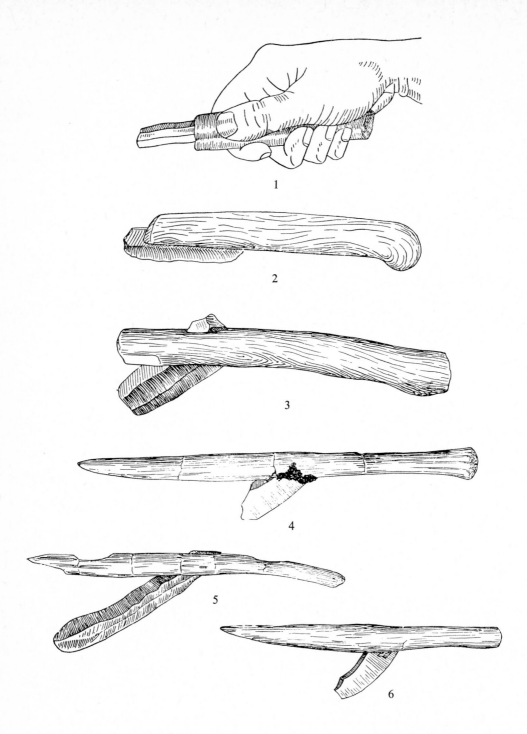

53 *1–3 various methods of hafting flint sickles on the basis of the late neolithic material from Luka-Vrublevetskaya (1 in end of handle; 2 in groove at end; 3 diagonally in a slot); 4–6 flint sickles mounted in wooden handles from Lucerne, Switzerland.*

In the upper layer of the south tell belonging to the Iron Age iron sickles were found, but the excavator did not recognize the stone sickles from early Anau.

The reaping implements of Anau corresponded in every way to the level of development of those of Tripolye agriculture; with few exceptions they were insert blades with toothed edges for use in composite sickles. Some of the inserts had been used on both edges as the intense wear on both sides indicated. Micro-analysis revealed the characteristic sickle wear on the flint with striations and holes of comet shape, their tails pointing to the left, that is to the working end of the sickle (fig. 54.5, 6).

Without a doubt the Copper and Bronze Ages are distinguished by a higher technical level of making flint reaping tools. Our studies of the composite sickles from Dolinsk station in the north Caucasus (dug by Kruglov) and the pre-Urartian settlement on the hill at Karmir-Blur in Armenia (dug in 1943 by Piotrovsky) dealt with objects retouched on both sides. Their large teeth were well made as on a saw, and intense polishing covered the toothed edge on one or both sides. Sometimes fresh facets could be seen on the teeth showing that they had been re-sharpened after the blade had been blunted. The

front insertions reached 80 mm in length. There is every indication that we are dealing with large sickles designed for harvesting cereals in big fields.

There is no reason to suppose that the composite sickle of the Bronze Age displaced the reaping knife made of a single flint fitted into a handle; we have a good deal of evidence for its survival until fairly recent times.

As examples flint sickles may be cited from the village of Mereshevka (Moldavian S.S.R.) and from a place called Gamarie (near Lenkovits in the oblast of Chernovitsk) found by the Tripolye Expedition in 1950 and belonging to the late Bronze Age. These are large triangular flint flakes whose working ends and edges are retouched (fig. 55.1, 2). The one from Gamarie has, in addition to retouch, a series of small teeth, and its concave blade is strongly polished. A peculiar feature of these tools is the method of hafting. The polishing begins at the narrow end and gradually increases to the broad end, extending over both faces in the shape of a triangle, from which it follows that the front was at the broad not the narrow end. When mounted in a longitudinal groove the blade's edge would lie at an angle to the axis of the handle, and so give the implement greater efficiency (fig. 55.2). Obviously these one-piece sickles were firmly

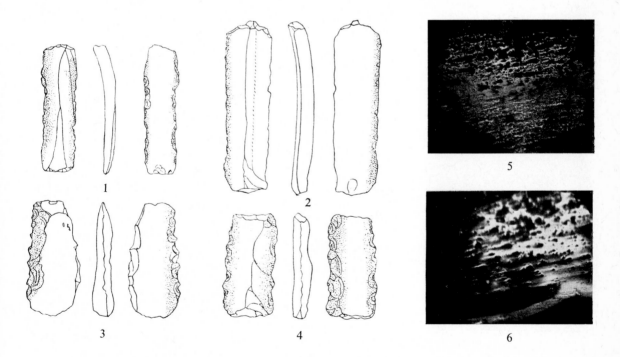

54 1–4 *Late neolithic flint sickles* (1 *and* 2) *and sickle inserts* (3 *and* 4) *from Anau;* 5 *and* 6 *micro-photographs of wear traces on sickle flints from Anau.*

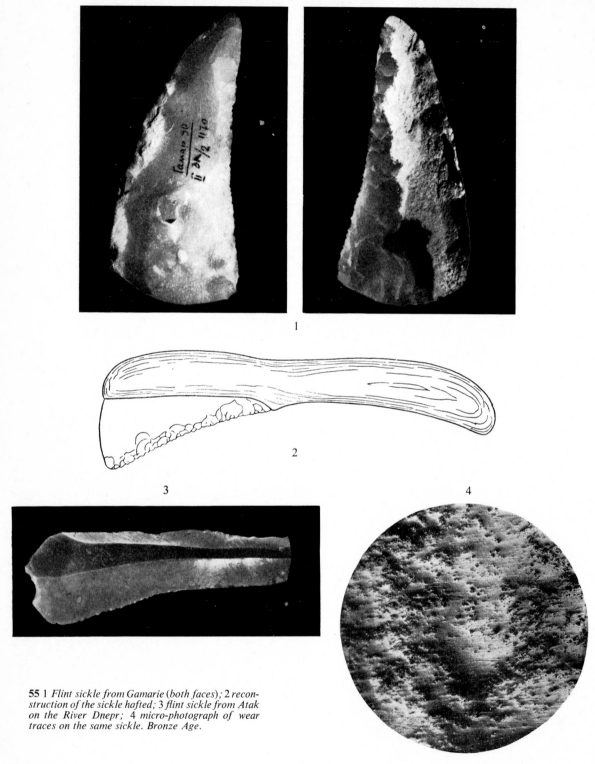

1

2

3

4

55 1 *Flint sickle from Gamarie (both faces); 2 reconstruction of the sickle hafted; 3 flint sickle from Atak on the River Dnepr; 4 micro-photograph of wear traces on the same sickle. Bronze Age.*

fixed in handles, and due to the considerable width of the blade it could be repeatedly trimmed without taking it out of the handle.

An example of a straight sickle is the dagger-shaped tool from the lower layer of Tyritace (Crimea) found by Gaidukevich (fig. 56), which has been made by bifacial pressure retouch and is almost symmetrical in shape. One edge is denticulated by interrupted retouch, and the teeth are slightly separated. The toothed edge is polished on both faces, and the micro-structure of the traces is that characteristic of stone sickles. The other edge bears neither teeth nor polishing. The sickle had been mounted in a side groove in its handle and had not had much use, as is proved by the moderate intensity of the polishing and the absence of traces of re-trimming.

Amongst reaping tools knives without a handle occupy a special position. They were not found amongst the very early tools of Luka-Vrublevetskaya, where we might have expected they ought to occur, but only in later industries. The first of such sickles was found in the collection from Anau, and consisted of a quartzite blade of rough prismatic shape with vague traces of retouch on

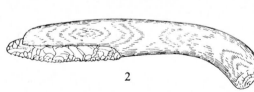

1

2

56 1 *Flint sickle of pre-Hellenistic period from Tyritace; 2 method of hafting reconstructed.*

one side. The opposite side had a thick butt and traces of rough trimming. It was about 70 mm long, 30 mm wide and up to 13 mm thick, with a blade roughly and unevenly toothed and intensely polished along almost its whole length (fig. 57). It would certainly have been difficult to insert a knife with such a thick butt into the

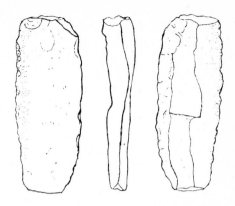

57 *Sickle from Anau used without a handle.*

longitudinal groove of a handle and this had not been the aim, even when it was made, for, as one can see, there had been no retouch to thin the thick butt.

A second example of a sickle used without a handle was found by the Tripolye Expedition in 1949 at Ozhevo in the Sokorensk area of Moldavia. It could not, it seems, be exactly dated, but, as fine denticulated inserts for composite sickles were found with it, it can probably be referred to the Bronze Age. It was a large blade of rough limestone flint, 115 mm long, 35 mm broad and about 15 mm thick. One edge was sharp, the other thick and blunted by steep retouch. On the front part of the thick side was a notch intended as a rest for the index finger when held in the hand, while typical polishing covered the working edge on both faces along its full length, being stronger at the front.

Analytical study of sickle blades indicates therefore that their shapes and methods of use were varied. Their traces of wear by disposition and micro-structure are unmistakable and cannot be confused with any other type of work. Consequently precise definition of sickles is possible without experiments. The latter can merely show the efficiency of this or that type and test the character of the wear, but is not a method of defining the real function of ancient tools.

We carried out tests in reaping with flint blades of the type found at Luka-Vrublevetskaya. These were done at Voeikovo near Leningrad, where unused blades from the site were tested on fields of barley and oats. One was mounted in the end of the handle, the other diagonally in a slot. The tests were done over one day in late August when the cereals were fairly ripe, and the stalks were cut at about 25 cm above the ground or higher. A handful of twenty stalks could be cut with one or two blows, although in rare cases it required three.

From the test we can understand the relatively high productivity of a flint sickle the length of whose working edge was only 50–55 mm and moreover not retouched. Some technical deficiency of mounting with the flint set in the end of its wooden handle caused it over a time to become loose and fall out, which did not occur with the knife set diagonally in a slot.

Traces of wear on the flints after only a day's work were weak, although a slight gloss could be detected with the unaided eye. The micro-structure of traces was typical for sickles, as we had identified it on ancient examples.

The tests give some basis for believing that wear traces on sickles reaching a mirror-like lustre could only be the result of prolonged use. Probably the long duration of use was due to the considerable areas of ground sown with crops by early agricultural communities.

j. An axe from Kostenki I and an adze from Pesochny Rov

The origin of chopping tools (axe and adze) is an important problem in the history of ancient technology. Hand chopping tools, used without a handle, undoubtedly have a very ancient origin, since they can be traced back to the Chellean period. The hand-axe is essentially an implement for giving blows, but it is impossible to concur with Vayson, who regarded them as having been mounted in handles in lower palaeolithic times.[1] Nor can the opposite view be conceded according to which mounting in a handle was much later and arose in neolithic times, when conditions of life in forests or close to forests made an axe indispensable. There can be no doubt that in the neolithic period, especially in the forest zone, there was an extraordinary extension in the use of chopping tools, but the axe and the adze came into use a good deal before this, as early, in fact, as upper palaeolithic times. At all events with regard to the axe we can say this quite positively.

A word of caution is necessary here. In both the western and Soviet archaeological literature on the palaeolithic period the terms 'discoidal chopping tool' or 'core-like chopping tool' are employed. These terms are used both of lower and upper palaeolithic implements, but they have only formal typological significance, and arose when bifacial dressing, found on Chellean and Acheulian tools, was loosely regarded as a sign of 'chopping' in all bifacially dressed tools. The terms can be regarded as conventional, created for classification and comparative dating, and not to indicate real functions.

The study of real functions of palaeolithic tools by traces of use has allowed us to recognize the existence of the axe in the upper palaeolithic period. In 1932 Efimenko found a flint tool of somewhat unusual form at Kostenki I (fig. 58). It was 120 mm long (or high),

1

45 mm broad and in the middle 25 mm thick, and in its manufacture the whole of an elongated nodule, or half of it but not a flake, had been used. This is proved by the presence of the nucleus and accretion rings in the nodule around which the flint had originally accumulated. The tool was worked bifacially into an oval shape, very like an Acheulian hand-axe, and then at the thick end three transverse blows produced an uneven platform by their scars, while on the opposite side four longitudinal blows gave the butt its present shape. Finally it had been trimmed by pressure and percussion retouch from different directions along its edge, and blunted along its middle convex part or arris by light blows and rubbing against stone.

In all its external features the tool does not differ from

[1] A. Vayson, *L'Anthropologie*, 30 (1920), pp. 479–82.

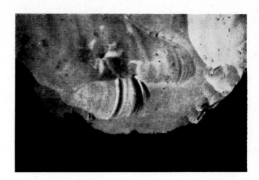

2

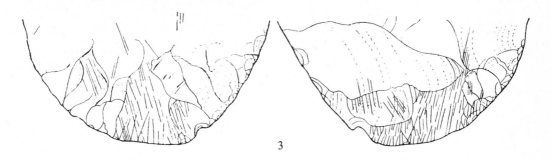

3

58 (AND OPPOSITE) *Upper palaeolithic flint axe from Kostenki I:* 1 *axe from left side;* 2 *both faces of the blade of the axe;* 3 *both cheeks of axe (4 ×) showing striations.*

the rest of the Kostenki I industry. The quality of the material, milky-grey patina with dove-grey specks and other features all show that it is of local origin.

Efimenko drew attention to its symmetrical profile, the presence of a blade and projections on its upper part suitable for securing to a haft, and identified the tool as an axe. However, Efimenko's deductions at the time were regarded as having insufficient basis, and Zamyatnin, Bonch-Osmolovsky, and Sosnovsky believed that the tool had some other function.

Our first microscopic examination of the tool's surface was made in 1937, but no traces could be found, as they were very faint. The binocular lens with its limited power could not detect them. We know now that we still had not had sufficient experience, nor perfected methods of preparing subjects for study. Not until 1948 were the wear traces identified with a binocular microscope, while today they can be studied even through binocular lenses of low magnification.

The observed traces were those characteristic of an axe (figs. 58.3 and 59.2). They occurred on the oval working end of the tool on both faces, and consisted of fine scratches or lines running upwards, inclined to the left at an angle of 20–25° to the vertical axis. Some striations lay at a different angle and intersected the majority. Probably they were produced at a time when the angle of fall of the axe blade was sharply changed; such traces occur on neolithic stone axes and contemporary metal ones. In the photograph of a chopper blade one can see the general background of striations regularly disposed running up from the blade-edge inclined leftwards in relation to the handle, but there are others deviating from this and going the opposite way (fig. 59.3, 4).

The basic mass of striations on the Kostenki axe are short cuts which appear to be straight. In reality they are tiny sections of the curved trajectory of the axe, small chords of its line of movement. Two features, the bifacial and diagonal arrangement of the striations, are the crucial functional criteria of an axe. It is quite obvious that this type of trace could only be produced by blows in which both faces or cheeks of the blade encountered uniform resistance from the worked material, which

123

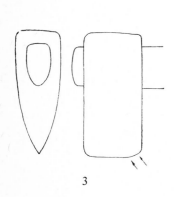

1

2

59 1 *Upper palaeolithic flint axe from Kostenki I; 2 micro-photograph of striations on right cheek; 3 modern steel chopper; 4 enlargement of striations on its left cheek.*

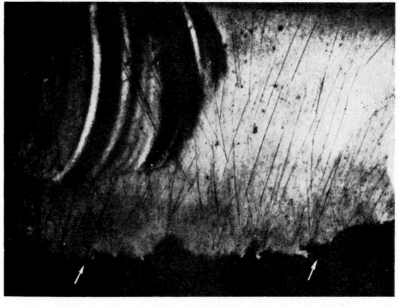

3

4

could only arise if the blade-edge, when the tool was mounted, ran parallel to the axis of the handle.

With an adze the traces arise in quite a different way. It is fixed to the handle with blade-edge at right-angles to it, while the tool's axis is at an acute angle to the handle, not a right-angle as with an axe. Consequently the wear traces on an adze are sharper on its front face away from the handle, precisely because this side encounters direct resistance from the worked material. In addition the striations lie, not diagonally, but more or less parallel to the adze's axis (fig. 60.1, 2).

From what has been said we may conclude that we can rely on the striations to distinguish an axe from an adze. Thus it is possible to attempt a reconstruction of the tool as a whole with its handle. The accompanying reconstruction of the Kostenki I axe (fig. 60.4) has taken into account, not only the wear traces, but also the shape of the butt, the general shape of the tool and its size. Axes would, of course, be lashed to the handle with thongs.

In our view every axe is connected with working wood. In all probability the Kostenki axe served this purpose also. All the same, study of the bones and mammoth tusks of such sites as Kostenki I, Gagarino, Suponevo, Eliseevich, Malta and many others (where numerous thin and thick tusks, shoulder blades, ribs, long bones and antlers bore signs of hewing or chopping) leads one to think that wood was not the only material worked with an axe. In a number of cases, for example, tusks had been chopped through not with an axe but with a special type of chisel with narrow working end. Ivory can be chiselled through more quickly than it can be hewn or chopped through. However, there are not a few cases where it has been hewn through with an axe, as revealed by traces of the blade on the material.

Examination of the different notches or cuts on the bones of large animals lends further weight to the contention that the axe existed in upper palaeolithic times. Some of the cuts on mammoth long bones from Kostenki I are noticeably bow-shaped (fig. 60.3). They are all curved one way, which indicates that the edge of the axe probably also was curved. Evidently this form was typical of the axe's working edge in upper palaeolithic times. There are some grounds for supposing that the technique of manufacture of the Kostenki I axe was not accidental, but had analogies elsewhere, albeit still not numerous. For example, the 'gigantoliths' discovered by Pidoplichka at Novgorod-Seversk in 1933

closely parallel the Kostenki I axe. The gigantoliths were made by bifacial dressing, one end formed by flat flaking, the other by longitudinal blows, and one midrib was partially taken off, as at Kostenki, or sometimes fully. The huge axes from Novgorod-Seversk were evidently secured by a handle on this side. The massive weight of these gigantoliths, reaching 8 kg, must have required great strength to use them, although we know of heavy mauls from early Bronze Age copper workings not exceeded in weight by the gigantoliths. Pidoplichka's view that these axes were used for hewing mammoth bones is plausible, but the matter can only be finally settled when the tools have been studied in detail.[1]

The development of stone axes in post-glacial Europe shows that the ground neolithic axe was preceded by an axe of unground flaked stone. The earliest may be regarded as those discovered in 1900 in the peat bog at Maglemose (Denmark) where there had been a settlement of hunter/fishers during the Ancylus stage of the Baltic area.[2] Mesolithic axes have been given the name of tranchet-axes, and are distinguished by a broad blade made by strong flat blows. Axes, known as picks, found on the same site, are longer and narrower with round blades, and sometimes oval bodies. Axes were still relatively rare at Maglemose, but occur in great numbers in Ertebølle kitchen middens and in the Campignian culture. In areas rich in flint, like northern France, such tools continued to be used into mature neolithic times (Fort-Harrouard) together with ground axes made of volcanic rocks.[3] They are also known in England. As examples the mesolithic sites at Flixton, Yorkshire,[4] and at Warren Oakhanger, Hants.,[5] with unground flint axes may be cited.

As axes occur less often in neolithic settlements than adzes the latter can be regarded as the more necessary tool in more frequent use. Hence it would be supposed that the adze had a more ancient origin than the axe. It is possible that further research will confirm this, but at present we have no evidence for the origin of the adze earlier than the mesolithic period. In the excavations at Pesochny Rov on the River Desna, Voevodsky found a flint tool which he took to be an axe. However, study of the surface has revealed that it was an ancient adze, not ground but worked by pressure retouch. It had a broad blade with rounded corners and was assymmetrical in profile, its flat face retaining traces of severe polishing. The butt was missing as the tool had broken during use (fig. 61.1). Examination of the polished area showed that

[1] I. G. Pidoplichka, *Materials and Researches on the Archaeology of the U.S.S.R.*, 2 (1941), p. 28.
[2] G. E. Sarauw, *Aarbøger* (1903), pp. 148–315. (For a much fuller account see: J. G. D. Clark, *The Mesolithic Settlement of Northern Europe*, Cambridge, 1936. T.)
[3] J. Philippe, *Cinq Anneés de Fouilles au Fort-Harrouard* (Rouen, 1927).
[4] *Proceedings of the Prehistoric Society*, 16 (1950), p. 103.
[5] ibid., 18 (1952), p. 32, pl. 1.

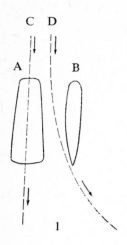

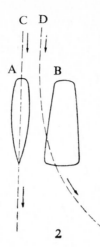

the tool had been mounted with its blade at right-angles to the handle (fig. 61.2). The linear traces in the form of fine lines were closely bunched and lay almost at right-angles to the working edge; such striations can be regarded as typical for an adze.

k. Traces of use on neolithic axes and adzes

Field researches have produced a great quantity of stone chopping implements from neolithic settlements, and certain areas of the Soviet Union have proved exceptionally rich. In the standard archaeological publications these tools are divided into axes, adzes, and chisels. An axe is recognized by its symmetrical profile, an adze or hoe by its assymmetry, and a chisel by its small size. Adzes can be straight or convex. Such a formal subdivision firstly does not by any means always correspond with the real purpose of the tools, and secondly does not take into account the specialized functions of different

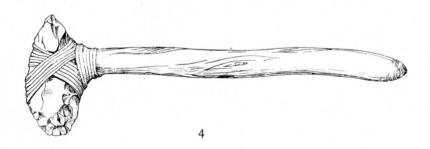

60 1 *Trajectory of an adze in frontal and sagittal planes; 2 trajectory of an axe in frontal and sagittal planes; 3 traces of blows with an axe on a mammoth tibia from Kostenki I; 4 reconstruction of axe from Kostenki I in its handle.*

chopping tools. Moreover, it is difficult on this basis to distinguish tools used as battle-axes. Commonly the latter are included in the category of working tools or vice versa, while some students call battle-axes battle-hammers or maces.

By merely considering the object's shape one cannot tell whether the tool in any specific case was an axe, a mattock, an ice-pick (tool for breaking the ice in winter fishing) or a pick. An example worth citing is three different opinions that have been expressed on the purpose of the pick-shaped tools from Karelia preserved in Moscow and Leningrad museums under the title of 'miners' picks' (*kail*). These tools, made of a dark fairly soft rock, are cigar-shaped with one side flat and one or both ends pointed (fig. 65.4). Uvarov[1] and Gorodtsov regarded them as hoes, Bryusov[2] as plough-shares and Tretyakov as ice-picks.[3]

Foss and Elnitsky wrote very fairly: 'Such a variety of opinion about the function of this tool has arisen because the older methods of formal classification made evaluation of the remains more difficult. They gave rise to the conventional terminology which still has not gone out of use. "Hoe" for example is the name given to certain tools regardless of whether they could have been used for agriculture. Even if the student denied the existence of agriculture in the period or area under discussion all tools of a certain form had to be called hoes for the sake of typology.'[4]

The observation of Foss and Elnitsky relative to the predominance of adzes over axes in neolithic remains is

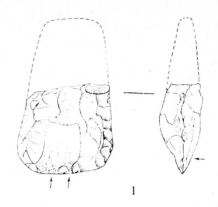

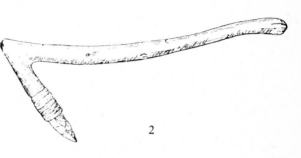

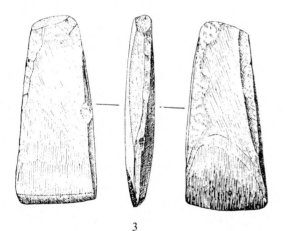

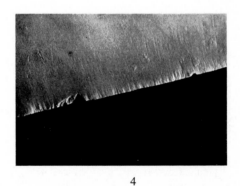

61 1 *Mesolithic flint adze from Pesochny Rov; 2 its hafting reconstructed; 3 nephrite adze from a neolithic burial on the R. Angar; 4 micro-photograph of the nephrite adze's blade.*

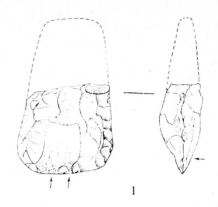

[1] A. S. Uvarov, *Archaeology of Russia* (Moscow, 1881), I, p. 351.
[2] A. Y. Bryusov, *Soviet Karelia* (Moscow, 1930).
[3] P. N. Tretyakov, *Journal of the State Academy for the History of Material Culture*, 14 (1932), p. 27.
[4] M. Foss and L. Elnitsky, *Materials and Researches on the Archaeology of the U.S.S.R.*, 2 (1941), p. 184.

1

2

3

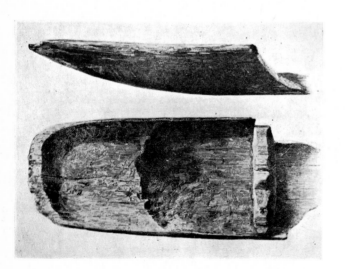

62 1 *Neolithic nephrite axe from Fofanov used in experiment; 2 the axe as hafted (stereo-photographs); 3 a fir tree of 25 cms. diameter after 6 minutes chopping; 4 part of dug-out canoe from the neolithic settlement on L. Ladoga.*

4

right; they explained it as due to the very wide range of functions accomplished with adzes in wood-working. However, from this accurate observation they draw an unjustified conclusion about the all-purpose use of stone adzes, writing thus: 'Comparative study has forced us to re-interpret a substantial part of these stone hoe-shaped tools as adzes. Relying on ethnographic parallels we must regard the basic striking tools, in particular adze-like forms, as to a great extent all-purpose tools; they would chop wood but could be used also, for example, for digging the ground. This is mainly because they were not used by one craftsman, a specialist in one branch of production (at this stage of development no such specialist existed) but met the fairly varied needs of the whole economy. This vagueness of function has left some marks of variability in shape, which we do not find later when tools become more specialized.'[1]

Such a conclusion about neolithic chopping tools, especially adzes, reveals that the authors had set too high a value on ethnographic parallels. As a result of examination of the traces of wear on adzes it has to be recognized that these tools were used only in rare cases as hoes, in fact only when they were no longer service-able as adzes. The combined functions of adze and hoe in one tool would be impossible, as the degree of wear on an earth-digging tool is very great, almost as much as when subjected to abrasive agents. An adze after use as a hoe could not be restored merely by sharpening, and moreover traces of wear on a hoe are very characteristic and occupy a good part of the tool's surface. Such traces are not found on the tools in question with the few exceptions mentioned, while with regard to specializa-tion in chopping tools this had already taken place in pre-neolithic times.

The opinion of the scholars that we have cited once again illustrates how the absence of reliable criteria for differentiating chopping tools deprives the archaeologist, not merely of the possibility of re-creating the details of past economic life, but leads to a distortion of the facts. A tool's shape must, of course, be taken into account, but to establish the real purpose of any chopping tool is only possible from the traces it bears, which show with certainty how it was used and on what material.

The wear traces characteristic of a stone adze were first identified in 1939 on material from neolithic graves on the River Angar excavated by Okladnikov.[2] Research showed that wear took place essentially on the front face. On an assymmetrical adze this side is convex and has no blade facet, which is on the back, flatter face. Usually the traces appear under magnification as grooves, thicker at the bottom and narrowing to fine

lines. As a rule the striations lie along the axis of the tool more or less parallel to each other (fig. 61.3, 4). This is due to the fact that, although the trajectory of the tool is curved while in the air, friction arises as the front surface of the tool reaches a vertical position. Then the front which is usually convex meets strong resistance from the material struck (fig. 63.1), while the rear face suffers less wear from the relatively slight parings and chips that have come off the wood. The form of the traces on the near face does not differ from those on the front, but the lines are shorter.

An axe wears quite differently. As described above, the striations occur on both cheeks of the axe and run diagonally, that is upwards from the blade edge and leftwards from the handle; the axe's curved trajectory leaves its mark on its working face as it sinks into the material.

Striations are easily detected on the ground surface of neolithic chopping tools if they have not been removed by secondary sharpening. Even then they can sometimes be seen somewhere on the blade or even higher up. If the tool has not been sharpened the striations often transect the lines of original grinding, or even obliterate them. The linear traces emerge most clearly on the blade itself.

The regular formation of wear striations on stone axes that we have described is confirmed by examination of them on contemporary metal axes. Both on a chopper and a bench axe striations occur on both faces running diagonally. Since splitting wood and cutting through it are rather different operations, the blade wear has its own special traits in each case. On a chopper the back angle of the blade wears quicker, on a bench axe the front part. This is due to the fact that the latter has a thin blade and is used for different work such as cutting wood, making grooves or angles, and is in some sense an all-purpose wood-working tool in which the front part does the main work. A chopper, on the other hand, is heavier with a thick blade designed for splitting wood with great force. During blows it sinks into the wood at its back, where the whole weight of the tool is concen-trated at the moment of striking.

The wear characteristic of contemporary choppers is hardly ever found on neolithic axes, since wood was not cut in this way, that is by imbedding the axe in the body of the wood to split off a piece. The neolithic axe flaked off the wood not by blows into it but by angle blows longitudinally along the surface. So in many neolithic axes the front angle is worn away, and the blade looks lop-sided.

This lop-sidedness of the blade cannot be regarded as a functional criterion of the axe, for the basic criteria are

---

[1] ibid., p. 186.
[2] S. A. Semenov, *Materials and Researches on the Archaeology of the U.S.S.R.*, 2 (1941), pp. 203–11.

still the wear striations. Lop-sidedness occurs not only on axes but also on adzes and even chisels. This feature which has been noticed by investigators has still not received an adequate explanation. It may be considered as due to the wear of a chopping tool used in a definite and quite rational way, that is by working wood with angle blows.

Probably by experience it was found that both axe and adze gave the most effective result if the whole force was applied in the blow without any bounce. In working with neolithic chopping tools bounce was considerable because of the wide edge-angle of the tool's blade. During a long period of work it might be noticed that bounce was reduced if the blade was made narrower (2–2·5 cm), which would allow the axe to penetrate deeply into the wood with full strength or only slight loss by bounce. Narrow-bladed axes and adzes commonly occur amongst neolithic tools, but as a rule they are small, like chisels. The mounting of small tools in a handle presented difficulties, however, and in addition they lacked the necessary weight. So the increased efficiency of tools with narrow blades was still not satisfactory. Probably they were used only for small jobs, while axes and adzes of medium size, 8–12 cm long and 4–5 cm broad, would have been useful for other work. For efficient results such tools would be used with angle blows, in which the whole blade did not penetrate into the material simultaneously. Although it all happened very quickly, one angle entered the material first and then the rest of the blade met the resistance from the material afterwards. In contemporary technology this principle is widely used in which the blade does not encounter the material along its full length simultaneously, and promotes high efficiency and smooth movement of the tool. The same principle is involved in the law about the action of a wedge.

Angle blows gave rise to uneven wear on an axe or adze, and so, by constant re-sharpening of the blunted part, the blade became lop-sided.

The account given above has been tested by working on wood at Voeikovo, near Leningrad, in experiments carried out in 1951 with a nephrite axe found by Okladnikov at the cemetery of Fofanov on the River Seleng (fig. 62.1, 2). Contrary to current views derived from ethnographic evidence, the great efficiency of a stone axe in working wood was at the same time revealed. A fir tree 25 cm in diameter was cut through in twenty minutes without any previous practice (fig. 62.3). The experiment fully confirmed the relatively high efficiency of the stone axe shown in earlier experiments in Denmark.[1]

Neolithic axes and adzes were extremely varied in shape, due to the properties and quality of the stone, method of hafting, customary practices in working and the special purposes of the tool. Gouge adzes, for example, were long ago correctly interpreted as tools for hollowing out troughs and dug-out canoes, that is designed to remove large masses of wood. This general picture, however, does not show all the necessary processes connected with this kind of work. Gouge adzes have the usual traces found on all adzes. On the latter, as was demonstrated on material from a cemetery on the River Angar, besides the polishing on the forward convex face there are vertical striations running along the axis of the tool, which gradually weaken and disappear away from the blade-edge. On the opposite face similar traces are weaker.

However, in addition to the normal run of wear traces, on some adzes others of quite another character are found. They occur not only on adzes but also on axes. These peculiar features are as follows: firstly, they are sharp, clear, and visible to the naked eye; secondly, they are equally strong on both faces; thirdly, their upper margin is very clearly defined, showing to what depth the tool penetrated into the wood (fig. 63.2, 4). They do not show as the usual streaks and scratches on the smooth surface of the working part of the axe or adze, but have a wavy pattern, small grooves alternating with ridges, one on top of another (fig. 64.3).

Originally it seemed that this feature was confined to nephrite tools due perhaps to some property of the rock, but later analogous traces were found on slaty rocks (from the Verkholensk burials) and even on crystalline igneous rocks. As an example we can cite the splendid cylindrical axe from the Volosov neolithic settlement exhibited in the State Historical Museum in Moscow. This type of trace in chopping tools depends, not only on the rock, but also on the properties of the worked material under certain conditions. Coniferous trees (spruce, fir, and larch) have very distinct annual growths of wood. In a radial section through the trunk there is a clear alternation of different hardnesses; lighter and softer in spring growth, tougher and harder in the summer wood. In a transverse blow with axe or adze there would be uneven resistance to the blade, and so the latter would suffer wear, at first hardly noticeable, but later more clearly corresponding to the texture of the wood. Even on metal axes such as choppers, not re-sharpened for some time, this plastic deformation becomes the more noticeable the longer they have been used. The angle at which the tool falls plays an important part in the formation of such traces. In cutting wood the angle at which the tool strikes the surface varies between 40° and 60°. The removal of a paring or

---

[1] O. Montelius, *Kulturgeschichte Schwedens* (Leipzig, 1906), p. 32.

chip takes place not just by cutting but by splitting also (fig. 65.2). The wood offers its strongest resistance when the tool falls at 90° to the surface, so the transverse cutting of wood and the hewing through of a trunk is therefore the most difficult part. At a time when saws were merely tiny stone objects transverse cutting had to be done with chopping tools. It is only this type of work which could have given rise to the very individual traces on nephrite axes from the area of L. Baikal, the neo-lithic diorite axe from Volosov, and others. Analogous traces on the adzes from the Verkholensk burials are probably due to transverse chopping of wood and hollowing out of dug-out canoes. The manufacture of dug-outs entails removal of the external part of the tree-trunk and of the internal wood between the trunk sides, which requires vertical chopping blows.

To judge by the oak boat found by Inostrantsev in Lake Ladoga, some dug-outs were made with massive

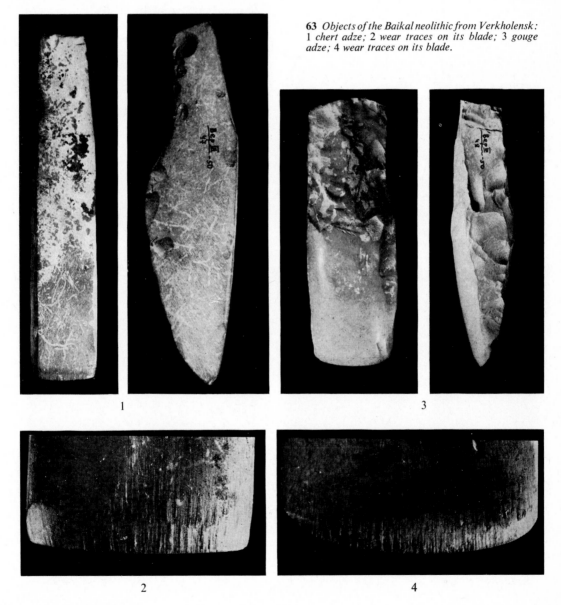

63 *Objects of the Baikal neolithic from Verkholensk:*
1 chert adze; 2 wear traces on its blade; 3 gouge adze; 4 wear traces on its blade.

1

3

2

4

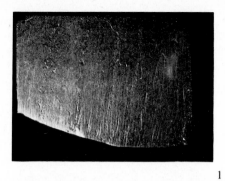

1

2

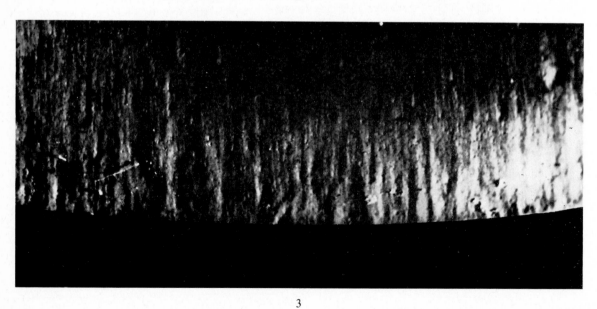

3

64 1 *Stereo-photographs of blade of a neolithic adze from Karelia (2 ×); 2 and 3 micro-photographs of blade along its edge (2) and back (3) of an adze from Verkholensk.*

bulkheads to strengthen the thin sides and of one piece with them.[1] In this example the bulkheads had been hewn into shape with straight vertical blows (fig. 62.4).

Study of the edge of an adze from Verkholensk gave results of no little interest. In spite of a high degree of wear on both faces it was clear that, although the tool had been in use for a long time without sharpening, it still retained its original keenness. Moreover, the binocular lenses revealed that the thin blade had, as it were, acted as its own sharpener (fig. 64.2, 3).

It would be difficult to give a complete explanation for this self-sharpening. One can only assume that the sharp blade in a vertical blow suffered friction in a very small part of its surface. The friction would mainly affect the part of the blade immediately adjoining the edge where the surface makes an angle of 55°. On the other hand, in a vertical blow on material much less tough than stone there would be no flaking, and so the blade did not bear the chip-marks that arise from a side blow.

Neolithic chopping tools achieved a fair measure of specialization. The Verkholensk burials yielded, in addition to the axes and adzes mentioned, adzes with broad blades and comparatively small blade angle, barely 40° if measured on the facet side. These were probably used for dressing the face of wooden objects, final shaping and levelling off the roughly chopped surfaces; in face dressing wood is worked by light blows with such a tool. The striations on them are typical of normal chisels.

A striking tool was systematically used as a hoe for agricultural purposes in neolithic settlements on the loess plains of Europe and Asia, although usually antler was used, less often long bone, and stone much more rarely. On many occasions they have escaped the investigator's notice because they lack well-defined morphological characteristics. There are cases where Tripolye peasants have employed axe and adze rough-outs or old and discarded adzes as hoes. As we have already observed, this can be decided by wear traces, which differ sharply on a hoe from those left by working wood.

A characteristic example of the prolonged use of an old adze as a hoe has been found in the material from the Tripolye site of Polivanov Yar. This adze had gone out of normal use as a result of severe damage to its working part which could not be eliminated by grinding. The tool was re-used as a hoe, possibly still in its original handle. The blade appeared severely blunted from blows against the ground. More than half the tool was polished; all the hollows and facets on the tool's surface not removed by earlier grinding had been rubbed, for practically every point of the tool's surface had experienced friction against the soft earth. The polishing and

fine wear striations showed that a fine-grained, almost powdery soil had been worked, although it had contained larger grains of silica sand. The striations did not run in one direction but intersected, showing that during use the tool's direction of fall had varied.

The special manufacture of stone hoes is still known to us only from the neolithic period in China. Diorite examples, ground or unground, and very practical and modern in shape, have been found at Lin-Si north of Peking. They are oval in shape and comparatively flat in section, with a short tang for hafting and a slightly pointed end (fig. 65.3). Photographs indicate that these hoes have been polished by wear.[2]

The basic criterion distinguishing a stone battle-axe from other axes is the absence of the traces of use found on the latter. This rather broad negative distinction needs amplification. There would have been a time when everyday use on the one hand, and warlike functions on the other, would have been fulfilled by a single tool. The appearance of a specialized battle-axe is evidently related to the initial disintegration of the primitive social system, when a physical and typological differentiation first took place.

As a classic example of a stone battle-axe the Fatyanovo axes may be cited. They are very variable in shape, but the most characteristic is the 'fan-curved' type of Gorodtsov's classification. The striking part of a Fatyanovo axe as a rule has a very individual curve, like a splayed chisel, which makes an excellent lethal striking weapon, but a poor instrument for working wood. In this peculiar shape the experience gained in angle blows with an axe or adze, described above, has been drawn upon. Here, however, the lop-sidedness has been carried to extremes.

The most important mark of a battle-axe is its method of hafting by means of a hole bored through the axe. The perforation required a substantial increase in the transverse section of the axe where it would be weakened by the hole, which caused the edge-angle of the blade to be considerably increased. Moreover, the round hole used in hafting made it stable in a direct but not in a sideways blow. In working tools therefore circular perforations were only resorted to as a method of hafting in the mallet and pick. The wood-working axe experiences a sideways thrust on its axis in a side blow and so cannot be hafted by a circular hole through the axe; it requires a square or oval aperture.

Thus three very important physico-technical factors rendered a perforated stone axe of the Fatyanovo type unsuitable for useful work: an exaggeratedly lop-sided blade, high angle on the blade edge and attachment by a

---

[1] A. A. Inostrantsev, *Prehistoric Man of the Stone Age on the Shores of Lake Ladoga* (St Petersburg, 1882).

[2] E. Licent and P. Teilhard de Chardin, *L'Anthropologie*, 35 (1925), pp. 63–74.

circular perforation. Strictly speaking one alone of these factors would have been sufficient to place a battle-axe outside the category of working tools.

The above observations are based on the study of a series of perforated axes of the Fatyanovo and other cultures. Their blades are generally blunt and on them one can detect traces of crushing and chipping whose origin is obscure. The typical signs of wear on tools from chopping wood are not present, although even when the Fatyanovo culture flourished and copper and bronze tools were already known, the normal stone axes and adzes of neolithic type continued to be used for everyday purposes.

l. Mortars and pestles of upper palaeolithic times for trituration of colours

Traces of mineral colouring are often found on upper palaeolithic sites. They occur as patches on bone or stone objects, or scattered about, sometimes profusely, throughout the cultural layer. They are found as lumps of ochre of various colours, iron concretions, pieces of bloodstone (limonite), manganese ore and pyrites.

The purpose of these colours is still not satisfactorily explained. Some students regard them as being used for colouring the body and tattooing, as with the modern Australians and Andaman Islanders.[1] If this were right, then we must suppose that body-colouring and tattooing among the people of the periglacial areas was confined to the face and hands, since we know that for more than half of the year people of this region went about fully clothed, and were rarely naked. It is well known that people of cold countries (Eskimos, Chukchy) do very little tattooing of the body and scarcely paint themselves at all, preferring to paint parts of their costume.[2] The problem of the purpose of the colouring in palaeolithic times must be regarded as an open one. Most probably they painted their costume, wicker-work and wooden objects, and, to judge by the west European evidence, colour was used also for painting the rock walls in caves.[3]

The tools used in the working of colouring matter were very varied both in shape and material. Archaeologists in western Europe regard circular or oval mortars made of granite, quartzite, and sandstone as preeminently used for this. Sometimes these were small boulders hollowed out. They are generally found in Magdalenian sites like Laugerie Basse, Gorge d'Enfer, and Laussel in France.[4] Sometimes hollowed stone plaques with traces of colouring matter have been noticed, while pestles are always being confused with striker-stones.

The study of colour grinders and pestles by wear traces has allowed these objects to be identified just where previously they had not been noticed.

During the excavations at Timonovka, Gorodtsov found a group of sandstone plaques which revealed no signs of hollowing out or shaping in any way, but on some there were obvious signs of rubbing and wear on the naturally rough surface. Gorodtsov noticed this and identified the objects as grinding plaques used for the grinding of bone tools. Some have been on view in the State Historical Museum in Moscow with this on the label, while the rest were preserved at Leningrad.

Examination of the sandstone plaques from Timonovka in the Museum of Anthropology and Ethnography of the Academy of Sciences showed that these were colour grinders, and not abrasive agents (fig. 66). The following signs of use were identified on the plaques:

(1) The maximum surface wear was at the centre of the plaque, and not at the edge, as would have been the case if they had been used for sharpening awls.

(2) The worn area had neither grooves nor deep scratches, nor any other kind of trace of friction by narrow objects; the rubbing on the surface is not strictly localized, but gradually fades away towards the periphery.

(3) On the rubbed area evenly ground quartz grains of eroded form, cemented in lime, were visible under low magnification.

(4) With side illumination from the Opak lamp parts of curved lines intersecting each other could be detected.

(5) In the hollows on the periphery where the rubbing was weaker traces of colouring matter of a deep carmine shade were visible.

Sometimes very small stone plaques were used as crushing slabs. For example, at Malta small uneven plaques of dark grey brittle shale not more than 20 sq cm in area were used for triturating colouring matter. Only a tiny pestle would have been used on these, for the worn area was even smaller and was roughly circular in shape. Traces of friction were sharper in the middle, and striations and streaks left by a circular movement of the pestle were clearly visible under the binocular lens, while remains of ochre survived in the interstices. The plaques had been broken and some fragments had not survived (fig. 67.1).

---

[1] E. H. Man, *Journal of the Anthropological Institute*, 12, p. 333.
[2] F. Boas, *Annual Report of the Bureau of Ethnology* (1884–5), p. 561.
[3] Since this was written palaeolithic rock paintings have come to light in Russia. T.
[4] J. G. Lalanne and J. Bouyssonie, *L'Anthropologie*, 51 (1947), pp. 121–2.

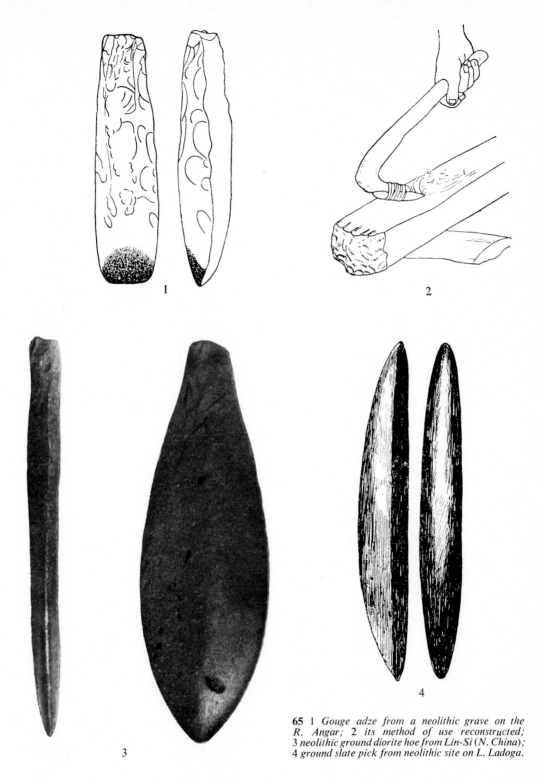

1

2

3

4

65 1 *Gouge adze from a neolithic grave on the R. Angar; 2 its method of use reconstructed; 3 neolithic ground diorite hoe from Lin-Si (N. China); 4 ground slate pick from neolithic site on L. Ladoga.*

135

1

66 1 *Sandstone plaque from Timonovka worn on the surface; 2 periphery of plaque showing weak traces of wear (12 ×); 3 centre of plaque with traces of wear visible as crushed quartz grains (12 ×).*

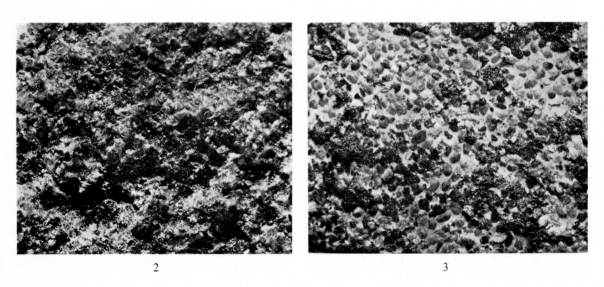

2   3

In Kostenki IV Rogachev found that the cultural layers within a long house were intensely coloured by ochre, not pulverized but occurring as lumps lying in holes. Pestles and crushing slabs were also found. Sandstone and slate plaques had served as mortars, while pebbles had been used as pestles (fig. 67.2, 3). Amongst the plaques a massive lump of dark green slate, recalling a mortar in shape, was especially noticed. For pounding up the ochre a hollow created by the splitting of a pebble more than 15 cm in diameter had been used, its edge worked by numerous blows to form the desired shape. The surface of the hollow, besides remains of ochre, showed traces of friction and blows by the pestles. Evidently it had been used not merely for trituration but also to some extent for breaking up the hard lumps of ochre. The working parts of the pestles also showed this, bearing traces of friction and blows in the form of chipmarks and holes containing ochre.

Pestles for pulverizing colouring matter were fairly varied. In Kostenki I a quartzite pebble had had its originally rounded surface worn to irregular facets by prolonged use; the wear traces were not confined to the narrow part held between index finger and thumb (fig. 68.1, 2). The worn surfaces were clearly visible on the pebble, but the granular structure of quartzite and the absence of polishing or grinding from friction made it impossible to investigate the movements employed. However, remains of colouring in the interstices of the quartzite and outside were clearly visible.

In Kostenki I crushing slabs for colour have not been found, but the site has yielded an extremely original bone palette. This was made on the short first rib of a mammoth whose broad end is spatula-shaped (fig. 87). The broad flat part of the rib was used for triturating the colour and during use the rib was held with the left hand at its narrow end. The external compact layer of bone had been obliterated and in certain places broken through slightly to become bowed in section. In spite of damage by roots the darkening of the surface from red ochre is clear, which occurs in the hollows, cracks, and crevices on the bone surface. It is well known that at Afontova Mountain bone colour grinders were found, made of ivory, whose identification presented no difficulty, as they were cup-shaped and had colouring in the bottom.[1] At Kostenki I a suitable mammoth rib was also used as a colour grinder, although it bore no indications of shaping, unless we except part of its flat end which seemed to be broken round.

Tools for pulverizing mineral colour are fairly often found on ancient settlements, but pestles are not always associated with pounding slabs and remains of colouring, or they pass unrecognized. Microscopic and macroscopic study of archaeological materials allows us to identify this kind of work from chance details and odd traces.

Illustrative of this is the mesolithic material from Shan-Koba in the Crimea excavated by Bonch-Osmolovsky and Bibikov. In the list of finds no tools for working colouring matter are recorded, although colour was worked on the site. A pounder consisting of a rosy sandstone pebble, pear-shaped but no bigger than an acorn (30 by 12 mm), was found in the Tardenoisian levels. By its size it is comparable to the microlithic flints from the site and, like the latter, reveals habits of very finicky work (fig. 68.3, 4).

We said above that on some pestles for triturating colours striations cannot be detected, since, although they suffered friction, the pestles were also employed for light blows on hard lumps. So the worn part of a pestle has a rough surface on which striations can be detected with difficulty and then only very fragmentarily. The

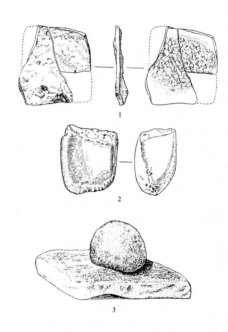

67 1 *Slate plaque (in pieces) from Malta (Siberia) bearing traces of grinding of mineral colouring; 2 stone pestle from Kostenki IV showing traces of crushing and pounding mineral colours; 3 pestle and plaque from Kostenki IV for crushing colouring matter. All objects upper palaeolithic.*

---

[1] G. P. Sosnovsky, *The Palaeolithic of the U.S.S.R.* (Moscow-Leningrad, 1935), p. 143.

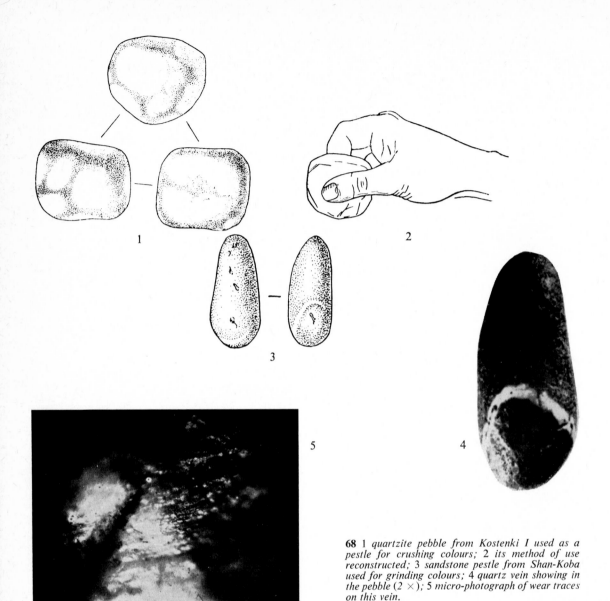

68 1 *quartzite pebble from Kostenki I used as a pestle for crushing colours;* 2 *its method of use reconstructed;* 3 *sandstone pestle from Shan-Koba used for grinding colours;* 4 *quartz vein showing in the pebble (2 ×);* 5 *micro-photograph of wear traces on this vein.*

tiny pestle from Shan-Koba of negligible weight would not have been suitable for blows and its use must have relied on friction alone. Wear traces are detectable on its convex base as circular lines, shown in the micro-photograph (fig. 68.5). They cross the white veins of the quartzite, which stand out on the photograph, while remains of colouring are visible in the pores of the rock.

On what kind of mortar could this small delicate pestle have been used? The character of the wear on the pestle itself supplies the answer. If it had been a flat stone slab then the pestle would not have had striations around its convex base, for that would have produced intersecting lines. Consequently the existing striations point to a cup-shaped mortar whose diameter would have hardly exceeded 40 mm. Such miniature mortars sometimes turn up on neolithic sites.

This example, like many others, once more confirms that wear traces on tools allow us, not merely to determine their working function, but beyond this to understand crucial details connected with the work being done.

The use of ochre as colouring in palaeolithic times

indicates the sophisticated needs of man at that time, who gave special attention to the search for mineral colouring matter in his environment. Besides ochre and other mineral colouring matters palaeolithic man undoubtedly made use of chalk, charcoal or soot for white and black colouring. Chalk is found in great quantities on certain palaeolithic sites, while charcoal and soot are the most readily available of all colouring materials.

There are grounds for supposing that palaeolithic man did not just work colouring matter mechanically by pounding and trituration, but that afterwards he dissolved it in water, and, in all probability, understood how to heat up ochre, wash it out and mix it up with grease and marrow. Heated over chopped charcoal ochre takes on bright shades of colour, while washing removes impurities, and grinding up with certain organic substances makes it more resistant to damp.

As an illustration of what colours palaeolithic man generally had at his disposal five samples were taken from the material at Eliseevich. Ground up in a china mortar, dissolved in a sugar solution and then applied to paper the samples gave the following shades: chestnut, brick, ochre, sand, and straw.[1]

m. Abrasive instruments from the neolithic graves of Verkholensk

In both our own and west European publications over many years stone objects have been figured that are semi-cylindrical in shape with a longitudinal groove on the flat side. Generally they have been found in pairs which fitted together look like a cylinder with a hole at one end. The ends are often narrower and curve inwards to give the cylinder a barrel-like appearance. Sometimes they are almost quadrangular in section, but the corners are strongly blunted and have been worked off. They are made predominantly of sandstone.

Gorodtsov personally found such objects in Catacomb graves in the Donets area,[2] as well as in Fatyanovo sites,[3] and identified them as moulds.

Even earlier such objects had been found in France, and by Shliemann in the lower layers at Troy. They have[4] also been found in Asia and America.[5]

In 1928 Dobrovolsky criticized Gorodtsov's identification and put forward an even less feasible proposal that the objects were thong stretchers.[6]

Other views have been expressed about them by Tallgren,[7] Artsikhovsky,[8] Iessen,[9] and Okladnikov,[10] who regarded them variously as burnishing tools or implements for straightening arrows.

Research on analogous objects from neolithic graves at Verkholensk in eastern Siberia has made it necessary to correct former views on the purpose of these objects. The series from this site consisted of five specimens: one whole, two damaged and two fragmentary. The whole example, which bore indications that it had never been used, was large: 22·5 cm long, 6 cm broad and (each half) 2·7 cm thick. The remaining specimens were about half the length and up to 5 cm broad. The grooves did not pass right through the object but starting with a broad bell-shape or funnel mouth they tapered away to nothing (fig. 69.1–6).

The objects were made of a fine-grained but porous sandstone with a lime matrix, rough to touch, and under the microscope the unworn state of the quartz grains could be seen. The angular particles took the form of regular crystals not united to one another but separated by a crumbly fragile mass of lime (fig. 69.8). Under pressure with even such a soft material as wood the quartz crystals were pulled out and fell away, a property which makes the sandstone one of the best abrasive rocks. The comparatively weak cohesion of the very sharp quartz particles does not allow the pulp of the worked material to choke up the pores.

As proof that this sandstone was used as an abrasive material are the whetstones found in the Verkholensk graves. They bear clear traces of being used for sharpening adzes, which are also found in the graves, as well as axes and ground knives of nephrite.

The sum of all the evidence on the objects under discussion is that they were abrasive instruments, although they were not whetstones for sharpening stone tools. Their working part was the groove, and the object being sharpened in it evidently had the same shape as the groove itself, that is it was pointed. In the grave material bone objects shaped like pointed rods were found in great numbers, mainly points up to 20 cm long, straight barbs of large composite fish-hooks and other pointed objects. Points made on large and small long bones of animals were noticed in the first instance (fig. 69.7). Examination of their surfaces revealed that in the final process of their manufacture they were not whittled but ground down with an abrasive instrument. There

[1] The colour plate, No. 69 in the Russian edition, has been omitted from here. T.
[2] V. A. Gorodtsov, *Proceedings of the Twelfth Archaeological Congress in Kharkhov* (1902), I, p. 194.
[3] V. A. Gorodtsov, *Report of the Russian Historical Museum for* 1914, p. 167.
[4] G. and A. Mortillet, *Le Musée Préhistorique* (1881), pl. LXI (593).
[5] W. D. Strong, *Smithsonian Miscellaneous Collections*, 93 (1935), p. 60.
[6] A. V. Dobrovolsky, *Anthropology* (Kiev), I (1928).
[7] A. M. Tallgren, *Eurasia Septentrionalis Antiquae*, 2 (1926), p. 118.
[8] A. V. Artsikhovsky, *Proceedings of the Archaeological Section of the Russian Association of Scientific Institutes of the Social Sciences*, 2 (1929).
[9] A. A. Iessen, *Journal of the State Academy of the History of Material Culture*, 120, p. 108.
[10] A. P. Okladnikov, *Materials and Researches on the Archaeology of the U.S.S.R.*, 18 (1950), pp. 361–4.

1

2

3

4

5

69 (AND OPPOSITE) *1–6 Neolithic abrasive instruments from Verkholensk (1 and 3 assembled, 2 and 4 in halves, 5 and 6 sectional view); 7 bone points from Verkholensk; 8 stereo-photographs of abrasive surfaces; 9 and 10, method of grinding points reconstructed.*

7

6

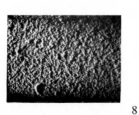

8

were no wavy traces on their surface characteristic of whittling or scraping with a flint blade, but instead straight almost parallel scratches running along the axis of the rod.

To judge by the traces of manufacture on these bone objects sharpening was done by straight movements through the hole in the instrument after the two halves had been put together (fig. 69.9). Such a method of work would give uniform grinding on all sides to the awl-like bone tools and ensure that they were straight. During sharpening done with a straight backward-forward movement now and again the hand would be twisted to left or right. The left hand would hold the instrument, and the two halves would be pressed together by the fingers, tightening or loosening (like a spring) according to when the bone tried to force open the two halves. Thus the left hand was not merely passively holding but actively participating in the work. The final operation would probably have been carried out with just one half of the instrument (fig. 69.10). Traces of such finishing

quite easy to restore the required dimension by grinding off part of the flat side on each valve, the rough friable sandstone lending itself to such adjustment of the aperture. An old worn example in which each valve is appreciably thinner than in a new example shows that this method of calibrating the instrument was used.

Tests that we did on sharpening bone and wooden rods with the abrasive instruments from Verkholensk confirmed our assumptions about their functions. Test pieces were quickly sharpened to the shape described. Moreover, it was established that the tip of the point required supplementary work to finish it off. Unexpectedly the abrasive instruments wore very slowly, almost imperceptibly. This was evidently due to the fact that almost the whole surface of the rod made contact simultaneously with the enclosing face of the groove.

In the light of the evidence yielded by the study of these objects from the Verkholensk graves it is possible to give a more precise definition of the other analogous or similar objects mentioned above. The 'mould forms'

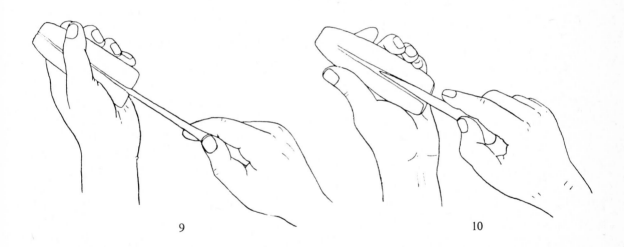

9   10

work can be seen on the valves: the grooves do not always have a regular semi-circular section and the depth of the grooves also is not always uniform in each part.

The invention of a bivalve instrument for abrasive work and its method of use illustrates the high level of technical knowledge in neolithic times. This method of sharpening rods to make awls has a considerable advantage over normal methods of sharpening on a flat stone. Not only did it speed up the work and enhance the straightness of the tool but it also allowed the calibration of the points by using standard grooves in the abrasive tools. If the groove became worn it was

published by Gorodtsov from catacomb graves in the Donets area differ somewhat externally and in the shape of the grooves. The valves in this case are straighter, almost quadrangular in longitudinal section, or slightly round at the ends and so more or less oval in shape. The grooves do not taper but pass right through. In transverse section the 'mould forms' are almost circular. So far as one can judge by photographs the grooves are even channels which could have been used for grinding completely straight rods, such as arrow shafts.

Very similar objects occur in Fatyanovo graves and Kitoisky burials from the area of L. Baikal, which also have continuous grooves and were used no doubt for the same purpose.

Hence it follows that the views of Artisikhovsky, Iessen, and Okladnikov about this category of abrasive tools were not far short of the mark. It is only necessary to add that the terms 'polishing', 'stretching' or 'straightening' do not properly describe an operation done with a sandstone abrasive. Grinding is distinguished from rubbing and polishing by the fact that it is an operation to smooth off a surface after whittling, to take off the unevennesses and complete the rough work. Polishing is the final stage of the work normally done with the help of an abrasive powder and skin. Whether polishing was always used in making arrows it is difficult to say. By 'stretching the shaft' one really means straightening it. In straightening arrow, javelin or spear-shafts heating and steaming would be employed, as is known from ethnographic descriptions.

Thus previous interpretations, which attributed to the tools under discussion a single pre-conceived function, were wrong. These are abrasive instruments used for making bone or wooden tools, a view based on the character of the material of which they were made (sandstone), on the shape of the grooves and the wear traces they bear from use.

First produced in neolithic times, these instruments remained in use in the Bronze Age and possibly even during later stages of the development of technology.

Section three | Bone

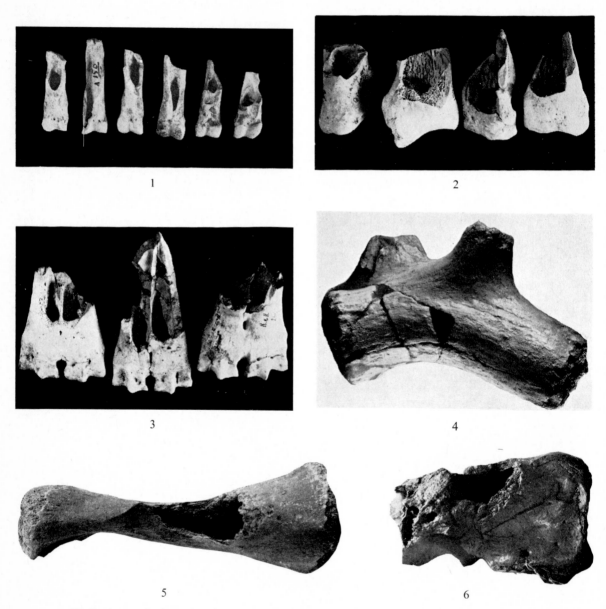

70 *Cracking and splitting long bones and chopping antler in palaeolithic times: 1–3 long bones split by Neandertal man in Crimean caves; 4 base of antler chopped with stone tool from Starosele, Crimea; 5 and 6 mammoth long bone (5) and skull of giant deer (6) trepanned by palaeolithic man.*

1. Basic methods of working bone in palaeolithic times

a. The simplest methods of working bone in lower and middle palaeolithic times

THE working of bone originally started with splitting it in order to extract the edible marrow. The methods of breaking long bones were not as simple as one might first suppose, if we may judge by the material from Crimean caves (Kiik-Koba, Kosh-Koba, Chokurcha and others). The long bones were not simply splintered with a stone so that the pieces of marrow could be picked out of the pieces. The epiphyses were skilfully struck off, so that the whole of the marrow could be obtained (fig. 70.1–3). Palaeolithic man sometimes extracted the marrow from bones of large animals by cutting a hole through the bone wall, that is by a kind of trepanation (fig. 70.5, 6). This method of cutting a hole was evidently a habit of upper palaeolithic times.

The oldest evidence for the use of bone is provided by the material from the cave of Chou-Kou-Tien, if we may judge by the observations of certain archaeologists.

The early Pleistocene inhabitant of China, *Pithecanthropus Pekinensis*, possessed both stone tools and fire, and naturally he was unlikely to neglect a material like bone, which could be put to good use without much effort. Usually he employed deer or gazelle antlers, but, inasmuch as fresh deer antler is difficult to break, he often used not only stone tools but also fire for working it, as Breuil has shown.

He used a very simple method. Having selected the spot on the antler where he wanted to sever it, it was first burnt and charred over a fire, and then the charred place was scraped with a piece of stone. The notch produced was like a Roman figure V, penetrating through the external compact layer into the spongy matter below. After this the bone would be broken without difficulty.

Attempts by Pekin man to notch bone with stone tools without fire are also recorded. They consisted of cuts on fragments of long bone probably caused in cutting off the meat and sinews from the bone.

He also employed one further method of working bone, percussion. In fact, skull, long and flat bones (shoulder and pelvic) had been worked by blows along the edge from a striker. For example, the frontal bone of a deer freed of antlers had very often been converted into a cup-shaped object, which, according to Breuil, could have been used for drinking water. Facets on the bone show that it had been worked from inside outwards, and the edges of some of the cups had been rubbed by use to a shine. When mandibles of deer, boar or hyena had been employed as tools a similar method had been used to strike off the upper projecting part. The working part of the jaw bone was at the front as revealed by traces on the edges of the tooth socket and the disappearance of some teeth, torn out during use.

In Mousterian times the use of fire in working bone continued. Burning and then scraping the burnt place with a stone tool is a very simple and quite rational method of working on such a hard and unyielding material as bone. For example, antler tools discovered in Java associated with remains of Solo man retained traces of the action of fire. These tools are shaped like picks and recall analogous objects used by Pekin man. However, the new Mousterian methods of working stone, which produced comparatively flat leaf-shaped flakes completed by retouch to form a sharp cutting edge, markedly advanced the techniques of bone-working. Such methods of work as whittling appear and also clear evidence of chopping bone. Amongst the bone material from Kiik-Koba there is one noteworthy object made on the left side of the mandible of a wild horse or donkey. On its thick rim traces of work with a thin-bladed tool are visible as short cuts running in a wavy line all along the edge. In the Mousterian deposits of the Crimean caves the basal parts of antlers have been found with traces of the tines having been chopped off (fig. 70.4).

In addition the inhabitants of Kiik-Koba used the metatarsal (*golen*) bone of horse to make a tool with a sharp end. First the proximal epiphysis was struck off and then the diaphysis was split longitudinally. When the marrow had been removed the bone was flaked to a narrow point, while the other end retaining its epiphysis served as a handle. The roughly shaped point could later be whittled and scraped with a flint tool (fig. 70.1–3).

The working of mammoth tusk by whittling has been

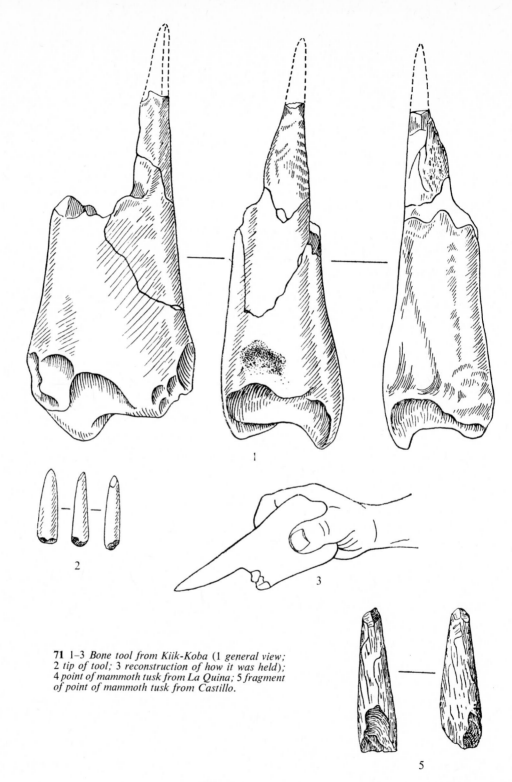

71 1–3 *Bone tool from Kiik-Koba (1 general view;
2 tip of tool; 3 reconstruction of how it was held);
4 point of mammoth tusk from La Quina; 5 fragment
of point of mammoth tusk from Castillo.*

observed among Mousterian tools at La Quina and Castillo. H. Martin identified and published two points (fig. 71.4, 5), one of which was fairly large and could have been used as a head for a boar-spear.[1] The diameter at its base was almost 5 cm and it was 26 cm long. When complete it had been longer, but both the point and base were broken off. Slanting cuts show the whittling, so far as we can infer from the illustration.

Fragments of ivory tools found in Chokurcha Cave (Crimea) had also been worked by whittling. Part of a curved rod and a point from this cave had been ground down after preliminary whittling into shape.

Important evidence showing that Neandertalers whittled bone and wood has been found on a flint tool from Volgograd.[2] This is a flat flake bearing cortex on its dorsal side of the nodule from which it was struck. Seen dorsally the right side is blunted by retouch, while the left side is slightly notched with the facet on the ventral face. The wear traces in the form of polishing and striations detected with the microscope are on the ventral side. The length of the striations reveal that bone was worked not by crude scraping but by whittling, when the blade is at a slight angle to the worked surface. It is true that amongst all the material from Volgograd only one tool with such traces was found, while the other flakes had traces indicating that the blade was held almost at right-angles.

Thus already in early palaeolithic times very simple methods of working bone had come into use: transverse division of antler by using stone tools and fire, and percussion-dressing of long bones. Whittling of long and flat bones and ivory emerged later during middle palaeolithic times.

b. Methods of working bone by striking (flaking, notching, and chiselling) in upper palaeolithic times

At the beginning of the upper palaeolithic period there was a crucial advance in the technique of making stone tools. The flaking of blades off cylindrical cores created a range of flint tools, including instruments suitable for cutting, which was the most important achievement of the new technology. Among implements that appeared in upper palaeolithic times the burin has a special place with fundamental significance for bone-working. Burin work on bone constitutes the most refined method, but in addition there were many others.

Amongst a variety of technical methods of working bone in upper palaeolithic times an important part was still played by percussion and splitting, which had arisen much earlier. On flat bones of animals (shoulder, pelvic and skull), on flakes of ivory and especially on long bones one often sees traces of blows along the edge in the form of rough angular facets, which gave the necessary shape to the bone. Such a rough percussion technique is to some extent merely a copy of the old methods of working stone.

At Eliseevich cup-shaped objects were found with traces of use for trituration, probably of food. Some of them have retouched edges. Blows given on the concave side had produced irregular scars on the convex side, which give the external edge of the object its broken profile (fig. 85).

An excellent example of dressed bone is the mammoth shoulder blade from Kostenki I already cited. Here at the same time cutting had been used to remove unwanted parts of the bone and percussion with suitable blows to form the edge. The cutting had been done with a flint burin, which, as in other cases, marked out the line along which the flat part was to be broken off (fig. 89.1).

Thus the cited examples show us that palaeolithic man wasted his labour as little as possible and worked as quickly as circumstances would allow. The picture that is presented in archaeology of all manufacturing processes in the Stone Age being slow and laborious is quite baseless.

A technique of striking was very often used in working long bones. The hard material of the diaphysis would be difficult to whittle and not always easy to cut with a burin. A diaphysis that had been split longitudinally could easily be worked by blows directed from the outside inwards, putting the splinter on a hard rest (fig. 72).

Traces of a percussion technique can be detected on mammoth tusk from its extraction from the alveolar socket up to its final shaping into a tool, that is varying from hard blows with a heavy stone to careful grooving with delicate hand movements and a suitable instrument.

The carcass of a mammoth would be brought from the point where it was killed to the hut already dismembered. A very valuable part was the ivory; sometimes the tusks were removed from the animal where it had been killed, pulled from their sockets after preliminary loosening by blows with large stones. The root of the tusk which was unsuitable for working because of its friability would be broken or chopped off.

Breaking off the root and severing the shaft of tusk into parts would have been attended by major difficulties; the large tusks of an adult mammoth, 10–15 cm or more in diameter, demanded expenditure of an immense amount of labour. To chop such a tusk would be possible only with a heavy stone wielded with both hands. Part of a large tusk examined from Kostenki I bore traces in the form of cracks and splintering from hard blows from

---

[1] H. Martin, *L'Anthropologie*, 42 (1932), pp. 679, 681.
[2] Materials from the site at Volgograd are housed in the Museum of Ethnology of the Academy of Sciences of the U.S.S.R. in Leningrad.

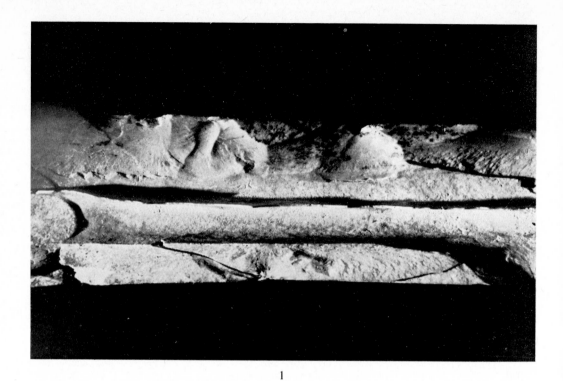

1

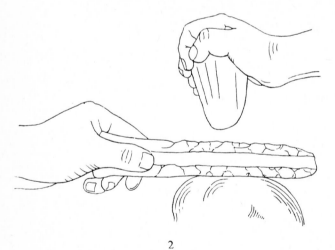

2

72 *A long bone worked by percussion: 1 horse long bone with traces of working by percussion; 2 its method of being worked reconstructed.*

a heavy stone which had shattered the outer layer of ivory. The crushing was at the root of the tusk on its concave side, and the break had a torn profile. It is very probable that tusks were broken, or rather chopped up with the large flint axes, 'gigantoliths', found by Pidoplichka at Novgorod-Seversk (see p. 125 above).

At Kostenki I a method of chiselling or notching for cutting up ivory has been identified on the material including the tusk mentioned. At the other end this piece shows traces of being chopped through by notching (fig. 73). The tusk is 16–17 cm in diameter and the notch 4–5 cm deep. The notch had been made with a narrow chisel-like instrument leaving marks 4–6 mm wide. After notching, the tusk had been broken through with an exceptionally powerful blow, possibly the tusk itself being raised and struck against a rock.

148

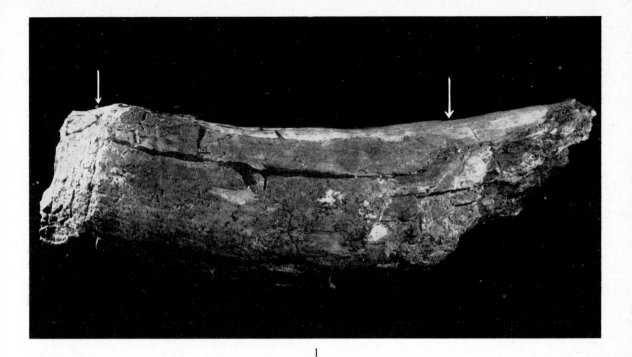

1

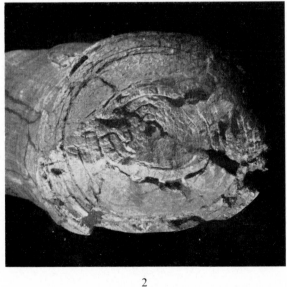

2

73 *An upper palaeolithic worked mammoth tusk from Kostenki I: 1 the root chopped off with stone tool; 2 sectional view of chopped end.*

With regard to the tool used to make the notch it is difficult to envisage its appearance. For operations of such a kind upper palaeolithic man had a range of possible implements, since any large pointed stone held either in the hand or mounted in a handle would be suitable (fig. 74.6). It is probable that flakes and blades were used as chisels and gouges. Such specialized tools (*pieces écaillées*) have been found on upper palaeolithic sites, consisting of flakes and even blades with wear facets on both faces. These facets as a rule have a wavy surface with sharp short flaking line and commonly a steep fracture. The character of the facets indicates that they arose not from pressure retouch but by direct blows into the flake in a vertical position on a hard base, and the facets are best regarded as signs of use, not as trimming. There are grounds for considering such flakes and blades as chisels or gouges for working bone and probably wood (fig. 75.7).

For transverse chopping axes were probably used as indicated by traces on the bone and the existence of axes themselves.

Transverse division of mammoth ivory by circular grooving is well exhibited on the bone material from Eliseevich discovered by K. M. Polikarpovich in 1936. At this site tusks of young mammoths were employed. An object that we examined was a cylinder 11 cm long and 4·5 cm in diameter, evidently a rough-out to be used for scupltural work (fig. 74.2). To judge by the traces the

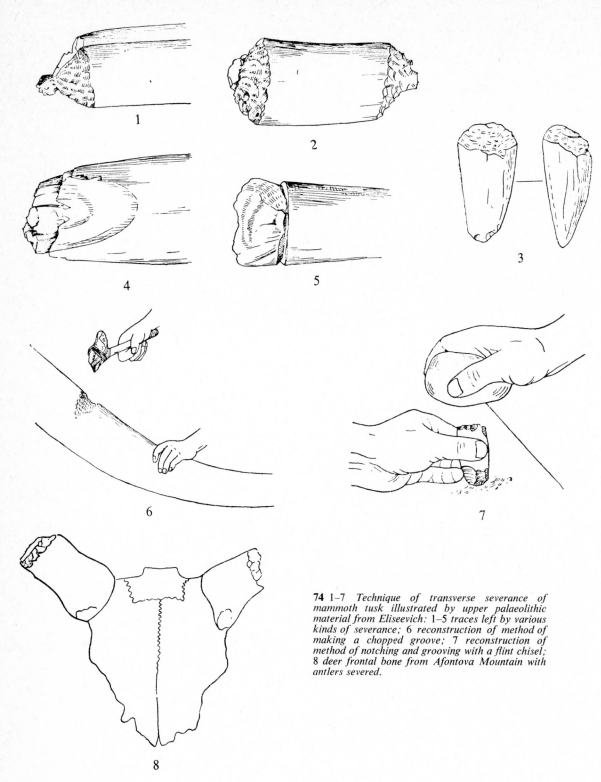

74 1–7 *Technique of transverse severance of mammoth tusk illustrated by upper palaeolithic material from Eliseevich: 1–5 traces left by various kinds of severance; 6 reconstruction of method of making a chopped groove; 7 reconstruction of method of notching and grooving with a flint chisel; 8 deer frontal bone from Afontova Mountain with antlers severed.*

notch had been made by a small chopping tool with a narrow working-end. Blow by blow the palaeolithic craftsman had hollowed out around the tusk a broad groove deepening towards the centre. When only a narrow neck of ivory some 15 mm in diameter survived the tusk had been broken across by a sharp blow.

On another example (fig. 74.1) the craftsman's attempt to break the tusk can be seen after only taking the groove two-thirds of the way round. As a result he has not produced the desired result, for the tusk did not break quite along the right line.

Circular grooving of tusk would have given a positive result even if the groove was not taken very deep; a rough-out from the same site (fig. 74.5) shows that a groove of 10 mm on a tusk 45–50 mm in diameter was sufficient for the tusk to break along the right line. Other specimens from Eliseevich demonstrate a similar ratio, but on some even a groove of 10–11 mm deep in a tusk of 60–70 mm in diameter caused it to break exactly on the desired line.

Probably the results of severance by notching with a small groove depended on the ivory's condition. Fresh ivory splits better than dried-out ivory in which imperceptible cracks alter the direction of the break (fig. 74.4).

However, fresh ivory would have been extremely difficult to break across merely by striking without a notch chopped or cut round with a burin. A part of a tusk from Eliseevich illustrates this, one end of which has been broken by blows, the other grooved round by chopping with an axe. This ivory had been grooved and chopped while fresh, as is indicated by the conchoidal fracture lines, and also by the absence of longitudinal cracking found on dried-out ivory. The results of the two kinds of work were very different. The grooved part gave a clean stump, but the battered end shows a large conchoidal flake scar, as a result of which an appreciable part of the material had been wasted.

The technique of notching, which testifies to the patient and methodical character of palaeolithic man's work, was not confined to dividing tusks, but had a wide general application. It was used in the plastic working of ivory, when the form had to be changed, such as a part removed or a hollow or a notch made.

The part of the object from Eliseevich called a 'clapper' (*kolotushka*) which might be regarded as its handle is covered by traces of chiselling by blows from an implement with a sharp and narrow end. The depth of the holes is very slight, for to avoid flaking the material the blows were light but numerous, producing bunched masses of holes. At first glance the ivory's surface looks gnawed or rasped, and it is very rough to the touch (fig. 75.1).

It should be noticed that the handle-part of tools made of ivory found at Eliseevich are covered with cuts, even when the ivory in the remaining part of the tool is unworked. When considerable force was used the roughening of the handle prevented these tools from slipping in the hand. Amongst the ivory tools at this site was a dagger made from the tusk of a young mammoth, which was 26 cm long and 4·5 cm broad in its handle part. The natural point of the tusk had been sharpened by whittling. The object was broken in the middle and lacked its tip, but the clear traces it bore could leave no doubt about its use as a dagger. The handle part was covered on both faces by small cuts, where the palm and fingers gripped it hardest, to assure a firm hold. The necessity of this precaution to prevent the hand slipping by artificial roughening of the surface is quite obvious; the handle part tapers down to the point (fig. 75.4, 5). Another example of chipping the handle of a tool is part of the tusk of a young mammoth used without additional sharpening. The cuts have been made on the two corresponding opposite sides, and as in the former case the smaller area is intended for the thumb (fig. 75.3).

As an example of plastic alterations to ivory by means of grooving or notching there is a problematical object from Eliseevich, a large flake struck off a substantial tusk. The greater part of its surface is covered by cuts which, as in the preceding specimens, are tiny holes of irregular shape (fig. 75.2). At one end a notch has been cut which passes right through the ivory to give the flake a sort of bifurcation. The edge of the flake has been carefully worked by this notching technique. It is difficult to say what intention the palaeolithic craftsman had when he did the work, which either he left unfinished or spoilt by mishap and abandoned.

The most simple method of severing an antler transversely in upper palaeolithic times was by chopping through it with a sharp chopping tool. Without falling back on the old lower palaeolithic methods of burning over a fire, a deep groove could be made all the way round by hard blows with a flint axe on the desired line of division, deep enough to reach the spongy interior of the antler, which would then break through. Without a deep groove fresh deer antler, which is extremely resilient, would be impossible or at all events very difficult to break.

The upper part of a deer skull with chopped-off antlers from Afontova Mountain illustrates two such very simple methods of severing antler. The right beam has been grooved all the way round and then snapped off very evenly, almost as if sawn. The left beam was grooved only half the way round and then broken off unevenly, so that in part of the beam which was not grooved some of the compact layer of antler has been split off beyond the marked-out line of division (fig. 74.8).

c. Sawing bone

In the daily life of upper palaeolithic people long bones

of such small animals as hare and polar fox were widely used. Hard and very tough in structure, they were employed for a variety of small articles: awls, needles, perforators, beads and so on. Yet small bones are very difficult to divide transversely with a burin, which had perforce to be done by sawing.

Examination of the material from Eliseevich confirms that transverse severing of bone objects was effected by sawing through with a retouched bladelet (fig. 76.1–3). The toothed flint edge was eminently suitable for this. In certain cases the bone has been sawn half or a third of the way through and then broken, giving an uneven toothy end to the broken edge (fig. 76.2). In order to get a smooth end the bone could be sawn through on all sides right the way round. After breaking there was only

a slight waviness on the inner edge of the bone wall; the end of the break otherwise was reasonably smooth. In the micro-photograph of the stump of this bone, five sawn grooves made one after another and the 'fringe' of unsawn broken bone, are clearly visible (fig. 76.7).

Palaeolithic man often used the mandibles of carnivorous animals with their sharp, sturdy canine teeth, as tools. A mandible for this purpose was broken into two halves with one canine in each half, the projecting parts being broken or chopped off, to give a beak-shaped tool. Implements made out of the mandibles of carnivores (bear, lion, tiger) were of considerable weight and size, and were commonly used for cracking long bones to extract marrow, which was practised up until the last century. Such a fact was noticed on the material from

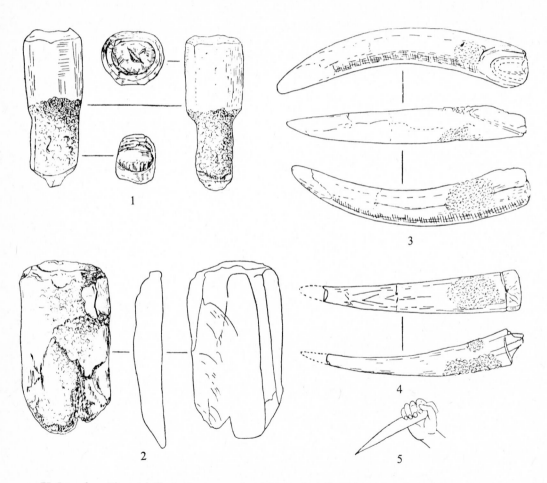

75 *Ivory from Eliseevich illustrating upper palaeolithic work: 1 'bell clapper' made with burin chipping technique (axe blows are visible on the upper cylindrical part); 2 blade of ivory with traces of chipping; 3 tusk of young mammoth with two patches of chipping to give purchase for the hand; 4 dagger of ivory with two patches of chipping; 5 reconstruction of how it was grasped.*

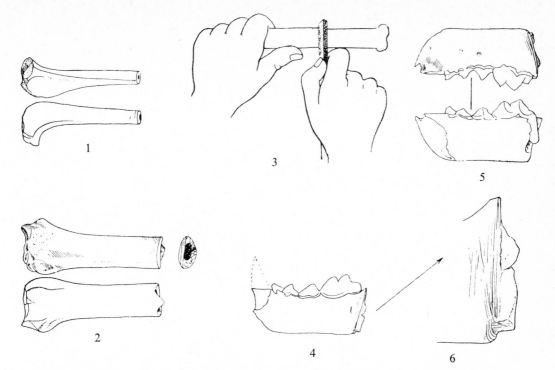

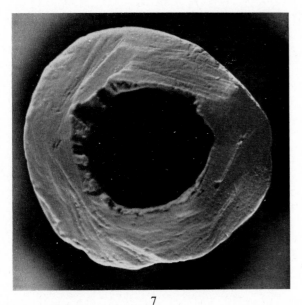

76 *Upper palaeolithic bone sawing illustrated by material from Eliseevich: 1 and 2 sawn long bones of small animals; 3 the sawing reconstructed; 4–6 wolf mandibles (traces of sawing (4) enlarged (6); traces of incising (5)); 7 micro-photograph of sawn end showing separate saw cuts.*

the cave of Hohlfels near Wurtemberg by Fraas.[1] In addition there are numerous ethnographic parallels for the use of mandibles of small carnivores as tools. For example, we can quote the mandible of cynadon and other fresh-water animals used by the tribes of Bororo in central Brazil.[2]

At Eliseevich several wolf mandibles were found worked by cutting and sawing (fig. 76.4–6). The projecting parts had been cut away by two methods: on one examination of the cut showed the use of a burin, on the other signs of sawing with a retouched blade were visible. The purpose of these wolf mandibles treated in this way is uncertain.

To judge by the material from Avdeevo and other sites the ribs of large animals were divided by sawing with a flint blade.[3]

d. Flaking mammoth tusk

The longitudinal division of mammoth tusk was achieved by palaeolithic man in several ways. The first and most simple was to strike off flakes by blows with a

[1] O. Fraas, *Archiv für Anthropologie*, 5, p. 173.
[2] K. Steinen, *Unter den Natürvolkern Zentral-Brasilien* (Berlin, 1897), pp. 200–1.
[3] M. D. Gvozdover, *Materials and Researches on the Archaeology of the U.S.S.R.*, 39 (1953), p. 196.

pointed stone tool on the tusk's circumference without a preliminary burin groove (fig. 77.3). In such cases the flakes produced were of irregular shape. The lamellar structure of ivory allowed longitudinal flaking even without preparatory grooving. At Eliseevich a flake of spatula shape (fig. 77.1), struck off a tusk in precisely this crude way, showed the following marks: (1) absence from the edge of the flake of traces of work with a burin; (2) presence on the left edge of four little dents from four blows with a stone chisel; (3) presence of a

large oval facet on the front flat end of the flake. The broad spade-shaped end had been polished all over from friction in use on a soft material. Its dark surface with intense lustre and good state of preservation prompted the thought that the flake had been saturated in fat and so protected from weathering. It is likely that it was some kind of spoon used in preparing a porridge-like food and also in eating it.

Commonly ivory flakes underwent a finishing process like a large flake from Eliseevich out of which a scoop

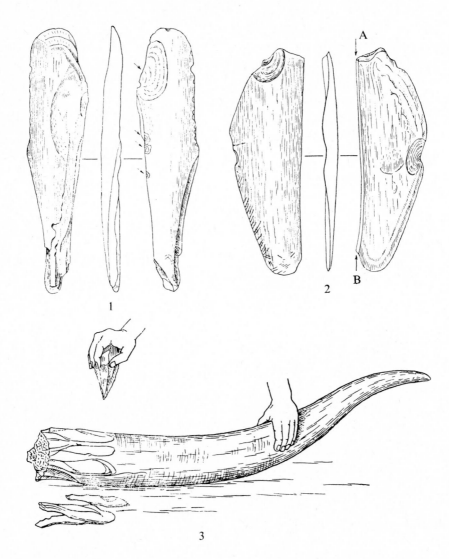

77 *Upper palaeolithic ivory from Eliseevich:* 1 *flake removed without preliminary grooving (arrows indicate chisel scars);* 2 *flake removed after preparatory grooving by burin along line* AB; 3 *reconstruction of flakes being struck off a tusk.*

was made. Its handle was formed by a notch cut out with a flint knife (on the right) and by a side flake off the narrow edge (on the left). In addition the projections on the inner layer of ivory on the working edge had been planed off. The scoop was 25 cm long, 8·5 cm broad and more than 1 cm thick, with a convex working edge rubbed from use. The edges are thin, particularly on the left, and have been broken in use. The handle has an unrubbed rough end where it had been held in the palm, contrasting obviously with the front end of the scoop, the thumb being accommodated in the notch. The scoop could have been used for digging and throwing out soil during earth-digging work with picks and mattocks, which were also discovered on the site.

Flakes struck off tusks after grooving with a burin achieved a more regular shape. One of these struck from a tusk after longitudinal grooving (fig. 77.2A–B) had two large facets on it indicating two hard blows with a chisel. One of these is on the external face of the ivory, and this raises the problem which blow actually detached the flake. Most of the indications suggest that the flake came off from a blow delivered at the bottom of the facet on the concave side of the blade.

e. Longitudinal and transverse division of bone with a burin

A more difficult, but technically more accomplished, method of dividing bone transversely and longitudinally in upper palaeolithic times was by cutting with a burin. The invention of the burin in this period, as mentioned above, can be regarded as a very great step forward in the field of technology. In order to appreciate this fact fully attention must now be turned to the full flowering of manufacture of bone tools in upper palaeolithic times, including artistic burin work on bone.

There can scarcely be any doubt that the burin was created by the need for more skilful division of bone. In upper palaeolithic times man invented an instrument and started a method of cutting which today is the basis of machine-engineering, as well as the whole of industry itself. In order to justify a statement that at first glance seems very rash it is sufficient to observe that almost all the basic and essential details of machinery and mechanism used for lathes, and in cutting and rolling steel mills rely on burins.

The presence of burin facets is the distinctive trait of burins, although only a single vertical blow was necessary to make the working end, which could be done on a simple blade. Even when we have a medial burin made

by two facets the working part may well be a corner angle produced by a single facet.

Eskimo burins used on bone are based on this principle. They have one working face, and are made of forged iron sharpened and then set in wooden handles. Different shapes are used for different kinds of work: straight burins for dividing materials, and hooked for making deep slots in bone objects.[1]

The mechanical principle of operation with an upper palaeolithic burin, made on a prismatic blade by a burin blow, amounts to this: the bone is not scratched but the burin angle takes a fine paring off it, in just the same way as a modern steel burin does in working on metals. Cutting bone with a knife as envisaged by Gerasimov[2] would be very difficult (fig. 78.1). A knife blade can whittle bone taking off a thin paring, but it cannot pass through its hard body in a longitudinal movement as, for example, it passes through meat or skin.

A burin was widely used for the transverse severance of ivory in upper palaeolithic times. In examining the material one is at once struck by shallow notches which pass a third or a half or the whole way round the circumference of the tusk. Usually they penetrated one layer of ivory, at most two, after which the tusk had been broken through. Instances never occur of the ivory being cut right through by the burin; undoubtedly this would have been superfluous, as the circular groove ensured a relatively straight break along the prepared line. The break would not be absolutely regular, but the main objective was achieved. As an example of notching a dagger handle from Eliseevich may be cited where the groove passed round two-thirds of the circumference. The fracture line in the inner layers of ivory makes a sharp zigzag (2 cm) on the side away from the groove (fig. 74.5).

Cases have been noticed when even a circular groove in the ivory did not give a regular line of division, but they are probably attributable to uneven drying-out through the tusk's section.

Very often longitudinal division of ivory was undertaken with the object of getting rough-outs.[3] A very remarkable specimen of longitudinal division along the whole length of a tusk by preliminary grooving with a burin may be cited from Eliseevich (fig. 78.2). Before us we have a long blade of ivory with traces of work on it. A long thin shallow groove, hardly penetrating beyond the ivory surface, extends practically along its full length. Approximately in the middle of the blade are traces of blows from a stone chisel showing the craftsman's

[1] J. W. Powell, *Annual Reports of the American Bureau of Ethnology* (1896–7), p. 81, pl. XXVI.
[2] M. M. Gerasimov, *Materials and Researches on the Archaeology of the U.S.S.R.*, 2 (1941), p. 73.
[3] A practically identical method of removing splinters from deer antlers was used in western Europe, although owing to the interior of antler being soft and friable blows were unnecessary to remove the splinter, as was the case with ivory; see *Proceedings of the Prehistoric Society*, 19 (1953), pp. 148–60. T.

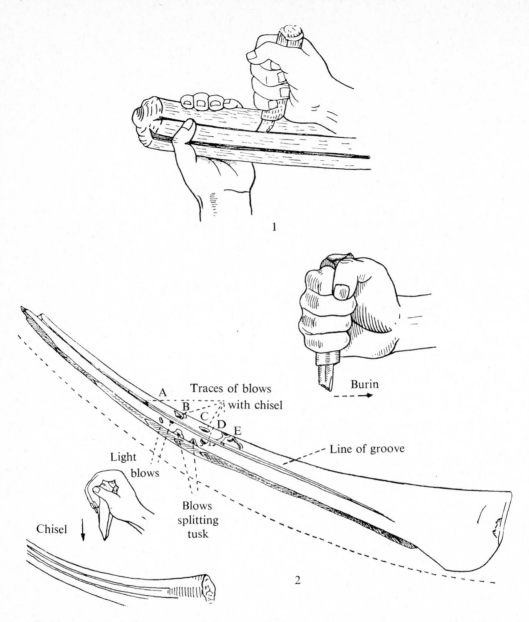

78 *Longitudinal division of mammoth ivory: 1 Gerasimov's reconstruction of cutting ivory with a knife; 2 fragment of mammoth tusk from Eliseevich with traces of cutting and splitting along a prepared groove.*

intention to strike in the line of the groove in order to take off a strip along its whole length. Of traces of ten dents visible two are not connected with detachments of this strip; they were due to blows used in detaching a previous one off the left side. Two small dents indicate blows of quite insufficient force. Five dents (A, B, C, D, E) are connected with this strip, but clearly show that the craftsman had not considered the matter sufficiently.

Of the five, four had not fallen on the proper line, only one being in the right place, but of insufficient strength. Work had then been abandoned on the tusk while still unfinished, so leaving interesting evidence for us today to study the methods of working bone used by palaeolithic man.

A fragment of tusk from Timonovka that has been studied deserves special attention for the signs of trans-

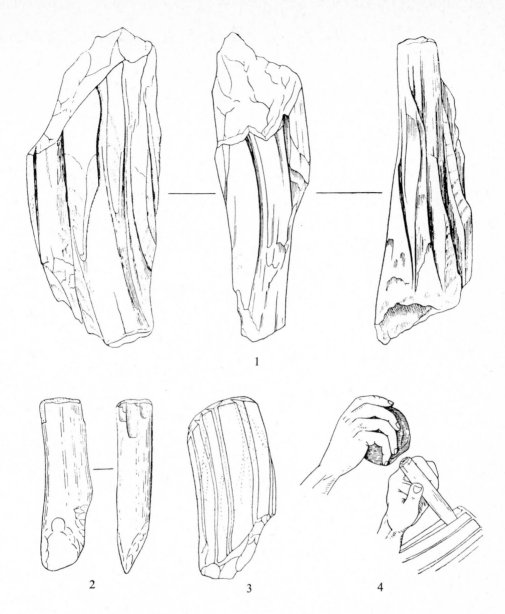

1

2   3   4

79 *Longitudinal division of mammoth ivory: 1 tusk fragment from Timonovka with traces of cutting and splitting; 2 antler chisel for splitting along a groove from Malta (Siberia); 3 grooved tusk from Malta; 4 method of splitting along the groove reconstructed.*

verse and longitudinal division that it bears (fig. 79.1). At one end the tusk has been hewn through without any visible traces of the use of a notch or burin; evidently the ivory was fresh when worked as indicated by the conchoidal nature of the fracture on the stump. At the other end it had been severed, using a very deep notch made with a burin.

Longitudinal grooving of the tusk was designed to produce regular strips by making deep parallel grooves at intervals of 15–20 mm, the rough-outs made in this way being employed for objects whose nature is uncertain. The secondary work was done with ivory that was fairly dry, after the lapse of some time since the transverse severance of the tusk.

After he had made the longitudinal grooves the palaeolithic craftsman had to split off the strip. How-

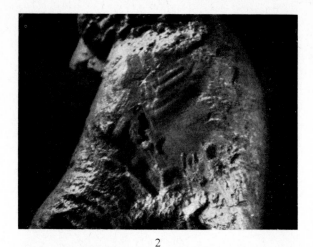

2

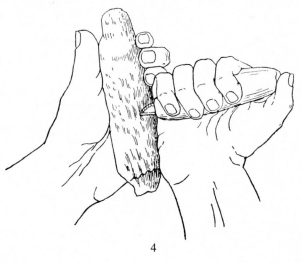

3

80 *Upper palaeolithic female statuette carved of mammoth ivory from Avdeevo: 1 general view; 2 traces of whittling with a flint knife at the head (enlarged); 3 traces left by use of burin on the back (enlarged); 4 method of carving reconstructed.*

4

ever, strips would not split off along their whole length but broke more or less centrally, in spite of some of the grooves being undercut, so as to differentiate the strip to the maximum and ease its detachment.

There are no grounds for believing that in splitting off the strip a single striker stone only would have been used. The reconstruction shows a lump of grooved ivory before the strip has been split off, assuming that a bone wedge was put into the groove (fig. 79.4); the Eskimos split walrus ivory in this fashion. The existence of a chisel of Eskimo type has been established in some palaeolithic sites (Afontova Mountain, Kostenki I, Malta). The chisels have a thick battered butt end with scars from blows on the edge and a wedge-shaped working end (fig. 79.2).

f. Plastic work with a burin

There are other facts showing the wider use of the burin by palaeolithic man; it was also used for sculptural work. A statuette from Avdeevo studied in this connextion has traces on its surface of whittling with a knife and clear furrows cut with the angle of a burin that show best on the body and legs (figs. 80.2–3). In this case a burin has been used not only for notches and hollows on the figure but also for removing surplus material, smoothing off the contours and modelling details (fig. 80.3).

The character and disposition of the furrows makes it possible to infer that the burin was held with the edge of the palm of the right hand pressing on the ivory, and short movements made by squeezing the fingers with slight assistance from neck and shoulder muscles (fig. 80.4).

Thus upper palaeolithic man made use of techniques of grooving and burin work for purposes as different as obtaining a bone rough-out on the one hand, and sculpture on the other.

g. Whittling

Traces of whittled bone indicate that this method of work was well understood in upper palaeolithic times. Two methods of whittling can be distinguished. One can be described as a sort of scraping with the flint blade held almost at right angles to the bone surface. The traces on the bone consist of parallel lines slightly wavy and at closely spaced intervals characteristic of this type of work. An example is an object from Kostenki I conventionally called a 'boomerang', which has been made from a mammoth rib with the curve taken out and the edge sharpened by whittling. In this instance the whittling was of a distinct kind, whose purpose was to take off an appreciable quantity of the material by means of a frequently repeated movement. The so-called boomerang from Kostenki I is of considerable length, about 80 cm, and its breadth in the middle is about 7 cm. In transverse section it is rhomboidal. The epiphysis has been removed and the edge sharpened by whittling. At this end on the concave side are traces of chops made with a stone axe, whose significance is uncertain.

In reality this object probably is not a boomerang but a throwing club for hunting birds, not one which returned to the feet of the hunter if he missed. In ethnographic souces there is widespread record of such clubs which have a circular flight and, used on a flight of birds, can kill several of them.

In upper palaeolithic times whittling was not confined to the method just described, that is a sort of scraping. Bone material extracted by splitting was used for rough-outs, on which there are very often all kinds of bumps and torn edges which had to be removed by the cutting type of whittling. An example of this kind of work is the working of wood with a knife and plane in contemporary peasant industries. On palaeolithic bone articles similar surface alterations are visible characterized by facets, notches, cuts, and hollows. It would have been impossible to carry out such work on bone without a whittling knife. Undoubtedly grooving and chopping with flint axes would also be used, but even then the final touching up required whittling to smooth off the chopped surface.

h. Softening bone

Almost all the methods that have been described of working ivory, antler, and long bones were employed by palaeolithic man without altering the natural quality of the material. Sodden bone, as is well known, possesses a fair degree of plasticity and viscidity, which given patience and skill would allow it to be worked with flint tools.

Undoubtedly there was no necessity to soften the bone of a freshly killed animal when splitting, grooving, incising, whittling or retouch were used. For splitting and retouch indeed slightly dried-out bone would have been better. This is particularly the case with deer antler, which is extremely resilient in a fresh state.

Ivory also is better split in a dried-out state, since the lamellae adhere less firmly and the tusk loses some of its monolithic character, but whittling and burin work would be very difficult on dried-out bone. This is easily confirmed by simple experiment, that is by using a flint or metal tool (knife or burin) firstly on a long bone that has been allowed to dry out for several months, and then on the same bone after it has been soaked in water for several weeks.[1] In our test the dried-out bone after soaking took up moisture that increased its weight by 7 per cent, demonstrating a relatively high degree of hydroscopicity. In this way working (whittling and burin work) on the bone was made appreciably easier; parings three to four times thicker could be taken off.[2]

There are grounds for supposing that palaeolithic man did not always resort to softening; he adjusted himself to the condition of the material and did what was possible with the normal methods of work. He worked

---

The translator can confirm by tests that this was also so with antler. In 1952 at Cambridge a section of reindeer antler was tested with a micro-hardness tester. Three sets of readings were taken diametrically across the antler: twenty readings on the dried-out antler, six after one hour's soaking at 80°C. and fifteen after 89 hours drying-out in still air. The mean hardness values were respectively 37·35, 19·9 and 31·13. Thus after an hour in hot water the antler's hardness dropped to 53 per cent of the original, but it returned to 83 per cent of the original after 89 hours drying. T.

[2] The translator might point out that softening of bone, antler and ivory, prior to carving, was generally practised on both sides of the Bering Straits, with urine among the Koryak and by boiling among the Alaskan Eskimo; see: *Annual Report of the Bureau of American Ethnology*, 18, pt. i (1897), p. 196, and W. Jochelson, *The North Pacific Jesup Expedition*, vi, The Koryak, pt. ii (1908), p. 647. T.

quickly, employing complicated and laborious techniques only of necessity, when normal methods did not give the required results.

There exist, however, undisputed facts demonstrating the softening of bone by steaming. In this connexion a diadem from a child's grave at Malta must be cited, which consisted of a hoop made of a thin strip of ivory. Fresh ivory could not possibly have been bent into a hoop thus, and it would have been difficult to flake off a strip like this because of its lamellar structure. In order to obtain such a strip it would be necessary to use dry ivory, and then force it into the necessary curvature.

Gerasimov with good cause considers that in order to obtain such shapes palaeolithic man resorted to steaming. If damp bone had been thoroughly heated it would be possible to give it a curvature. In order to make dry bone elastic it must be heated in damp conditions to prevent it cracking.

In contemporary peasant techniques the softening of bone is carried out by steaming in a damp medium at a temperature of 120°C or higher.

Palaeolithic man not having the use of clay vessels probably first soaked the bone for a long time and then heated it up over a fire.

Gerasimov's experiments showed a very feasible method of softening ivory: 'After thorough soaking for five days a lump of ivory was wrapped up in a piece of fresh skin, itself also soaked until it was swollen. The skin with fur inwards was twisted round the ivory three times, and the whole packet was put into the camp fire and kept there until the skin had completely charred, which took one hour forty-five minutes. The soft skin wrapping was completely charred falling to pieces at a touch, and the temperature of the bone was so great that for some time it was impossible to hold it in the hand. It could be freely whittled with a knife with flint blade giving long spiral-like parings. An ivory strip could be easily bent after steaming in this way.'[1]

2. The manufacture of bone points in the settlement of Luka-Vrublevetskaya

THE study of traces of use on artefacts permits us to detect the consecutive stages of manufacture of this or that object, even if only fragments of it have survived.

An example of this is the manufacture of bone points studied in the material from the early Tripolye settlement of Luka-Vrublevetskaya.

The points were made out of long bones: first one epiphysis was knocked off, and then grooves were cut with a burin along the shaft of the bone so as to make four rough-outs from each bone. The bone was split into narrow strips along these grooves for their full length including the remaining epiphysis. The thickened end of the latter served as a handle, which was trimmed only after the final work on the tapering part of the tool. The next step was to work the rough-out on a rough stone block to remove superfluous material and grind the bone into shape. The final stage was to sharpen up the tip on a fine-grained stone plaque, a touch-stone.

The stages enumerated are represented in traces of wear shown in the photographs. Traces of longitudinal grooves are visible in the front and side edges of the bone (fig. 81.1, 3). They start at the epiphysis and run as parallel lines gradually deepening; their number indicates the number of movements made with the burin, which very often penetrated the interior of the bone at first cut.

Traces of the rough grinding are visible in the microphotographs (fig. 81.4) as diagonal lines intersecting at a slight angle. They are situated on the side edges of the rough-out previously marked by the parallel lines of the burin movement. Evidently grinding against a stone was very efficient and the bone wore down very quickly, so there was no necessity to resort to whittling.

The final work of forming the tip was done more carefully on a stone of finer grain, as shown by the regular lines which hardly intersect (fig. 81.6).

81 (OPPOSITE) *Methods of manufacturing late neolithic bone points at Luka-Vrublevetskaya: 1 traces of splitting along prepared grooves cut in the diaphyses; 2 bone strip with traces of grinding on an abrasive stone; 3 traces of parallel cuts for grooves; 4 micro-photograph of traces of grinding on a coarse-grained stone; 5 finished points; 6 micro-photograph of traces of sharpening a point on a fine-grained stone.*

[1] M. M. Gerasimov, op. cit., pp. 70–71.

1

2

3

5

4

6

3. Some methods of working bone among the ancient Eskimos bearing on the problem of the growth of their settlements

IT has already been explained in the examples cited of palaeolithic and neolithic bone-working that traces of work reveal not only technical devices, the sequence of operations as well as the amount of force applied, but also disclose features of the tools applied to carry out the work.

The possibility of identifying the character of the tool, that is the shape of its working part, the angle of its blade-edge and its depth of penetration into the worked material, gives an opportunity to recognize its qualities and properties, and indeed the material of which it was made. This is a crucial matter if an archaeological site yields artefacts only, and the working tools are slightly represented or entirely absent. It goes without saying that not all artefacts allow us to identify the tools used to make them.

Research of this type on the harpoons of the ancient Eskimos of the Bering Sea from Rudenko's excavation of 1946[1] has given definitive results, because these objects were well preserved. The excavations were undertaken at a series of points in the Chukotsk peninsula, where different stages of Eskimo culture were represented, from the Uellen-Okvik stage up to remains of contemporary Eskimos.

It is well known that the history of the Eskimos, especially the problem of their penetration into the Arctic, has been studied by American and Danish archaeologists over the course of several decades. On the basis of numerous excavations made over a great area from western Alaska to Greenland Collins worked out a periodization of the history of the Eskimos starting from well back in the second millenium B.C. and going up to contemporary times.[2]

Before this, the prevailing opinion among American and European archaeologists, a view to some extent still surviving, had been that Eskimo settlement of the Arctic was of much greater antiquity. Relying on the resemblances between upper palaeolithic cultural remains with those of the Eskimos the latter were regarded as the descendants of the former, who would have been compelled to migrate into the Arctic regions following the retreating herds of mammoth and reindeer at the end of the Ice Age. With the passage of time the ancestors of the present Eskimos staying in the Arctic changed over from a palaeolithic to a neolithic culture. They continued at this level until the appearance of Europeans.

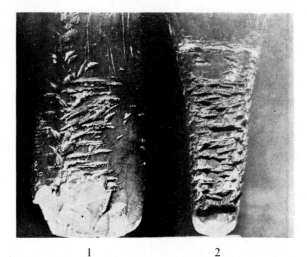

1   2

Nobody disputed the neolithic level of culture of the Eskimos. Danish and American archaeologists with Collins at their head never considered the possibility that these Arctic hunters of marine animals used metal in the very early stages of their history as revealed by the excavations. Yet study of their bone tools has shown that metal was known to them already in the oldest cultural periods, the Uellen-Okvik and Ipiutak cultures.

Artefacts of walrus ivory, including harpoons and other items of hunting equipment, of the ancient Eskimos are conspicuous for their exceptionally fine workmanship. Everything that we know about palaeolithic bone objects, including artistic pieces, does not cause surprise with regard to the methods of manufacture employed. Every movement of a flint blade was witness to the unyielding nature of the material, the fragile flint blade or edge, the necessity to supplement every cut with trimming, cutting and scraping. In the shaping of objects and surfaces, especially in making grooves, perforations, and notches the bone responded poorly to a flint tool, often leaving an uneven ragged working part, chipped from the work and in general a complete absence of standardization, because the shape to an appreciable extent was a matter of chance.

There is no need to guess as to the techniques of working bone in neolithic times. Stone tools impose a

[1] S. I. Rudenko, *Ancient Culture of the Bering Sea and the Eskimo Problem* (Moscow-Leningrad, 1947).
[2] H. Collins, *Smithsonian Institute, Miscellaneous Collections*, 100 (1940), p. 536.

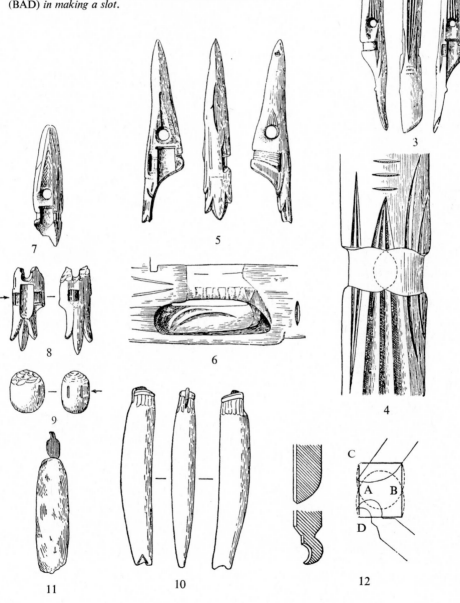

82 (AND OPPOSITE) *Eskimo tools: 1 handle part of wedge of walrus ivory roughened with a stone adze; 2 bone handle for stone adze roughened with metal adze; 3 toggle-head harpoon of walrus ivory with slots for stone point and line; 4 schematic drawing of groove for line (in plan); 5 toggle-head harpoon; 6 schematic drawing from side of slot for line with traces of work by burin; 7 and 8 harpoons with slots for line; 9 walrus ivory ball with slots; 10 bone handle with remains of an iron burin from Cape Baranov; 11 contemporary claw-shaped burin; 12 movement of straight burin (BAC) and claw-shaped burin (BAD) in making a slot.*

3

7

5

8

6

4

9

11

10

12

163

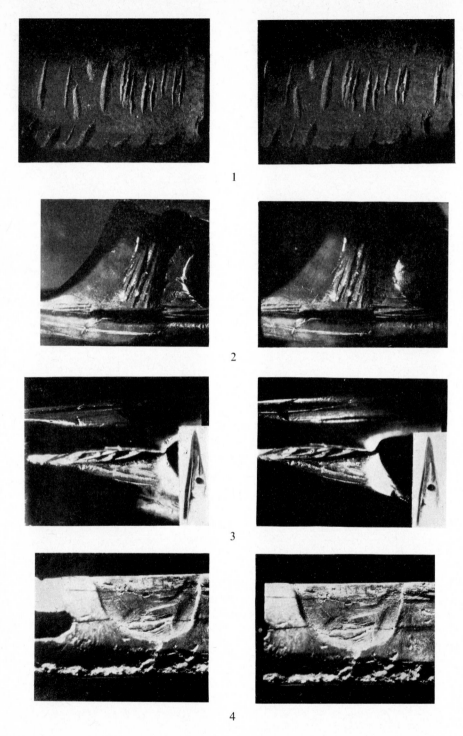

83 *Stereoscopic views of bone objects of the Old Bering Sea Eskimo: 1–3 chipping done with an iron adze (1) and grooves made with an iron burin (2 and 3) on harpoons of walrus ivory (2 ×); 4 slot in a handle of walrus ivory.*

certain limit technically beyond which the work cannot be taken. The edge angle of a blade or point of stone had always to be large perforce on account of the brittleness of stone. The cutting edge of a burin could never be a perfectly regular shape, while it was almost impossible to make a perfectly cylindrical bore because of the difficulty of controlling the direction of drilling with flint. In particular it was impossible with brittle stone to give the working part of an instrument a regular shape. Ground axes, adzes, chisels, and knives of the neolithic period are only a big step forward in wood-working (albeit within certain limits) by comparison with the preceding period; as far as bone is concerned ground tools offered practically nothing new or an advance on what could be done before.

Bone tools of Eskimo manufacture present quite another aspect (fig. 82). The grooves on rough-outs, made for longitudinal or transverse division of bones, are very deep and perfectly regular. Chop-marks or cuts on even a very hard material like walrus ivory reveal a very small edge angle on the blade used. Flat cuts have a regular shape without crushed angles, and there is no trace of repeated movement of the tool over the same point. Each movement of the knife or burin was an effective one. Scraping, rubbing down, and scratching through are hardly visible; the very shape of the objects is distinguished by symmetry and clear planning of details.

These are only general impressions from studying Eskimo tools, but closer examination of individual aspects and details reveals, not only a high level of skill, but extreme specialization of methods employed. The investigator's attention is mainly held by the working of the grooves, slots, perforations, and sockets on the small bone objects, particularly on the toggle-head harpoons (fig. 82.5–9).

Deep slots were designed to hold the line by which the head was fixed to the shaft whose end sits in the open socket in the middle. These slots are an extension of a transverse groove on the head (fig. 82.2–5). Due to the slot and the groove the line did not project from the surface of the head at the moment of impact and penetration into the animal's body.

The proportions of these slots are surprising. They are not only up to 10 mm deep, but are also extremely narrow, often not as much as 1 mm, and 4–5 mm long. Examination with the Epi-lamp and binocular lenses makes it quite clear that they were not made by burning or boring; in no instance were there traces of this. All slots, even the most tiny, had been cut out with a burin and show the regular geometric cut of its working edge.

Stone burins whether made of flint or obsidian cannot have a regular cutting edge, since they were made by a burin blow which produces a conchoidal fracture. Moreover, stone would have quickly splintered in this type of work. Stone burins are in general not suitable for making deep, narrow, and short slots, which cannot be made even with a metal burin of the normal shape with straight cutting edge whose front face was held vertically on the surface being cut. The normal burin will not penetrate deeply into the material, because it takes off a paring with each horizontal movement gradually deepening by taking off a little more from the point where the groove was started. So the ends of the groove are always sloping or even stepped. For this reason burins normally have a wide edge angle to permit very great pressure on this small area, although this broad cutting edge prevents deep cutting into the material. On the other hand, a burin with low angle at the edge could not be held vertically on the cutting surface, since a stone burin with narrow working part will snap at the first horizontal movement and a metal one bend. These rules are well understood in contemporary methods of working metals and their theoretical basis worked out.[1]

A narrow angle on the cutting edge is only practical if the edge of the burin is not straight but claw-shaped, only possible that is with a shaped burin.

Among palaeolithic tools stone claw-shaped burins are known to us, but these have been made by fine retouch and were probably intended only for cutting shallow grooves in linear ornament on bone objects, in other words scratching. The undercut edge of these burins is small and the cutting edge sharp. Such shaped burins, having regard to the brittleness of flint, could bear only a very small load, quite inadequate to cut bone.

Shaped burins of claw form with regular cutting edge could only have been made of metal. The unbreakable qualities of metal as well as the possibility of sharpening it allowed it to be given any form necessary for fine and precise operations requiring appreciable force. Examination of the slots on Eskimo harpoons shows that the burins employed were claw-shaped with a sharpened point. Stereo-photographs of traces of work within the slots of these harpoons clearly show each separate act of cutting done either with the side or the edge of the burin angle (fig. 83.2, 3). In many cases semi-circular movements of the burin are clearly visible (fig. 83.4) and its gradual penetration into the material.

Prolonged experiments in cutting bone with flint and metal burins of different shapes have achieved results conforming with those observed in the traces and with

---

[1] A. M. Vulf, *The Cutting of Metals* (Moscow, 1944).

the theoretical aspects of cutting known to science. Only claw-shaped metal burins were suitable for producing slots like those found on the harpoons and other objects of the Eskimos. Metal burins with a working facet at right-angles to the cutting plane, that is normal burins, were not suitable for such work, since they penetrated into the material (within the limits of the short slot) only to a very shallow depth. They were prevented from penetrating more deeply, as we have said, by the wide angle of the working edge (fig. 82.12).

The ethnographic evidence in its turn confirms the deductions made relative to the possible kind of metal burins used for working bone. In the nineteenth century both the Asiatic and American Eskimos still made bone harpoons with stone or iron heads. For bone-working especially on walrus tusk they had different kinds of burins. Straight burins were used for longitudinal or transverse splitting of bone, for making cuts, grooves and other work. In addition they had burins shaped like a claw or eagle's beak (fig. 82.11) with which they made small slots, open or solid at the back, and various perforated lugs on bone objects including harpoons.

On bone objects of the ancient Eskimos there are traces of chopping and chipping and small cuts to roughen certain parts to provide purchase for lashed thongs, which give us a clue to the sort of tools they had at their disposal.

The chop marks on walrus tusks, which have been used as mattocks and ice-picks, reach 8–10 mm in depth and have been made at an angle of 75–80° without any signs of splintering on the bone. Cuts made at a low angle on different objects have retained the chips which have been only slightly bent or broken off. The internal angle of such cuts averaged 15° to 18°, which indicates a very small edge angle on the adze or axe. Among stone chopping tools an edge angle of less than 40° is practically unknown. By the term edge angle we mean not the general angle of the profile but the angle along the narrow facet specially ground on the very blade edge, sometimes also called the angle of sharpness. Using an axe or adze with such an angle of sharpness it is quite feasible to roughly work wood, as chops or cuts made by such a tool in a vertical line break the wood fibre. On bone vertical cuts are very shallow and inclined ones look broad, because the chip does not stay, but is almost entirely removed by the blow (fig. 82.1).

The difficulty of obtaining metal forced the ancient Eskimos to continue to make ground stone adzes, which they used for many purposes both on wood and bone. The existence of stone chopping tools among the Eskimos caused American archaeologists to refer their

ancient culture to the neolithic period. The angle of sharpness of the stone adzes from the ancient Eskimo settlements of Chukotka averages 55°–60°, which is relatively wide.

Traces of the use of a stone adze have been identified on a fair number of objects. The character of these traces (notches and cuts) is sharply distinguished from traces of work with metal adzes which can best be understood by comparing the two. The thin blade of a metal adze which penetrates bony matter leaves a fine line about 0·1 mm broad; cuts adjoin one another very closely sometimes at intervals of barely 1 mm or even less (fig. 82.2; fig. 83.1). The traces left by a stone adze are widely separated and, as already described, are very broad (fig. 82.1). If the blows were delivered vertically and their marks are bunched closely the bone surface has a splintered look and the individual lines merge into each other.

The features of work traces from metal and stone tools described above can leave no doubt that the ancient Eskimos, as well as stone, were acquanted also with metal, and knew how to use it for working bone. This deduction was made in 1946. In the following year Okladnikov dug an ancient Eskimo settlement on the shore of Sarychev Bay (Cape Baranov), where objects of bone and wood had survived exceptionally well. The bone harpoons were of the 'Birnik' type, which would place the site in the first century A.D., using Collins's scheme, that is more recent than the Uellen-Okvik culture. The slots on the harpoons at this site are indistinguishable from those of the latter culture. In Hut I of the settlement two iron objects came to light; one was a knife made on an oval piece of metal and fixed in a bone handle, the other the remains of an iron burin also mounted in a handle. The iron was covered with corrosion excrescences. The knife had been mounted in a side groove in the same way as short neolithic knives were mounted, while the burin was seated in the end of the handle (fig. 82.10).

Confirmation of this deduction about the use of metal by Eskimos in early periods is offered by new material from America. In 1948 the work of Larsen and Rainey appeared describing material from the settlement at Ipiutak in northern Alaska dug before the war.[1] Amongst this was an iron burin, again only a fragment.

In order to test whether the iron was of meteoritic origin it was submitted to spectrographic analysis. This showed that the iron had been obtained metallurgically and consequently was evidently an import.

This unexpected discovery led to a sharp change of opinion among American archaeologists about the

---

[1] H. Larsen and F. Rainey, *Ipiutak and the Arctic Whale-Hunting Culture* (New York, 1948).

antiquity of early Eskimo cultures. On the new classification of these cultures put forward by Larsen and Rainey Ipiutak would be identified as the most ancient site and would date from the first centuries A.D. The Okvik, Old Bering Sea, Birnik and Pumuk stages would follow with diminishing antiquity. Thus the whole history of the Eskimos would now be confined to two millenia. Yet even these dates arouse doubts. It is difficult to believe that iron which even in China appeared only in the first centuries A.D. could at this time already have thoroughly penetrated the extreme north. There is no evidence for direct trade connexions between China or Japan with the Arctic in the first centuries A.D. or even later. The first outside influence on the Greenland Eskimos was by Europeans, by Norsemen in the thirteenth to fourteenth centuries. Archaeological confirmation of this is provided by the settlement of Inugsuk in the district of Upernavik, where Scandinavian objects have been found. In the seventeenth century Russian traders and colonizers appeared on the shores of the Bering Sea, who entered into trade with the Eskimos, as is revealed

by iron and glass objects on late Pumuk sites. This exhausts the archaeological evidence which tells us with certainty as to how the Eskimos could have obtained iron.

The possibility cannot be excluded that in the thirteenth, and even before the tenth century, the Eskimos had irregular contacts with the outposts of Chinese culture and with Japan, from where they could have got iron. Such contacts could hardly have extended back to earlier than the fifth to sixth centuries A.D., although this is still merely an assumption.

In the light of the facts just set out the question of the settlement of the Arctic by the Eskimos can receive a new interpretation, provided new archaeological evidence of settlements earlier than Ipiutak, and of undisputed neolithic age, does not emerge.

The study of techniques of working bone is very important for the chronology of those remains which lie on the borderline of changing from stone to metal, but which, in the absence of direct evidence for the existence of metals, have been referred to the neolithic period.

4. Identification of the functions of bone tools and objects

a. The use of broad and flat bones in palaeolithic times

TRACES found on broad and flat bones must be described first. Skull, pelvic, and shoulder bones of large animals, as the marks indicate, were used by palaeolithic man, who had no pottery, as vessels and as other articles of everyday domestic use, from very early times. Amongst the bone material from Cave I at Chou-Kou-Tien (the cave of *Pithecanthropus*) deer frontal bones may be mentioned. From the descriptions and published photographs three important types of work on them can be distinguished:
  (1) Frontal bones with antlers removed that are cup-shaped.
  (2) Edge of the cup retouched by blows as shown by facets on the outer edge.
  (3) Edge of the cup rubbed to a shine.

Needless to say the problem of these bone vessels of Pekin man can only be worked out by specialist study of the traces of work on the objects in question, which can only be done when they have been examined in the laboratory.

Amongst the bone material from the cave of Kiik-Koba in the Institute of Zoology of the Academy of

Sciences of the U.S.S.R., part of the left side of the lower jaw of a wild horse has been found hollowed-out and shaped like an elongated vessel. The signs of use observed on the bone were as follows:
  (1) The external compact layer of bone on the concave side had been destroyed together with the internal spongy matter; this only survived on the edges.
  (2) Friction by a hard, probably stone, object had produced strong wear on the surface.
  (3) On the thick edge of the worn surface traces of whittling down with a sharp flint blade were detectable.
  (4) No signs of colouring matter were observed.
  (5) The external bone surface of the relatively flat side of the bone bore no traces of friction and had not been interfered with (fig. 84).

What material had been ground up on this object is still not known, although it evidently had some connexion with everyday use. So far finds of this kind have not been made on other Mousterian sites.

Upper palaeolithic material has also provided some evidence on the use of flat bones. At Eliseevich three complete cup-shaped fragments and about ten others with traces of grinding on the concave side were found. The complete ones had been made from the pelvic bones of a young mammoth, while the fragments were parts of skull, pelvic, and shoulder bones (fig. 85).

The whole objects are rather roughly and carelessly shaped. In two cases part of the pelvic bone has been broken off on its concave surface and used without further trimming, as a good part of its edge is ragged and projecting, which would give a grip for the left hand. In a third instance part of the bone has a regular almost hemispherical hollow made by strong blows whose facets show on the reverse convex side. Traces of wear on the convex side from prolonged friction can be clearly detected by contrasting the state of the compact layer in the centre with the edge. On the edge faint impressions of friction on the lamellar outer compact layer have survived.

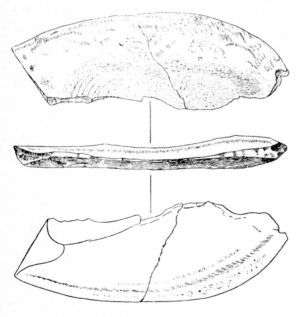

·84 *Middle palaeolithic object from Kiik-Koba; left back part of the mandible of wild horse bearing traces of prolonged friction.*

Additional traces of friction, as shown in fig. 85(4), reveal two facts: firstly, the friction has impinged on the rolled over edge of the bone; and secondly, the section illustrated here indicates that the strongest wear took place in the centre of the bottom of the cup.

Inasmuch as the worn bone surface bears no traces of colouring matter it may be presumed that the matter crushed up in it related to food, and was of plant or animal origin.

Kostenki I has yielded examples of the use of broad bones, besides the first rib of a mammoth used as a palette for mixing colours which we have already described (fig. 86), also bones put to other everyday uses. Mammoth shoulder bones found on this site sometimes have groups of scratches or grooves reaching 10–15 cm long. The movements of the pointed tools with which they had been made ran down and away from the articulation. The grooves occurred in groups of several dozen, the lines sometimes intersecting at a slight angle, and their individual width varied from 0·1 to 1 mm (fig. 87). According to information from K. M. Polikarpovich the mammoth shoulder blades from Eliseevich were thickly covered by small grooves or scratches.

The origin of these traces has not been finally decided. It may be suggested as a working hypothesis that skins were cut up with flint cutters on the bones, but we still know very little about such tools. We are only acquainted with stone skin-cutters from neolithic times, that is the ground elbow-shaped knives of northern Europe. Amongst the flint tools from Kostenki I only one has been observed where micro-analysis confirmed its identification as a skin-cutter (fig. 88.2, 3).

In its general shape this tool had nothing in common with the elbow-shaped knives of northern Europe. It was made on a blade triangularly prismatic in section, one end rounded to a spatula-shape, whose sharp edge had been blunted by use. This small blade has scarcely any signs of retouch, apart from slight trimming on the working end (fig. 88.1).

Besides the traces mentioned other remarkable indications of use were noticed on the shoulder blades of an adult mammoth found in a hut at Kostenki I. One was more than 70 cm long, and bore both traces of working and of use. The broad flat parts as well as the mid-spinous process had been removed by two methods. First grooves had been made with a burin, but then, instead of completing the work this way, the flat part and process had been struck off by strong blows with a stone. The blows were given from the outside into the hollow of the scapula as the scars on its inner edge indicate (fig. 89.1).

Traces of use survived at various points on the surface (fig. 89.3), whose analysis revealed the following:

(1) The articulating area of the epiphysis, shaped like an oval hollow, was mottled by transverse lines and scratches.

(2) Its raised part was worn and battered and so reduced in height.

(3) On one part, the most worn edge, striations indicating the direction of movements occurred, which took the form of transverse grooves across the raised circular edge.

(4) From the epiphysis half-way down the bone had been intensively rubbed, in places abraded and polished. This wear was confined to the external convex part of the bone hollow, especially on the retouched edges. The lower part of the scapula was entirely free from this, but it had decayed badly and the external layer was friable and cracked. It should be mentioned that the scapula had been broken in the middle, just on the division between upper and lower halves whose state of preservation so sharply contrasted with each other.

At the beginning of research it looked as though the scapula had been set vertically in the ground with epiphysis downwards and the other end projecting above the surface, and so weathering and breaking off. This

85 1–3 *Fragments of mammoth pelvic bones from Eliseevich used as vessels; 4 and 6 drawings of 1 and 2; 5 profile of 3.*

was a guess, apparently reasonable but quite irreconcilable with the traces left by man on the bone. The traces on the epiphysis half, and more particularly on the articulating area could only have been formed, if the scapula had been buried in the ground with epiphysis uppermost (fig. 89.2). Moreover, it had been set up in the floor of the hut and not outside, since there was no evidence of weathering on the epiphysis end. With regard to the other half its surface suffered more because the floor of the hut, littered by organic material from objects used by the inhabitants, was a medium of intense chemical activity. Furthermore the better preservation of the other half, once it had been broken and buried, would have been enhanced by the greater resistance of the rubbed bone surface.

What could have been the purpose of this object in

1

2

86 1 *First rib of mammoth from Kostenki I used in upper palaeolithic times as a palette for colours; 2 broad end of rib with traces of crushing of colouring matter.*

the domestic life of palaeolithic man? Rising 35–40 cm above the hut floor the epiphysis would reach the level of the chest of a seated man. He would evidently sit with the concave side towards him, as this is the side where the articulating area is worn. Probably the object served as a kind of work bench, and possibly also could have been used in eating because of its hollowed-out platform. Subsequently this piece of domestic furniture was broken off almost at ground-level.

Mammoth scapulae worked in an analogous way, as shown on the plan of excavations at Kostenki I, numbered about a dozen. Some of them occurred in positions that fully confirm our deductions that the scapulae were dug into the ground inside the hut with the articulating end upwards.

As auxiliary items animal bones played a great part in ancient manufacturing. Already by Mousterian times, as material from the Crimean caves of Kiik-Koba and Kosh-Koba testifies, man made extensive use of bone in making stone tools. Mammoth foot bones found on these sites (carpal, lunar and cuneiform bones) bore traces of use as anvils,[1] and there were many fragments of long bones of wild horse and donkey used as retouchers (figs. 90, 91, 92).

Thus in this Crimean material the basic stages of manufacture of stone tools can be followed. Traces on the middle of the articulating surface of a lunar bone show that cores had been flaked on it; the impressions are sharp and angular (fig. 90.1). At one point on the edge a series of narrow marks are visible, like the impressions of a roughly retouched toothed point made by percussion retouch. These traces are clearly related to work on the edge of the bone and disappear in the centre. Just the same type of mark can be seen on the edge of a carpal bone (fig. 91.2). On a cuneiform bone marks on the right side of the picture are due to percussion retouch, this time not of points but of scrapers or tools of that shape (fig. 91.1).

Pieces of diaphyses of long bones were used by the inhabitants of Kiik-Koba for more delicate subsequent work: retouchers for trimming edges of flint cutting tools by pressing in the hand without use of a support (fig. 92.1–3). By studying bone retouchers very interesting observations have been made on the work of Neandertalers. In some cases traces of pressure retouch have the form of broad grooves one on top of another, in others very slight dents hardly detectable with the naked eye. From these run almost microscopic grooves like very tiny scratches, which show the tearing of the blade when worked by extraordinarily careful and fine retouch.

87 1 *Part of a mammoth scapula from Kostenki I with traces of cutting on its surface; 2 part of the surface with traces at half natural size.*

---

[1] S. A. Semonov, *Short Reports of the Institute for the History of Material Culture*, 49 (1953), pp. 143–7.

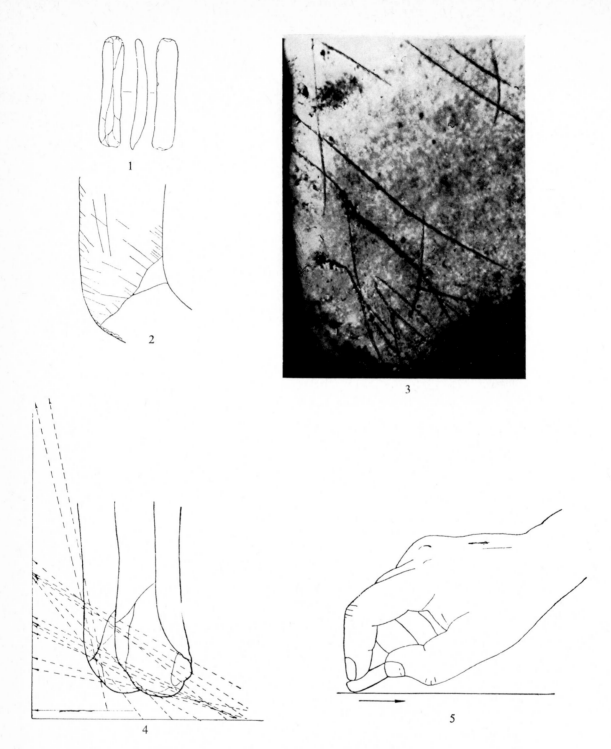

88 1 *Upper palæolithic flint skin cutter from Kostenki I; 2 micro-drawing of wear striations on the flint; 3 wear traces enlarged 100 ×; 4 angles of inclination of tool during use; 5 method of operation reconstructed.*

These facts prove that the hand of the Kiik-Koba Neandertalers possessed fairly delicate qualities and sensitivity in spite of its great muscular strength. They lend no weight to the conclusions reached by Bonch-Osmolovsky on the paw-like nature of the hands of Neandertalers at Kiik-Koba and on the feeble development of their motor system.[1]

Furthermore study of the disposition of the dents on bone retouchers from Kiik-Koba and Teshik-Tash confirms that in working the right hand of the Neandertaler played the predominant part, for he held the retoucher in the right hand and the flint being worked in the left. We can infer this because the dents on the convex side do not lie at right-angles to the axis of the retoucher, but at a fair angle, which indicates that the axes of the retoucher and the tool being retouched met at angle of some 75–85°. Thus the upper group of dents on the wide retoucher were made from the left and the lower from the right (fig. 92.1).

Had the Neandertaler held the retoucher in his left hand, then the dents would have been in the reverse position.

Bone retouchers for working blade edges appeared in Mousterian times and continued to be used into the upper palaeolithic period, as the material from Kostenki I (fig. 92.4) and other sites indicates.

b. Bone and antler handles in palaeolithic times

In the course of studying palaeolithic bone tools the nature of the oldest handles has become somewhat clearer. The technical role of a handle is very significant: it multiplies several times the mechanical strength and efficiency of a tool. In striking tools (axe, hoe) a handle amplifies the mechanical force of the blow by increasing the radius of the swing; in cutting tools (knife, burin) it amplifies the mechanical force of the pressure by bringing more powerful muscles of hand and arm to bear. Thus the invention of a handle was the first significant step in prehistoric life towards the mechanization of work.

In lower palaeolithic times a handle as a special attachment for a tool was unknown. The archaeological evidence shows that at this period a tool, stone or bone, consisted of one unit which included the handle. Amongst the material from Kiik-Koba there is a tool shaped like a pointed dagger made from the long bone of a wild horse, the epiphysis serving as the handle. The use of an epiphysis as a handle on a bone tool, which is a crude but practical achievement, appears first in Mousterian times or even earlier, and continued through the Stone Age into the early period of metals.

It is well known that bone tools rarely had a separate handle, chipping of an unworked part to provide purchase for the hand being most common. This probably also was an ancient device, but it has not been recognized from before upper palaeolithic times. At Eliseevich there were small tusks of young mammoths, and also daggers cut out of tusks, with such chipping at the base to serve as a handle. It is very curious that the chip-marks do not cover the whole of the holding part, but are concentrated in two patches: a small one for the thumb of the right hand, and a more extensive area for the remaining fingers and palm. The same thing can be seen on Eskimo bone tools.

Handles as an independent attachment to tools to complete them appear in upper palaeolithic times.[2] On the existence of handles for such striking tools as axes and hoes we could speak with full confidence, once the presence of the distinctive traces of use of these tools had been established.

Bone handles for stone cutting, drilling, and perforating tools are also known. Malta has yielded a very crude form of bone handle, where a flint knife was deeply embedded in the spongy mass of an antler cylinder, which provided a very simple immovable seating. Such a method of mounting had one major snag; if the tool broke, as often happened when it was of flint, it would be very difficult to extract the stump. Therefore there appeared already in upper palaeolithic times a much more accomplished handle, a sort of clip open at both ends for ejection of the flint stump. Such a changeable handle is known from Eliseevich made of a deer long bone and probably used for burins. The clip consisted of the diaphysis with two perforations in the articulating end of the epiphysis for ejection of the stump. However, as a material for handles deer antler considerably preponderates over long bone; the circular shape of a long bone did not always lend itself to the form of the flint tool, and the walls of the diaphysis were brittle.

Two examples may be cited of changeable handles of deer antler: one for end-scrapers in the material from Afontova Mountain, and another for burins from Mezin, which is technically very accomplished.

The handle from Mezin is very small with the sides of the clip partly cut away, so that it could be held with the fingers rather as we hold a pencil today with the finger near the point. These indications and others allow us to see that this handle was not designed for a simple burin, but to be used by a palaeolithic artist for incising his lines, which are so well represented at this particular site.

A more accomplished example of bone handle-making with provision for changing the tool is provided

---

[1] S. A. Semenov, *Short Reports of the Institute of Ethnography of the Academy of Sciences of the U.S.S.R.*, 11 (1950), pp. 70–82.
[2] S. A. Semonov, *Short Reports of the Institute of the History of Material Culture*, 35 (1950), pp. 132–8.

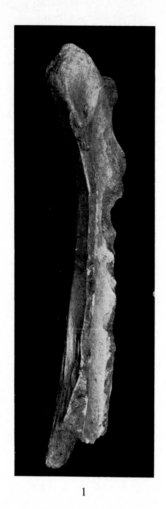

1

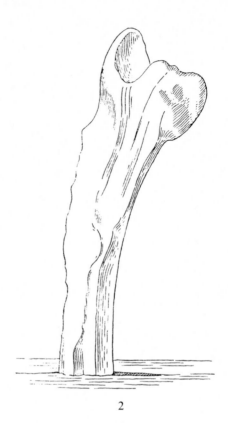

2

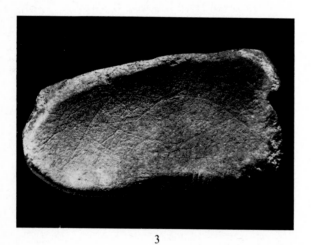

3

89 *An upper palaeolithic worked mammoth scapula from Kostenki I: 1 traces of percussion and grooving on edge of scapula; 2 position of bone imbedded in the floor of the hut; 3 articulating area of scapula bearing traces of human interference.*

naturally by the Eskimo technique. For ejection they used an elongated cut in the side at the bottom of the clip while a cylindrical hole is bored through the back end for suspension from the belt. Such handles are for the most part made from the rib of a marine animal.

c. Bone tools for burnishing skin in the upper palaeolithic period

Bone mattocks from Eliseevich and Pushkari I and tools similar to them with a flat section, bent shape and convex end, as is well known, have been classified as 'burnishers' (*loshchila*) (tools for rubbing skin). All bone objects resembling this have been referred to this category, but in fact the tools which are really 'burnishers', although they look like mattocks, differ in their proportions and traces of wear.

Two series of bone burnishers have been studied in detail from Kostenki I and Avdeevo. Those from the former site are made out of deer and mammoth ribs and ivory. For the most part they survive as fragments 40–200 mm long; they had broken during use as a result of relatively strong pressure. The working part of these tools is flat and rounded. The animal ribs of which they were made had been first split along their length, the

tool being made of one half of the rib as the exposed inner spongy structure of the bone on one side indicates It is curious that it is precisely the latter side which was the working one to judge by the wear and striations from use. In profile the burnisher is slightly bent, the working and spongy side forming the external part of the bend. The actual working end, curved with the spongy mass cut away, is often not only rubbed and polished but even ground down by use and sharpened like a knife blade.

The burnishers from Avdeevo are better preserved, some complete ones being over 300 mm long. Besides burnishers of the Kostenki type at this site there is a special variant of the tool (fig. 93.3). It is also made of rib, but the kind of wear is very distinct, for its end has a sort of curved bevel on it, and not the gradual tapering off as at Kostenki I. The end gives the impression of having been ground down, but the curvature of the ground facet clearly shows that we are not dealing with sharpening against a hard object, but with attrition on a more or less yielding material into which the burnisher's end sank slightly.

The character and direction of the striations also have their special traits on each type of object. On the first the striations, beginning at the edge of the working end, run

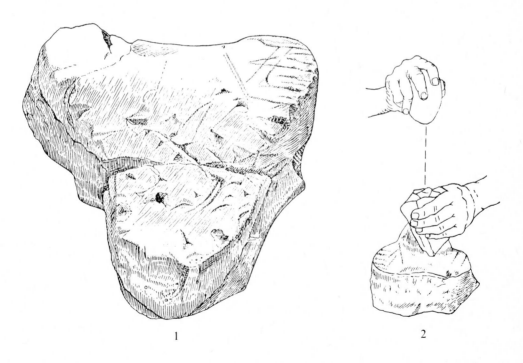

90 1 *A mammoth foot bone (os intermedium dextra) from Kosh-Koba (Crimea) bearing traces of use by Mousterian man as an anvil; 2 its method of use reconstructed.*

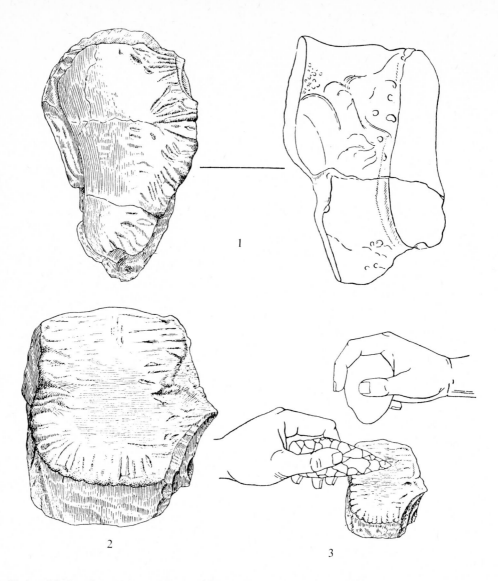

91 1 *and* 2 *Cuneiform and carpal bones of mammoth employed by Mousterian man at Kosh-Koba as anvils for percussion retouch;* 3 *method of use of carpal bone reconstructed.*

slightly diagonally and thereby prove that the operator pushed forward on the tool not along its axis but slightly to the right of it (fig. 93.1, 2, 4). Working with the second type he pushed strictly along the axis, pressing hard on the skin's outer surface (fig. 93.5). Moreover, in the first case the angle at which the tool was held in relation to the worked surface was considerably less than in the second one.

The change-over to this new method of work, that is to the burnisher of the second type, was in all probability caused by the fact that the implement often broke under pressure on its end when held at a low angle.

The length of the tools, their position in work and the degree of wear reveal that the rubbing was done with both hands. The right hand held the base of the tool and controlled the angle made to the worked material, while the fingers of the left hand (index and middle fingers or thumb) pressed from above on the forward working part (fig. 93.4, 5).

Rubbing the outer face of skin is one of the essential

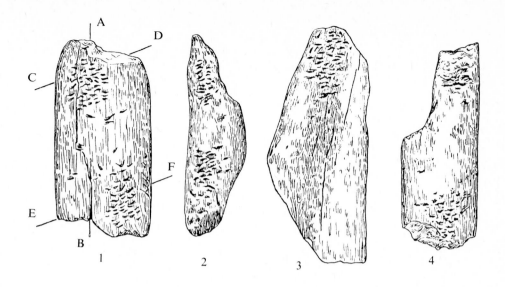

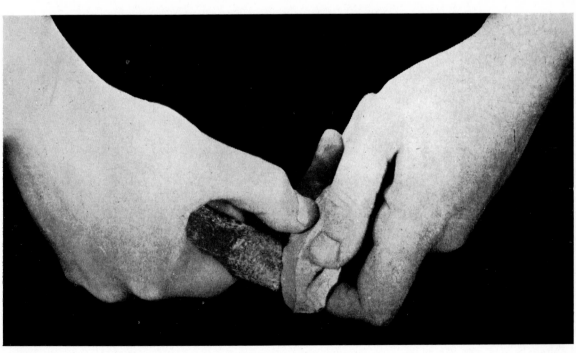

92 1–3 *Retouchers of long bone from Kiik-Koba (middle palaeolithic)* (CD *and* EF *show the inclined angle of the tool in the hand,* AB *its vertical axis); 4 upper palaeolithic retoucher of long bone from Kostenki I; 5 method of using bone retoucher.*

operations in skin-dressing. Almost all skins undergo this treatment in the contemporary industry on special rubbing machines, in which the basic instrument is an agate or glass roller. The rubbing compresses the skin, its outer layer acquiring a lustre (sheen, gloss), which makes it not only prettier but tougher and more impermeable. The major part of half-dressed hides undergo rubbing after greasing and colouring.

On some palaeolithic burnishers traces of colouring (ochre) occur, although the majority do not bear such traces. Sometimes in the palaeolithic period burnishing would have been combined with greasing, that is rubbing fat into the pores of the skin to make it elastic and impermeable. Such a combined operation in skin-dressing can be seen among the Eskimos.

What is especially noteworthy is the rational nature, the calculation, if one can use the expression, of the palaeolithic bone burnisher and its method of use. In a contemporary rubbing machine, although, of course, on quite a different scale, the principle is the same as in the bone burnisher: to produce a great pressure over a small area on the treated material. The compression of the skin and the polishing to a sheen on its outer face is only possible by concentrating the pressure on a limited area,

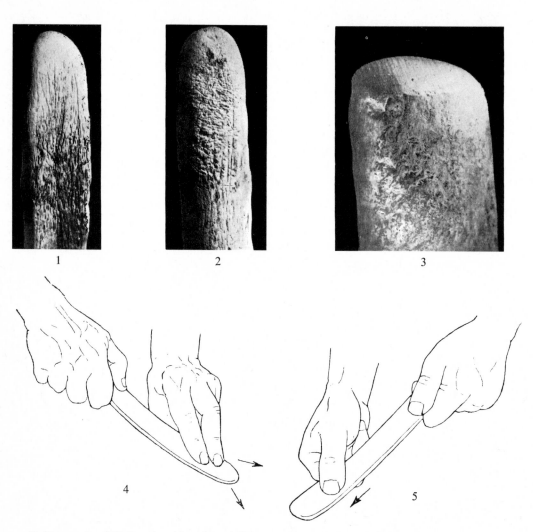

93 *Upper palaeolithic bone burnishers from Avdeevo: 1 and 2 working part of tool of first type (1 inner side and 2 outer side bearing traces of use as retoucher); 3 working part of tool of second type; 4 and 5 method of use of first (4) and second (5) type.*

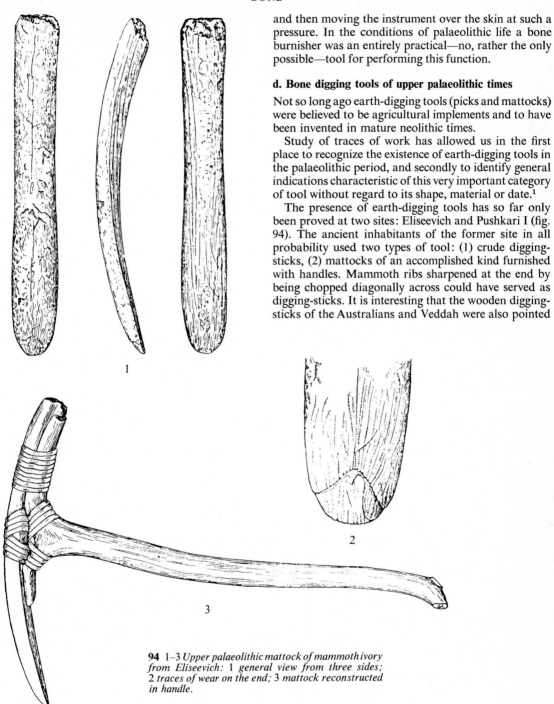

and then moving the instrument over the skin at such a pressure. In the conditions of palaeolithic life a bone burnisher was an entirely practical—no, rather the only possible—tool for performing this function.

d. Bone digging tools of upper palaeolithic times

Not so long ago earth-digging tools (picks and mattocks) were believed to be agricultural implements and to have been invented in mature neolithic times.

Study of traces of work has allowed us in the first place to recognize the existence of earth-digging tools in the palaeolithic period, and secondly to identify general indications characteristic of this very important category of tool without regard to its shape, material or date.[1]

The presence of earth-digging tools has so far only been proved at two sites: Eliseevich and Pushkari I (fig. 94). The ancient inhabitants of the former site in all probability used two types of tool: (1) crude digging-sticks, (2) mattocks of an accomplished kind furnished with handles. Mammoth ribs sharpened at the end by being chopped diagonally across could have served as digging-sticks. It is interesting that the wooden digging-sticks of the Australians and Veddah were also pointed

1

2

3

94 1–3 *Upper palaeolithic mattock of mammoth ivory from Eliseevich: 1 general view from three sides; 2 traces of wear on the end; 3 mattock reconstructed in handle.*

[1] S. A. Semonov, *Soviet Archeology*, 16 (1952), pp. 120–8.

by being cut diagonally across. The digging-sticks from Eliseevich were not of uniform size; besides small examples 20 cm long made by splitting off a length of rib, there were others 50 cm and more. They all had strongly worn and blunted ends, with their faces and angles worn by attrition. Striations, that is scratches due to friction against sand grains, were either hardly noticeable or quite absent, and so indicated that the stick was not used in a definite fixed manner. It would be sunk into the earth vertically and then act as lever by pressing the body against it. Sometimes the user would pick at the earth and break up the ground with it, and also give frequent blows with the hand at ground-level, like the Australian women do when they are ripping open an ant-hill.

The mattocks at Eliseevich are made of the tusks of young mammoth, but at Pushkari of ribs of the same animal. In both cases the natural curvature of the bones has been made use of, but, while the larger mattocks of

tusk bear traces of more preparatory work, because half the tusk had to be removed longitudinally, those of rib, which are smaller, only had to be sharpened at the digging end. In both cases this end is convex. The traces of use on mattocks have a definite individual character; distributed mainly on the front face they take the form of clear lines and scratches, caused by contact with sand grains, running vertically up the blade from the working edge, and are similar but more weakly expressed on the back face (fig. 94.2).

The character of the wear and striations on bone mattocks can easily be recognized by comparison: firstly by placing these marks beside those on mattocks in ethnographical collections, and secondly by comparing them with the traces on contemporary metal mattocks.

Examination of Eskimo bone mattocks, as well as steel mattocks from the field equipment of the Leningrad Department of the Institute of the History of Material

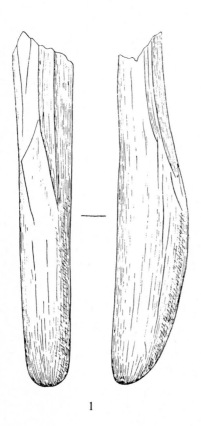

1   2

95 1 *Working end of an Eskimo pick of walrus ivory from Chukotka; 2 traces of wear on the pick (2 ×).*

Culture of the Academy of Sciences of the U.S.S.R., has confirmed inferences made from the archaeological material.

Traces of use on bone mattocks have allowed us to draw conclusions not only about the degree of wear and duration of use of the tools, but also about the character and properties of the ground on which they were used. Splintering of the outline, sharpness and depth of the striations on the working end will testify to the presence of ballast or grit in the ground. As an example of such a mattock an Eskimo pick of walrus ivory may be quoted, found by Rudenko at Chukotka with other similar tools in 1945 (fig. 95).

Even wear on the mattock and very fine and slight striations will reflect a dust-like (loess) or fine-grained consistency of the soil. An antler mattock found in the settlement of Pechor dug by Artamonov in 1947 is an example of this (fig. 96).

e. An antler shovel from Shigirsk peat bog

An antler object that bears wear traces very characteristic of a shovel is a tool discovered in the Shigirsk peat bog (Ural area) and now housed in the Archaeological Section of the Ethnographical Museum at Leningrad with the label 'paddle' attached to it.

The shovel is oval in shape and has three pairs of perforations down its centre for the attachment of the handle (fig. 97.1, 2). It is made from the wide palmation at the bottom of an elk antler, and is 30 cm long, 15 cm broad with a very thin section, 5–6 mm. Since one face consists of compact antler and the other of spongy matter, it is evident that the base of the antler had been very skilfully split sectionally along the interior spongy matter.

Traces of working which are best studied on the sides of the perforations indicate that the shovel was made with a metal tool. This is revealed by cuts made accidentally on the surface of the compact layer with a tool of very low angle of blade-edge. The perforations have been cut out by a knife with a sharply pointed narrow end.

The oval shape of the shovel, its vaguely ladle-like appearance and very thin section caused it to be identified as a paddle. Such an identification seemed the more probable because paddles are known to exist in this period. Wooden paddles of excellent workmanship have been discovered, for example, in the Gorbunovo peat bog.[1] The blade of an antler shovel was also found on this site, but of a different construction from the Shigirsk specimen.

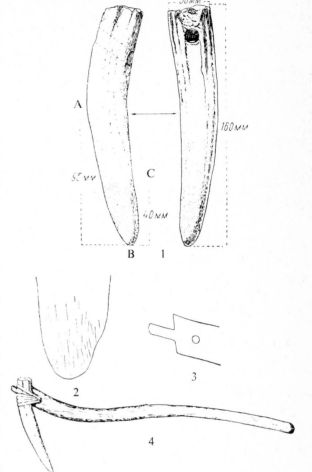

96 1 *Early Bronze Age antler mattock from Pechor (S. Podolia) with lateral perforation (AB working part worn by use); 2 striations on end of hoe; 3 and 4 conjectural form of handle and hafting of hoe.*

Wear traces on the latter are very clear and lie for the most part on the edge of the back face of the blade. The striations reveal a movement parallel to the implement's handle (fig. 97.3), and analysis has shown some special features of the wear. On the front face of the shovel, whose surface is rough, wear also occurs near the edge. The traces take the form of rubbed, slightly shiny patches on the raised parts of the surface. All the traces

---

[1] D. N. Eding, *Engraved Sculpture from the Ural Area* (Moscow, 1940), p. 27.

1   2

3

97 1 *and* 2 *Views of both faces of an early Bronze Age elk antler shovel from Shigirsk peat bog;* 3 *traces of wear on its front edge (enlarged).*

are distinguished by a texture different from those on the normal earth spade with its marks of the action of sand and gravel; the working part of the Shigirsk shovel has been worn and even polished by meeting resistance from a yielding and crumbly material, which could only be friable soil, soft sand or snow. One did not dig with this shovel, but threw out soil that had already been loosened with an antler mattock; antler mattocks have been found on the site.

It should be observed that digging in the contemporary sense, when the spade is pushed into hard caked ground with the full weight of the body, that is cutting the earth, only developed later with the appearance of metal spades.

5. The use of long bones in ancient technology

I N some branches of manufacture the use of bone tools was of long duration, as is underlined by the essential part of long bones and antler in the technical processes, not only of prehistoric society, but even in much later times. The examples that follow of the use of long bones of boar, ox and horse from final neolithic times, the Classical period and the eighth to thirteenth centuries A.D., show that society was extremely reluctant to give up some primitive methods of work, even although in other branches of manufacture they had long since been abandoned. On the other hand the examples cited may prompt field workers not to dismiss material which on first sight looks doubtful or meaningless.

a. Burnishing bones from Luka-Vrublevetskaya

The settlement of Luka-Vrublevetskaya has yielded bone tools with wear traces very characteristic of working the spherical surfaces of clay pots (fig. 98).

A series of boar long bones bear very indicative traces on their diaphyses. At first glance they look as though they have been cut longitudinally on several sides by some kind of sharp instrument without giving them the appearance of very useful tools. In places the whole surface of the diaphysis has been cut away, but the cuts, or rather facets, are of irregular shapes. They are rather hollow or even spheroid, and one's first impression is that such working of bone is frankly impossible. A further difficulty is that they are not complete long bones but only halves, each with a spheriod hollow of different diameter. Evidently originally the entire bone was used, but as a result of wear all along it on several sides it broke into two, just as happened with the bone rasps from Olbia. However, at the present site they continued to be used even after the break.

To solve the problem of their purpose recourse was had to study of their wear striations. In the hollow surface even the unaided eye could detect lines showing the direction of movement during use, which ran along the axis of the diaphysis and generally were parallel to each other.

In spite of these lines the hollowed surfaces were smooth and finely polished, and the arrises between the different facets were sharp. With regard to the epiphyses they had no wear traces except an even rubbing.

The observed marks allowed us to draw the following conclusion.

Since the hollow worn surfaces were spheroid they would only have been produced by friction against spherical or almost-spherical objects, and as the striations were almost parallel (fig. 99.1), then the friction must have arisen by horizontal movement, normally in one direction, for two-way movement always produces a strong confusion and intersection of lines. By a one-way forward movement the whole of the curvature on the bone would come into contact with the worked object. The absence of traces of work on the epiphyses and their even polishing on all projecting parts indicate that they served as the handle for the tool. The sharp arrises between the facets indicate that the object being worked was fairly hard, while the scratches detectable by the naked eye indicate the presence of small hard particles in the surface of the worked object.

Detailed study of the hollow areas on the bones has shown that they could not be due only to friction against the spherical object; evidently the hollows had been scraped out previously on the bone with a flint implement which had a convex retouched blade. Traces of scraping out remain as wavy lines on some of the facets (fig. 99.2).

Thus the working areas on the bones had been made originally with a flint tool, and made to correspond with the diameter of the spherical object before they were ready for use.

All the signs enumerated have allowed us to regard these bones as burnishing tools used in the manufacture of clay vessels. The nature of the ceramic material from

Luka-Vrublevetskaya has confirmed this inference: a vast proportion of the pots found here have a dark burnished surface of shades varying from black to grey. Some of the sherds had a radius corresponding to the radius of the concave area on the bones. Under magnification the burnished surface of the pots showed the working was done by horizontal movement; the striations on the surface show this. The lustre had been produced after the drying of the clay, and in some decorated pots the burnishing had been done over the ornament.

The whole process of producing a burnished surface

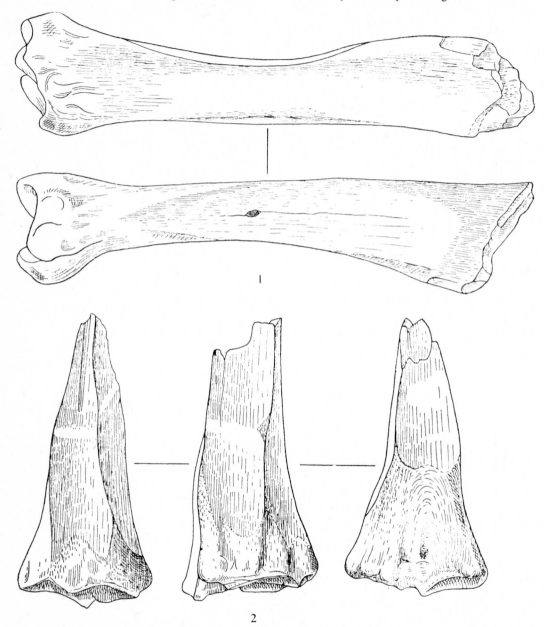

98 *Late neolithic pot burnishers from Luka-Vrublevetskaya: 1 whole bone with concave area on diaphysis; 2 broken bone with four concave areas.*

on ancient pots is still not properly understood, and the technique, especially the application of a wash which gives the impression of glaze, is one of the secrets of ancient firing methods. The use of bone burnishers during this process is not, however, a matter for doubt.

In pre-Revolutionary Russian peasant manufacture of pottery antler or bone burnishers (smoothers) played an essential part in the work. They were used both on the dry surface of the shaped pot and after drying. 'The finer and greasier the paste the better in the firing will it maintain its lustre from burnishing', wrote M. Novgorodsky.[1]

99 *Late neolithic tools for burnishing pots from Luka-Vrublevetskaya: 1 micro-photograph of wear traces on a bone; 2 micro-photograph of surface of bone whittled by a flint tool; 3 sherd of burnished pottery; 4 method of burnishing reconstructed.*

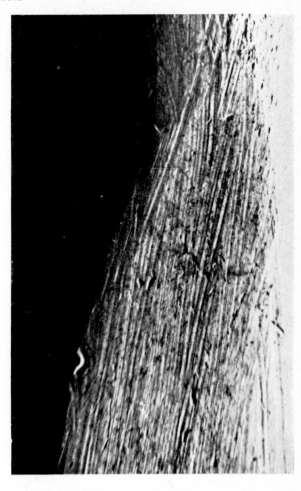

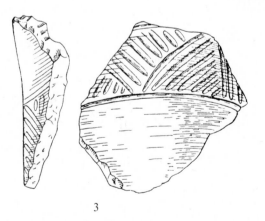

2

1

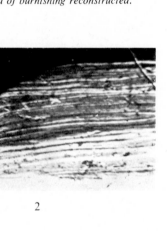

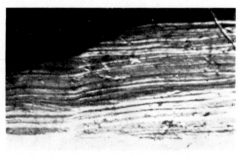

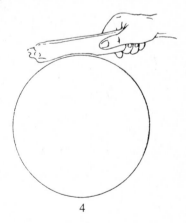

3

4

---

[1] M. Novgorodsky, *The Kiln* (St Petersburg, 1908), p. 49.

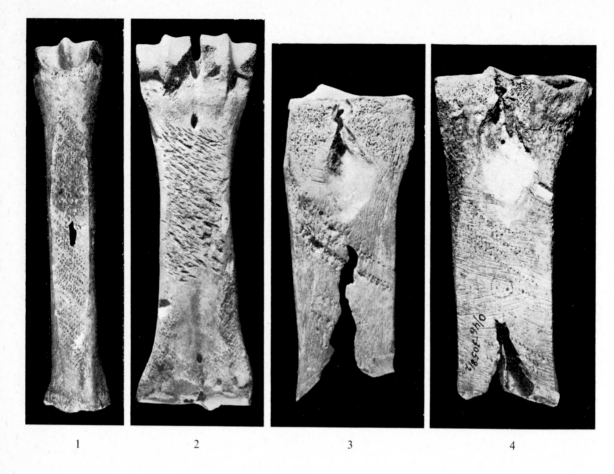

100 *Bone rasps from Olbia: 1 worn bone with toothed notching visible on surface; 2 bone with cuts made by axe (not by use); 3 and 4 fragmentary tools worn and broken in use showing notching and wear striations.*

b. Rasping and polishing bones from Olbia

The use of animal bones as working tools continued when metals had been introduced. A clear illustration of this is the long bones of ox and horse found by the Olbia Expedition of 1947 in layers of the Hellenistic period.[1]

These bones are of no little interest for us. Apart from Olbia they are known from Scythian Neapol and Thanagoria, and reveal a new technique in building in the Graeco-Scythian area around the Black Sea, and perhaps even beyond it in other countries of the Classical world.

A large series of bones were studied, about fifty specimens, which had clear wear traces and were in varying states of preservation. All these bones had been worked before use with metal tools, as the following marks indicate: (1) the diaphysis had been whittled down on two or even four sides, altering the cylindrical section of the bone to a quadrilateral one; (2) each face of the diaphysis was covered by small grooves or cuts running diagonally (fig. 100).

That we are dealing with working tools and not ornamental or cult objects was obvious at a glance, but to have explained their purpose without studying the traces of work would have been impossible. The traces revealed that the work had been on a hard and very resistant material, as the scratches on the bone shafts are very sharp and numerous. They also tell us that great

---

[1] The bones were found by S. I. Kaposhina in holes in building debris.

physical force was used and that the objects were worn out fairly quickly; evidently they were related to something produced on a large scale. The overwhelming majority of the bones had been worn through and abandoned only after they had broken in the middle by the force of the pressure on them.

It was also evident from the marks that during use the bone was held with both hands at the epiphyses, which acted as natural handles, with the left hand slightly forward, just as nowadays we hold a plane or rather a rasp. The direction of the striations indicated this, for in almost all cases they ran in the same direction as the cuts, that is diagonally (fig. 102.1, 3).

It had become increasingly evident that what we were dealing with was a sort of Classical prototype of the modern rasp. However, serious doubts arose on this, for the hardness of a long bone is inadequate even for rasping wood. Yet the traces indicated a very hard material

and apart from everything else it was not clear why the cuts had been made.

As is well known, with a modern steel rasp the main work is done by the numerous teeth or projections produced by grooving the steel in a soft (tempered) condition with a grill. Teeth made by cutting bone could serve no useful purpose, since they would break off and fall away.

The problem was only resolved by study of the texture of the wear striations. The scratches or furrows running over the face of the diaphysis, as mentioned above, indicated a very hard, lacerating material with a rough surface, such as only certain stone surfaces could have had. Moreover, these furrows, 1 mm or less in width, had certain peculiarities, which could not have arisen by direct use on stone. No rock known to us would leave such a texture of traces, not to mention that the friction of bone on rock seemed very improbable. The furrows

1

2

101 1 *Bone polishing tool from Olbia (both faces);*
2 *stereo-photographs of spongy matter in this tool;*
3 *the tool's method of use.*

3

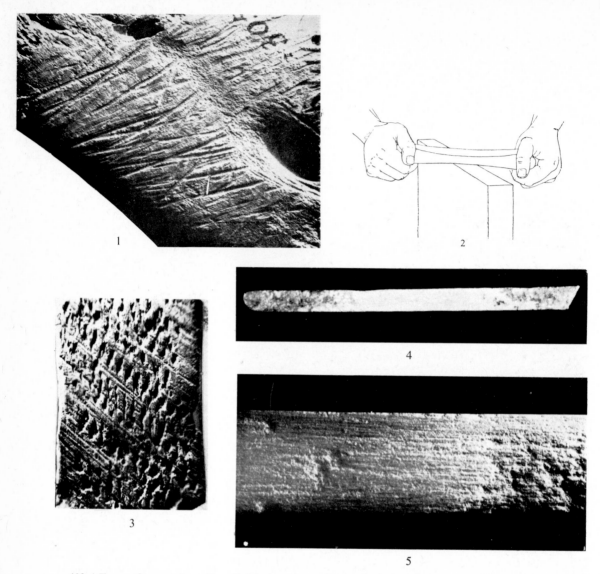

102 1 *Traces of wear on the surface of a bone rasp due to abrasion (2 ×); 2 method of work reconstructed; 3 relation of notching to wear striations on bone surface; 4 and 5 face of a marble slab worked with a bone rasp in an experiment.*

were very clear and sharp, showing all stages of wear on the bone by crystals with one or two cutting angles (fig. 102.1). Such furrows looked as if they had been made with microburins. Some even were rounded in section. It became quite obvious that these traces were produced by large grains of silica sand used as an abrasive agent with bone rasps.

Once this was understood the cuts also became intelligible: they were triangular holes designed to receive and contain for a period the sand sprinkled on the surface of the material being worked. Cutting holes on the bones was an extremely practical device, since with a narrow rasp it was necessary to keep sharp its small and perhaps sloping surface from which the sand would quickly fall off during use. Cutting the holes was probably done with a claw chisel, well known to Classical masons. The cutting was not done just once, but had to be repeated as the holes were worn off by attrition.

Few silica grains still remained in the holes, which

is understandable, since firstly they fall free from it very easily, and secondly the bones had been scrubbed after excavation.

When research started and the use of an abrasive material had not been recognized it seemed doubtful whether it was technically feasible to grind even such soft and friable rocks as Black Sea limestone with bone. However, there are reasons for supposing that not only hard limestones but even marble and other tough materials would have been worked with these tools. To verify this tests were carried out. A bone rasp made by the ancient method was employed on grinding the face of a block of hard marble. The experiment gave positive results (fig. 102.4, 5).

A bone without cuts and sand was worn by the friction which scarcely affected the marble; the rough surface of the latter seemed to choke up with bone pulp, became smooth and the friction was lost due to slipping. A bone with cuts but without sand wore more quickly than the stone, but after the addition of sand the marble was ground more quickly than the bone was worn. An uneven face on a block 23 mm wide and 12 mm long was smoothed in ten minutes' work. The wear striations on the bone used in the test looked identical to those on the ancient bones.

Thus the bones studied from Olbia can be regarded as tools for the secondary working of stone, that is for the grinding and shaping of architectural details and all kinds of small surfaces with the help of an abrasive agent (sand).

The working of stone by means of a long bone and silica sand represents a rough grinding of the hewn face, similar to what in contemporary technology is called 'rasping'. Subsequent excavations at Olbia produced bone objects which allowed recognition of yet another kind of tool used for working stone. In 1951 Kaposhina found an object consisting of half the epiphysis of a bone of a large animal (fig. 101.1). To judge by the marks the epiphysis had been chopped off with an axe and then sawn in half. On one side was the external compact bone, on the other the porous matter of the spongy interior. On the latter side were traces of prolonged friction in the form of rubbing, not only on the hard exterior bone, but on the spongy matter itself, in the pores of which were remains of chalk. As is well known, chalk is a delicate abrasive material used to produce a shine in stone-polishing, as are other fine-grained powders.

The use of the spongy matter of the bone for polishing is easily understood. It is tough in a fresh condition and its porous structure holds the abrasive material for a long time, preventing too rapid application but dispersing it on the surface being treated. In contemporary burnishing and polishing special instruments like wooden circles or balls enclosed by a soft porous material, such as bast, felt or skin, are used to hold the polish powder.[1] The use in this way of pumice, which has a porous structure, is also known.

In the ancient Graeco-Scythian techniques of grinding, burnishing, and polishing decorative stone, not only the bones of large domestic animals, but also deer antler was used. At Olbia a semi-cylindrical object has been dug up made from the sawn-off base of an antler. The saw cut had been made with a metal saw with fine blade and delicate teeth, as was evident by the traces. The spongy interior had been exposed longitudinally. Although no traces of use were detected the spongy interior of antler is a tough material and in all probability it was the rough-out for a polishing tool.

c. Thong-stretchers from Rodanov hill fort

Study of the thong-stretchers from Rodanov was our earliest attempt to apply to bone the method of studying the functions of ancient stone tools from their traces of use. Started in 1941, work was renewed in 1945.[2]

The trial was made on new material from a very recent period, the so-called 'large ground bones' from Rodanov hill fort found in the excavations of M. V. Talitsky. The site is dated to the eleventh to thirteenth centuries A.D. These ground bones are not newcomers to archaeology, since identical objects were published almost half a century ago under this name by A. A. Spitsyn in his 'Antiquities of the Kama Chud' based on the Teploukhovie collection.

A considerable series of long bones of large animals found at Rodanov, mostly horse metacarpals, bore these marks. Firstly each distal epiphysis had been trimmed with a metal axe, as revealed by broad flat scars. Secondly the diaphysis was marked by deep traces of wear, looking at first glance rather like that found on rough wooden axles. However, the traces differ from one another both in depth and shape (fig. 103.1–4).

Some inferences could be made about the purpose of these objects, the most plausible being that they were axes about which an object or something on a hinge had rotated.

Analysis of the wear traces demonstrated that there could be no question of rotation or hinging; the structure of the bones would not have allowed it, since in section they are not round but flattened, nor were there any indications of an intention to make them round. Moreover, the wear extended in many cases over

[1] G. R. Tkhiladze, *The Working of Decorative Stone* (Moscow, 1950), p. 156.
[2] S. A. Semonov, *Short Reports of the Institute of the History of Material Culture*, 15 (1947), pp. 138–42.

the epiphyses which had been given an almost quadrangular section by chopping. The marks of wear tend to concentrate on one side, and in some examples the diaphysis has been worn over four-fifths of its face from one side, while on the remaining part, for holding, there are no traces whatever.

The general impression given by these bones, that they had been ground on one side by a lathe, is a deceptive one. In fact, the one-sided friction has been produced by the sliding of a narrow object of some kind not moving simultaneously on the two edges of the bone. The grooves passing round more than half the circumference do not coincide, that is they do not join up, as is quite clear if the lines are projected on to a flat surface.

Study of the structure of the traces has shown that the surface wear took place slowly with weak attrition,

which technically in surface working is called 'burnishing'. However, this burnishing took place under considerable pressure, as more than half the bones had broken along the lines of deep wear.

Undoubtedly the material that produced such wear was thin and elastic, taking the shape of, and bending over, the rigid bone. This can be inferred from the fact already noted that the flexible object had embraced half or more than half of the bone shaft, just as rope, for instance, embraces the fixed axle of a pulley as it slides up and down. Here, however, the sliding took place with some horizontal slip, as shown by the narrow grooves lying together on top of the bone.

What, in fact, were these bone tools? There could have been two possible answers. Originally we thought that they were a device for stretching cord or twine

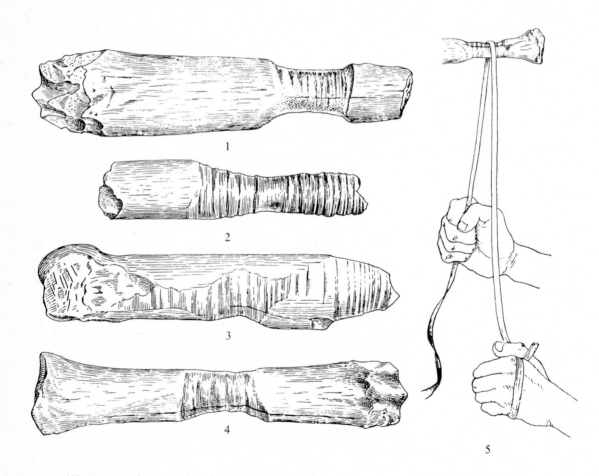

103 *1–4 Bone thong-stretchers from Rodanov hill-fort worn by use; 5 reconstruction of a thong being softened and stretched over one of these bones.*

190

material used in the daily life in hill forts of the Chud. However, the structure of the traces cannot be entirely reconciled with this conclusion, and subsequent examination has caused us to change our mind. The traces are flattish or circular, or even quite flat, and could only have been left by thongs. This indicates the existence of thong manufacture, as does the aggregate of the other traces.

Thus these bones can now be regarded as thong-stretchers for softening and stretching thongs, probably sewn ones, used in the making of sheepskin and fur clothing, harnesses, saddles, and footwear (fig. 103.5). In the north they are used with sinews at the present day. By measuring the traces on the bones we can work out the width of the thongs worked; on some they were 2–3 mm and on others 5–8 mm wide.

The deductions that have been made are quite consistent with the technical basis of skin industry, and can be verified by archaeological material from the Nenetz, Chukotsk people and Caucasians, illustrating implements for stretching thongs. A point arises here that is of great importance in the study of functions of bone tools.

The traces are of fundamentally the same character, but in their shapes the thong-stretchers have nothing in common. The Nenetz thong-stretchers are of very individual shape, made of deer antler with an aperture cut through them. In order to stretch and soften the thong both the aperture, through which the thong is passed, and the tines, over which it is stretched, are made use of. The Chukotsk people also use a perforated instrument but of a special kind, while in the mountains of the Caucasus they used a wooden hook strengthened with a cramp. Subsequently other variants of this tool, not resembling one another either in shape or material, have been elucidated.

Thus once more the proposition put forward in the study of stone tools has been confirmed: tools different in shape may have one purpose and, conversely, identical tools in many cases were used for different purposes. Relying on this crucial principle research must not concern itself with formal indications, but instead seek out the traces of use on all bones generally, and particularly on the nameless mass of material which has still not found recognition amongst certain categories of tools or artefacts.

d. Traces of use on the 'skates' and grooved bones at Sarkel

Amongst numerous bone objects in the fort of Sarkel (White Tower) dating from the tenth to twelfth centuries,

found during the excavations by M. I. Artamanov which concluded in 1953, were a large series of so-called 'skates'. Long bones of horse and ox, which have had one side trimmed and ground to produce a regular smooth face, have been widely given this name. 'Skates' are found comparatively frequently in sites dating from last millenium B.C. onwards. They are known from the south of the European part of the Soviet Union (urnfields and at Olbia and Sarkel), as well as the north (Staraya Ladoga).[1]

The 'skates' from Sarkel are made on metacarpal and metatarsal bones of ox and horse, occasionally on the radius. Generally the smooth area is on the frontal side of the bone, where an epiphysis has been trimmed off, so that the bone has the appearance of a sledge runner or skate (fig. 104.1–4).

In studying the surfaces on this series it became clear that the facet bore traces of wear in every case except one, where there was only preliminary trimming of the diaphysis. The bones were worn variably: some slightly rubbed, others worn all over or even through to the centre of the bone.

In rare instances they had been used without trimming, but generally after preliminary trimming the frontal face of the bone had been ground on an abrasive stone, which converted the rough chopped surface into a geometrically regular area (fig. 104.2).

Other specimens of 'skates' occur made in a different way, with not only the frontal side but three or even four sides chopped and ground, which makes them square in section. These bones are perforated at one end (fig. 104.3). In all types, however, the wear is only on one face.

A noticeable feature on almost all the bones is the rubbing not only on the face side, which was the working part, but also on other parts and particularly on the dorsal side. Here one or two patches of denting occur (fig. 104.4), which on bone tools was usually meant to give purchase either for the hand or for lashing.

The purpose of the 'skates' cannot be regarded as finally settled, although their study has brought us very close to a solution. First of all it is necessary to deny the proposition that these bone objects were used for skating on ice. A whole series of facts militates against this contention. First, the hollow part of the bone has no perforation with which to tie it to the foot. Secondly, friction against ice would leave recognizable traces on the ground areas: the edges would have been rounded, the sharp angles rubbed off and dulled, and the ground area would have lost its geometrical regularity. Thirdly, the striations would have reflected the movements of a

---

[1] It is of interest that they are also found on English sites; the translator has handled examples found on a Tudor site at Crowland, Lincolnshire. T.

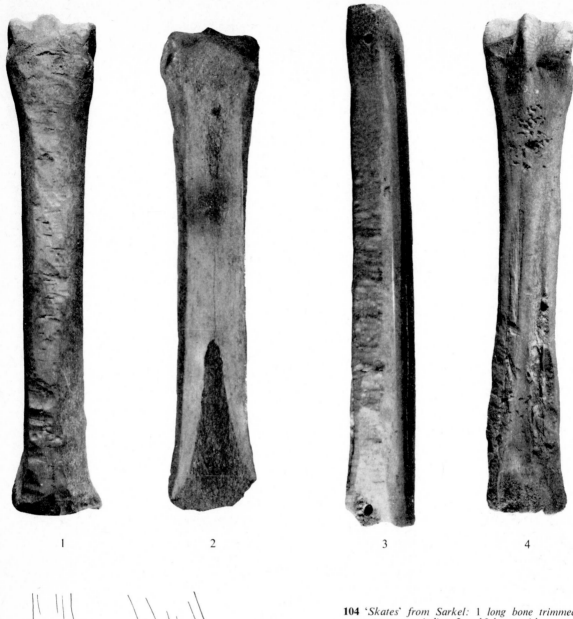

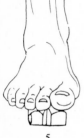

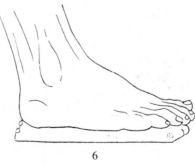

1   2   3   4

5   6

104 '*Skates*' *from Sarkel:* 1 *long bone trimmed preparatory to grinding;* 2 *and* 3 *bones with ground down area on front face worn to a hole in the end;* 4 *bone with two patches of chipping on dorsal face;* 5 *and* 6, *reconstruction of use of the bones with the feet as cloth pressers or smoothers.*

skater, which is not straight forward, for in order to propel himself he presses sharply on the pointed edge of each skate in turn to acquire momentum, when the skate itself does not move forward but gives slightly to one side under the weight of the foot. So on steel skates the wear lines cross the main axis at an angle of 70–80°. Fourthly, on real skates one can always see non-linear traces (abrasions and dents) produced when the skater stopped or walked on the ice. Dents and abrasions arise from the fact that ice is not of uniform consistency, since it contains foreign matter (sand, gravel and small pebbles). Fifthly, not all the 'skates' from Sarkel have a raised part above at the end. The ground areas on some bones in spite of traces of strong wear are perfectly straight right along. Such 'skates' could not have slid on ice without hitting each unevenness.

Thus the wear on the bone objects from Sarkel cannot be regarded as consistent with their use as skates. The ground areas have regular shapes, while the striations as seen under the binocular microscope have the appearance of very fine lines oriented in one direction, parallel to the axis of the diaphysis. Consequently in use these objects slid straight forward. The area on which the sliding took place had just the same degree of regular flatness as the ground areas of the bones. The rub or gloss on these areas indicate that during use friction beneath the 'skates' occurred through a thin and soft material, otherwise the bone would not have had a glossed surface. The intervening material could not have been of fluid or powder consistency, because there is no trace of it in the spongy structure of the bone, and it could only have been a textile or thin skin. It is possible that it was a textile which required finishing work after being taken off the loom. This is especially necessary in the case of silks, which are teased, sponged, and ironed on rollers (calenders) or under a press or rubber. In the Middle Ages, when machinery was in its infancy, such operations were produced by hand with the help of 'smoothers' (*gladilniky*).

E. A. Tseitlin has put the matter thus: 'The difference between a rubbing machine and a calender was that the former had as its object the creation of a gloss on an already finished piece of cloth. For this purpose the working part of a rubbing machine consisted of polishing (half-oval) stones acting like the roller in the calender. A second type of such an apparatus which we have already met in linen manufacture was the screw-press for dressing. Finally sometimes a cruder method of rubbing was employed—smoothing by pressing the material on a table with a polished stone (or lump of metal).'[1]

In antiquity evidently the differentiation of function in the preparation of cloth between calendry and rubbing did not exist; both operations were done with one and the same smoothing tool.

The bone smoothers from Sarkel, to judge by all the indications identified on the surface, were used not with the hand but with the feet. Especially indicative of this was the polishing on the dorsal side, which in the majority of cases was not trimmed and retained the anatomical shape of the bone. Moreover, on this side the craftsman sometimes had made dents with an axe edge, which, as already mentioned, was a favourite device on bone tools for giving the skin firmer purchase when it had become slippery. On the 'skates' there are two clusters of dents near both epiphyses, the distance between them roughly corresponding to the distance between the centre of the calcaneum and the distal head of the metatarsal bone on the sole of a human foot. The instrument was probably operated therefore with bare feet (fig. 104.5, 6) or only wearing soft shoes, the smoothing bones with an aperture in the epiphysis being lashed to the foot with thongs.

Work with the feet would be more effective in such simple operations as smoothing a length of cloth or skin, since it would permit the use of considerable muscular force and the full weight of the body.

The use of the strength of the legs played a part in other operations of ancient textile manufacturing: 'In 1208 in a London fullery a request of the urban fullers was considered that the fulling of broadcloth at a river mill outside the town be suppressed because it was depriving them of their earnings, since their "tools" (legs) had neither the strength nor quickness of fulling mill-stones.'[2]

Another series of long bones from Sarkel has different traces of working and wear (fig. 105.1–4). The marks of working are of two kinds. First are the marks, often found on long bones, of the epiphysis having been trimmed down in order to level it off with the shaft. The trimming has been done with a metal axe, well sharpened and with a low angle-sharpness. Secondly, deep straight cuts or grooves have been made on the diaphysis which intersect one another at different angles, the shapes made by the intersecting lines being square or rhomboid. The majority of the grooves have been cut with a knife, but in one instance on a tool with grooves of varying width the broader ones have been hollowed out with a narrow chisel. There is one example made out of deer antler instead of long bone. On one bone the channels do not intersect, but lie diagonally side by side, and on it traces of whittling are visible designed to trim the working

---

[1] E. A. Tseitlin, *Outline History of Textile Technology* (Moscow-Leningrad, 1940), p. 137.
[2] ibid., p. 68.

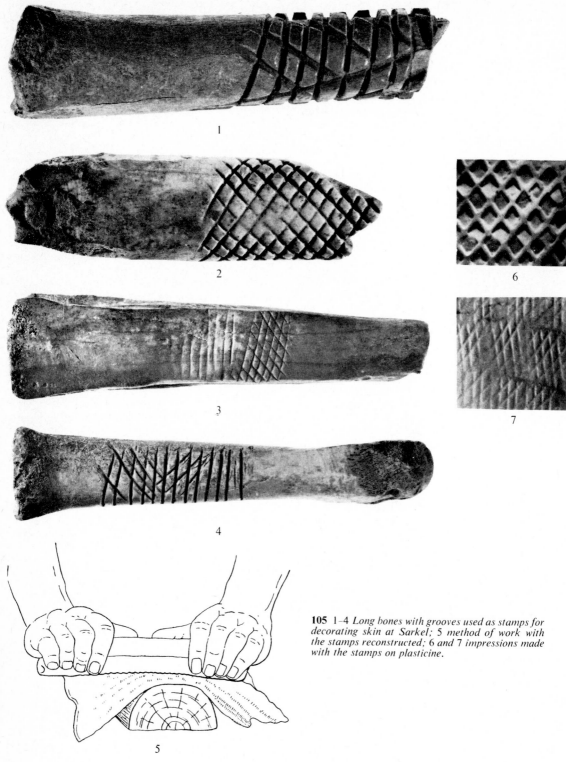

105 1–4 *Long bones with grooves used as stamps for decorating skin at Sarkel; 5 method of work with the stamps reconstructed; 6 and 7 impressions made with the stamps on plasticine.*

surface or take off projections, as had been done also on the others. Almost all the tools, with one exception, have broken along one of the deep grooves, where the resistance would be weakest.

The surface of these tools is rubbed to a shine or even polished in the area of the grooves. No traces from a hard or sharp implement can be seen on them.

In certain cases the relief of the squares and rhombs is not only polished to a lustre but also partially or completely worn away by prolonged use. However, study of the polished surface under binocular lenses has not revealed wear striations going in any definite direction. A series of small scratches visible on the projections of the squares and rhombs run in different directions, and so cannot serve as an indication of the horizontal movement of the tool. They could have arisen from various causes and give no clue to the tool's movement.

In addition signs of another order are noticeable: the edges of the squares and rhombs are damaged, blunted and rounded. A definite impression is created that the material on which the work was done partly filled up the interior of the grooves. Wear of such a kind could not arise by displacement of the tool on the surface, but only by pressure on the material causing it to penetrate the excised areas on the bone.

It seemed very important that the area of strong wear did not cover the whole of the excised pattern on the bone, but was confined to a small part. This indicated that the pressure exerted at one time did not extend over a considerable area. The broken tools reveal the very great mechanical force applied in the moment of pressure on the worked object, as also does their severe wear.

Taking the whole lot of marks into consideration, and especially the deep excision of the geometrical pattern on the sides of the long bones, the strong wear and polishing on it, the indication of vertical squeezing on a soft material and the small area of pressure with great mechanical force during pressing, one is bound to conclude that the tools were designed for stamping patterns on a plastic material.

Yet this material could not be clay, paste or anything like that, and on the face of it was likely to be skin. Stamped skin, as is well known, occurs since the times of the early nomads.

The designs from these tools stamped on plasticine give a positive impression of the design on the stamp (fig. 105.6, 7).

Section four | Regularity

Regularity in the development of the basic tools of the Stone Age

THE results set out above in the study of ancient tools permit some general conclusions to be drawn about the regularity in their development, that is an attempt to work out the fundamental tendencies, as it were, observable in the evolution of tools during the early stages of the history of society.

This is due to the fact that all tools, including the most ancient, are a means of acting upon objects of the external environment with the intention of altering them in a way necessary for man. In concrete terms the fundamental processes of work carried out with tools are directed towards the alteration of the external form or physical consistency of an object taken in its natural state, be it stone, earth, wood, bone, animal or vegetable, principally by dividing the whole into parts, separating one or many particles from the whole or reducing the whole to small parts. These alterations are achieved by cutting, chopping, splitting, scraping, boring, grinding and so on.

In correspondence with such tasks, and in so far as their completion derives from a preconceived plan, the main tendencies in the development of tools have been directed towards reduction in the resistance of the materials of which objects in the external world are made, raising the productivity of work, and trying to bring within the cognizance of society all new natural materials. The following basic tendencies can be discerned in the evolution of tools.

Firstly, to improve the manufacturing processes in which the tools were used prehistoric man changed them by reducing the edge angle of their working part. This applies to all kinds of tools with blades or points intended to penetrate into a plastic material like meat, skin, wood, earth and so on.

Secondly, man changed the same category of tools by giving them a smoother and more even surface on the working part contiguous to the tip or blade, in order to reduce friction against the worked material.

Thirdly, man improved his tools, especially striking ones, by raising the force of physical action on the object of work, or in other words he increased their mechanical power.

Fourthly, he worked out methods of increasing the rapidity of movement of the tool during the working process.

Fifthly, he expanded manufacture by differentiation of function and specialization, creating tools of new shapes, dimensions, and material.

Obviously these five tendencies in the development of tools do not exhaust all aspects and directions taken by the alterations and improvements. Yet it can be clearly seen that these five are the fundamental directions of change characteristic of the early stages of development. In later periods the number grows, as for example the subsequent acquisition by man, with the progress of technology, of means of raising the resilience and toughness of the tools themselves by altering the physico-chemical properties of the material of which they were made. However, this tendency only assumes exceptional importance with the adoption of metals, and as far as stone tools are concerned man from the beginning was employing a material not susceptible to internal change. Only with the so-called insertion technique in which stone and bone were united did man achieve some success in raising the potentiality of the material. It is true, of course, that we have in this only a mechanical combination of two qualitatively different materials, leading to a mutual reduction of their weaker sides without any alterations of the properties of the materials themselves.

It should be noted that, in order to enhance the practical use of natural matter, men in very early times began to try to change the physico-chemical properties of necessary objects by employing the action of fire, sun, and water. The first and most important achievement in this field was the cooking of animal and vegetable food with the help of fire; roasting and baking arose at the same time as fire was mastered. Besides cooking man very early tried to use fire for working his tools in wood and bone. Charring of wooden points in boar spears, clubs, and javelins, in order to increase their toughness and hardness, took place already in palaeolithic times. Then followed steaming and soaking of bone and antler to soften them and make working easier. The hardening of arrows by heat was rather later. However, problems of the use of physico-chemical methods of work (fire, water, sun) fall outside the scope of this book, which is concerned only with mechanical tools and mainly with stone ones.

Crucially significant in the development of ancient tools were not only the reduction of friction by making smooth (sliding) surfaces, but also the opposite tendency to increase the friction on tools designed for working hard materials (abrasives) or trituration of colouring and food matter (pestles, colour-mortars, and querns).

The category of abrasive tools received a definite extension in the later stages of development of pre-historic technology. In palaeolithic and neolithic times man employed as abrasives (pestles, colour-mortars, querns and various grinding tools) granite boulders, pebbles, and plaques, which retain traces of work but have not themselves undergone working (shaping and cutting out of the working surface). However, during neolithic times a tendency is already noticeable towards a significant alteration of the natural shape of abrasive stones (sandstones or cystalline rocks) for a more effective use of the mechanical properties of the granular rock. Gradually man enlarged the working areas (the friction surfaces) on pestles, colour-mortars, and plaques, which on whetstones and grinding tools took on a shape corresponding to that of the worked object, giving higher efficiency in terms of time and quality of work. An excellent example of such an accomplished abrasive is the grinding tools from Verkholensk.

Another phenomenon that is noteworthy in the development of stone tools again was intended not to reduce friction but on the contrary to increase it. This is the perfection of a tool with toothed or saw-like edge made by bifacial retouch. Such tools were spear- and arrowheads, knives for dismembering animal carcasses, gutting fish and cutting meat, flint sickles and saws. All these were designed for use on elastic and fibrous matter; the teeth bit into the fibres and tore them apart. However, to some degree this tendency ran contrary to that mentioned of reducing the edge angle of the blade. For example meat knives with very thin blades easily cut animal fibre, but at the same time they were very brittle.

The development of tools with a toothed blade received new possibilities at a relatively late stage with the adoption of metals, when first bronze and then iron saws for use on bone came into use, and finally wood-working saws.

Very close to the line of development leading to a decrease[1] of the resistance of the material is the burin, in essence a one-toothed saw for working bone, which appeared in upper palaeolithic times. In neolithic times

it fell behind by comparison with chopping tools (axe, adze), but after the appearance of metals the role of the burin gradually became more important and it took on major significance as a result of the development of mechanical working of bone, wood, stone, and metals.

It is necessary to draw attention to the tendency towards an increasing economy in the use of material with the aim of reducing dependency on it because of the difficulty of obtaining it. Some archaeologists have noticed this.[2] In the present work attention is mainly devoted to the tendencies in the evolution of prehistoric technology which were most important for mechanical tools of the Stone Age, and which can serve as objective principles for assessing the development of ancient tools. For the sake of brevity we will call the first tendency reduction in the angle of sharpness; the second, reduction of friction; the third, increase in the force applied; the fourth, increase in rapidity of movement; the fifth, specialization; and the sixth, economy of material.

With regard to lower and middle palaeolothic tools (Chellean, Acheulian, and Mousterian) there is not much to say, as the functions of the tools have not been studied. Nevertheless some general characteristic can be discerned. The angle of sharpness of these tools is very great, but some diminution is detectable between Acheulian and Mousterian tools. The amount of friction in use (cutting or whittling), particularly with tools made by bifacial percussion, was great because the working edge of such tools was formed by large uneven conchoidal scars. Hand-axes of Chellean type could be used in that kind of mechanical work which made use of their weight, that is striking actions. Such would be hewing bone, breaking rotten wood to get insects, making nests in hollow trees and in the ground, cutting off knots and young branches for wooden tools (staffs, clubs, boar spears) and so on.

The reduction of the angle of sharpness in the blade in Acheulian hand-axes as against Chellean ones is quite obvious.[3] In the latter it is 70–75°, in the former 30–50°, while the angle of the point in profile is 70–90° and 30–90°, and the facet angle 75–95° and 30–50°, in the two cases.

The blades changed in shape, retouch smoothing them out and getting rid of the zigzag. This change took place in the blade and point because in all types of plastic work on wood and bone the Chellean kind of implement is unsuitable, like all tools with a wavy edge. They would not have been practical as side or end-scrapers and would never have been used for cutting up carcasses, cutting fibrous plants and so on. The greater part of

---

[1] Russian text has 'increase'. T.

[2] G. A. Bonch-Osmolovsky, *Chelovek*, 2–4 (1928), p. 182.

[3] F. Bordes and P. Fitte, *L'Anthropologie*, 57 (1954), pp. 1–44, pl. I–IV.

these functions was probably carried out with flakes, which accompany hand-axes in abundant numbers and varied forms on Acheulian sites.

An extensive use of flakes and a permanent demand for them called into being the so-called Mousterian technique, that is the technique of flaking such flat rough-outs off a pyramidal core. The leaf-shaped flakes so produced, of course, required finishing work, but as tools they were distinguished by great possibilities, including a reduction in the angle of sharpness of point and blade. They could be retouched on one face, from ventral on to the dorsal side, which would reduce friction in working bone or wood. There were no facets on the slightly convex but smooth ventral face.

It was precisely in the Mousterian period that a more accomplished method of thin pressure retouch was adopted, well known from points, scrapers, and bone retouchers of this period. Fine pressure retouch made it possible to strengthen the relatively weak edge angle, and also to sharpen the tip.

An economy in material is noticeable with the appearance of the core. Repeated flaking of leaf-shaped flakes from a core made it possible to get a considerable number of rough-outs from a single flint nodule.

The birth of the Mousterian technique was not accidental; a technique of flaking off rough-outs from a core developed gradually and side by side with bifacial working. If on the one hand the prototype of manufacture was the flaking of a pebble or nodule leading to the Clactonian, Levallois, and Mousterian forms of tool, mainly used as knives and scrapers; then on the other an initial stage is represented by the rough sharpening of a pebble at one end, subsequently converted into bifacial working. In both cases a striking technique (percussion) was employed.

As regards a growth in productivity and specialization of the tools we still have little analytical evidence for firm judgment. Preliminary study of material from the caves of Kiik-Koba and Kosh-Koba and from the site at Volgograd makes it reasonable to consider that in Mousterian times man already had several types of tool at his disposal. Of course, the real existence cannot be accepted of such tools as bolas, 'disks' used as axes, 'choppers' and other conventionally named tools, classified by western archaeologists not by their purpose but by their shape. Obviously Mousterian industries contain stone strikers, stone and bone retouchers, bone rests or anvils, pointed flint knives for cutting up carcasses, knives made on flakes for cutting meat and whittling wood or bone, side scrapers for working skin, perforators, bone and stone heads for boar spears and other tools, not to mention wooden clubs, boar spears, devices for making fire and so on.

From the point of view of increasing the force and speed of movement of tools, no important achievements are recognizable in middle palaeolithic techniques. That the physical potential of Neandertalers was used irrationally can be judged by the fact that all the stone tools were held in the hand without separate handles. This explains the strong development of the width of phalanges (particularly the ungual phalange), as we can see by the skeletal remains from Kiik-Koba, Krapina, La Ferrassie and other sites.

Javelin-throwing, which requires a high degree of flexibility of the spine and free movement of the shoulder joints, was probably unknown to Neandertalers, and at all events cannot be proved. We can only speak confidently of the use of a non-throwing spear (the boar spear). European palaeolithic sites have yielded evidence of boar spears: Clacton-on-Sea, La Quina, Castillo and so on.

Very often lower palaeolithic and Mousterian man must have made use of the kinetic force stored up in the weight of stone, wooden and bone tools (choppers, clubs, antlers and so on). Strong muscular development is testified by the prominence of the projections on the bones to which the sinews were attached.

The change to the upper palaeolithic is marked by great achievements in all aspects of development in tools. Especially noteworthy is the new technique of making tools based on flaking off blades from a prismatic core, which made it possible to overcome several difficulties simultaneously.

Firstly, the angle of sharpness of the blade-edge of all categories of cutting tools was sharply reduced thanks to the flat section of prismatic blades; it now fell to below 20°. In addition greater opportunities revealed themselves for making every type of pointed tool (points, awls, perforators, drills), penetrating plastic materials with more facility because of the elongated shape of the blade.

Secondly, each blade consisted of a ready-made two-edged tool, whose sharp edges required blunting rather than sharpening. This led to the general development of two types of dulling retouch: fine (on the edge) and steep retouch in depth.

Thirdly, the prismatic blade allowed the creation of a new tool, the burin, thereby bringing into extensive daily use bone, ivory and antler, materials with high technical merits.

Fourthly, a significant economy in material was achieved by contrast with the preceding period, thanks to the new technique of blade-making, which to some extent eased man's dependence on the material. A person using a small quantity of flint could now achieve a significantly greater result.

Two difficulties arose with the new technique which man overcame with advantage to himself. One of these was that narrow two-edged tools were very often impossible to hold in the hand; they required handles, whose appearance in this period represents an immense technical conquest.

The second difficulty was that prismatic blades are bow-shaped in profile, a feature that impeded their employment for daggers, heads for javelins, darts and other tools with a straight axis. A solution was found by the application of flat pressure retouch (Solutrean retouch), which permitted the removal of fine slivers from the blade in order to get straight but slightly shortened heads and knives.

Thus bifacial working was re-created in upper palaeolithic times, but now on a much higher technical basis. This bifacial pressure retouch was especially valuable when good nodular flint was lacking and man was obliged to use low-grade varieties, like the tabular material which we met in the lower layers of Kostenki I.

As regards reduction of friction of the tool against the worked material here also were obvious improvements. The reduction of the angle of sharpness of blade-edge and point thereby implied some reduction of friction, but the main achievement of the period was not in this way. The technique of blade-making was such that the blade produced was, as it were, ground smooth automatically; the flat belly and the three facets of the back had level and smooth surfaces. These and particularly the belly were already slippery and as a result reduced the resistance of the material as the tool encountered it.

Man systematically and persistently sought out more rational ways of working and reducing friction, even if he did it mainly by trial and error in the course of the work. Traces of wear show that blades used as knives for whittling wood and bone were grasped in the hand in such a way that the belly and not the back of the blade faced the material. Exceptions to this rule have hardly ever been detected. Blades of whittling knives are hardly ever retouched to ease friction, and, when they are, as a rule it is from the ventral side on to the back, not vice versa.

The increase in manufacture and specialization of tools in upper palaeolithic times became more evident. The requirements of a society of hunters in the periglacial zone of Europe and northern Asia made necessary new branches of manufacture, for which the previous range of tools was inadequate. Different operations earlier performed by one tool were now carried out with several. For example, there were meat and whittling knives each with its own shape and method of use, and besides this there were known: end-scrapers for dressing skin, burnishers, perforators and awls, bone needles, drills, burins, stone saws, side-scrapers for use on bone, chisels, axes, bone wedges, mattocks, pestles, mortars, pounding slabs, retouchers, pressers, spearheads, harpoons, javelins, handles for various tools, and other tools.

Study of traces of use reveals that in upper palaeolithic times there was still no very sharp division of function between tools. Sometimes whittling knives were used for cutting meat, strikers as retouchers or pestles, and so on. Nevertheless division of function was one of the characteristic traits of the period; the properties of tools, for example flint blades, had become such that a mixing of functions in one tool was becoming more and more difficult. Whittling knives would require a blade either unretouched or barely trimmed from the ventral side, that is not toothed, but it was not essential for the blade to be straight; while on the other hand for meat knives straightness and a toothed edge were very important.

In upper palaeolithic times an increase in force of application of tools was achieved without any increase in human physical potential; indeed, it is possible that man then was physically weaker than Neandertal man. Nevertheless he was certainly higher in a social sense or in terms of technology.

Due to the use of the handles in which he mounted his knives and burins the application of useful energy was two to three times as great. This happened because a firmer grasp in the hand could make use of the muscular strength of the shoulder and upper arm to a much greater extent than when, as previously, a cutting tool had been used without a handle.

Handles on digging striking tools (mattocks) and chopping tools (axes) made it possible to increase significantly the coefficient of useful action of muscular energy, since the elongation of the handle made the movement more rapid. The increase in rapidity of movement was especially significant in projectiles, which were first adopted and brought into general use in upper palaeolithic times.

In the life of the most ancient periods of humanity hunting played an important part, but the advantage of humans over the animals they pursued was not great. It lay mainly in collective action, in the organization of drives of game, but once man was in a position to strike the animal from a distance by throwing a javelin his advantage was greatly increased. The sling, bolas and even the boomerang were not known everywhere, but javelin throwing became almost universal. It was precisely in this field that the principles were first realized of how to increase the rapidity of movement of objects over a distance.

The average flight of a light spear (dart) if we rely on the ethnographic evidence is 35–40 m; its average flight propelled from a spear-thrower[1] (woomera of the

---

[1] D. N. Anuchin, *Proceedings of the Fifth Session of Archaeologists at Tiflis* (Moscow, 1887), p. 333.

Australians) is 70–80m. This is a measure of the increase of distance obtained by palaeolithic man by means of increasing the rapidity of movement of his tools by a practical mastering of some elementary principles of ballistics.

Soon after the javelin, or perhaps at the same time, man explored the possibilities of more complicated ballistic devices by the creation of the sling, bolas and throwing club, whose flight is circular. The evidence as to whether these were employed in palaeolithic times is not known to us in a convincing form, but apparently they existed, although not everywhere.

Thus the most important technical advances in palaeolithic tools coincided with the cultural divisions in Europe: Chelles, Acheul, Moustier, Aurignac, and Solutré. The period known as mesolithic has been evaluated quite differently. This period in the evolution of the Stone Age has been regarded as an intervening stage without independent significance, merely serving as a link between two cycles of development, a sort of unconformity between geological layers. Not long ago some students still regarded the mesolithic period as one of decay and degeneration; study of technology of the period lends no weight to this view.

It cannot be merely chance that it is precisely in mesolithic times that man attempted in a considerable way to overcome one very weak side of stone tools that impeded further development in their use. This weakness consisted in the brittleness of stone and its inability to withstand pressure in movements and blows, and it was exacerbated by the fact that the angle of blade or point sharpness had been reduced, while at the same time the length of the working part had been increased.

In spite of all their other merits upper palaeolithic prismatic blades are very brittle rough-outs due to their narrow section. On sites of this period we encounter huge quantities of broken tools. Undoubtedly javelin and dart heads generally broke at the moment of impact against the animal's body; possibly many broke the first time they were used.

This feature is revealed by the broken shouldered points from Kostenki I and the leaf-shaped heads from Telmansk. On these sites a series of fragments have been found, not tips but stumps of the head. Evidently they had been brought home by the hunters with the shafts, but the tips of the heads would have been lost in the bodies of wounded animals.

The technique of insertion therefore was of immense significance. It was a new way of improving a tool to increase its toughness by uniting stone and bone in one construction.

The first steps in the manufacture of composite tools were made at the end of upper palaeolithic times, but systematic and varied application of the new technique falls within the mesolithic period.

Flint inserts were mounted in grooves in bone rods without steaming, the bone evidently being just soaked. It is true that by the action of water bone swells only very slowly, but, owing to the lime in it, it dries quickly and grips.

The advantage of a composite tool lay mainly in the fact that it offered greater reliability in a blow or other cases where it was subjected to stress; if individual inserts broke or fell out they could be replaced. It gave weapons a longer life. Composite tools such as heads for spears, knives, daggers or harpoons could be made of variable length, which might exceed the length of prismatic blades.

They could be made absolutely straight without regard to the curvature of a complete blade. There was no need to resort to the laborious Solutrean pressure retouch, which required large cores or tabular flint.

The manufacture of so-called micro-blades once more reduced the angle of sharpness, reaching the thinness of a razor and left without retouch on the working edge. Only with a bone mount could a small thin brittle blade be brought into practical use.

Moreover, in this technique the principle of economy of such an important material as flint was carried to its practical limit, a circumstance with important consequences. A society possessing such a technique was no longer confined to the area of deposits of high-quality chalk flint. In any case many of the deposits of such flint had been destroyed at the end of the glacial period. For making inserts any material of the quartz family was suitable; pebble flint, agate, hornstone, chalcedony, and jasper, even if they occurred only in very small nodules. Flinty minerals, however, occur as pebbles (river, lake, and marine) in abundance almost everywhere.

All these merits of the insertion technique were so important that, after its appearance in mesolithic times, it continued into neolithic and even to some extent into early metallic times. An excellent example of composite tools in the neolithic period can be cited in the beautiful Siberian specimens from graves in Isakov, Serov, and Rasputin published by Okladnikov.[1]

In the history of tools very great significance is attached to the invention of the bow, first brought into widespread use in mesolithic times. It became possible because man by experiment had reached the point where he grasped the value of the potential energy stored in elastic bodies, pre-eminently wood, with which he had had constant dealings. He had only to notice the strength of a bent branch or sapling.

---

[1] A. P. Okladnikov, *Materials and Researches on the Archaeology of the U.S.S.R.*, 18 (1950), pp. 183, 214, 365, 366.

Hunting society of mesolithic times because of the bow made a great advance in the increase of rapidity of movement of tools. The speed of an arrow exceeds by two and a half to three times that of a cast javelin, due to the brief impulse received from the bow string. The greater the speed the greater is the force and suddenness of the blow.

As regards distance of flight it was twice that of a javelin hurled from a spear-thrower, and three to four times that of one hurled from the hand. For example, the Veddah bow (Ceylon) tautened with the feet, according to the reports of K. G. Seligman and F. Sarasin, will shoot an arrow 300–350 m (free flight), which gives a practical wounding range of 150–200 m.

Yet the range of an arrow released from a bow and even its speed would have little practical importance without one essential feature of this hunting weapon, precision in back-sighting. Up to then not a single projectile (neither javelin, nor spear-thrower, nor sling, nor bolas, nor throwing club) had any kind of back-sight. The methods of throwing were learnt with great difficulty and were almost impossible to pass on by teaching. A bow allowed the arrow-shaft to be directed over open sights at the level of the hunter's eye, and so greatly simplified discharging missiles at game. On top of this the hunter could take a large supply of arrows with him because of their slight size and weight.

In order to appreciate the invention of the bow more fully it is necessary to remember that the principles of its mechanism were later employed very effectively in various types of cross-bows, which with traps and snares were the origin of ancient 'automatic' devices.

Ancient spear-, stone- and fire-throwing machines of Classical and early medieval times (cross-bows, catapults and so on) relied on the same physical mechanism, the elasticity of a piece of matter. Moreover, the technique of torsion is merely a specialized use of this physical property; the essential element here is a tightly twisted cord of ox sinews or woman's hair. The ballista, the Roman stone-throwing machine, is a typical specimen of torsion artillery.

Thus by the time all the possibilities within the principle of the bow had been exhausted society had practically entered into the fourth socio-economic stage, capitalism; the bow and cross-bow played some part in Europe even in the seventeenth century.

The cutural and technical achievements of the mesolithic period, besides the introduction of composite tools and bows and arrows, included also the invention of the adze and domestication of the dog. At this time and connected with great geological and climatic changes settlement began over new territories in all five continents. Finally it has to be noted that in mesolithic times agriculture started in the sub-tropical zone of the Mediterranean and tropical belt around the world.

A main feature of the development of neolithic tools which it is very important to notice is the fact that during this period society reached the limit to which the useful properties of stone, as the main technical material for tools, could be exploited.

With regard to the angle of sharpness no real advances can be discerned, but with regard to reduction of friction by means of grinding axes, adzes, chisels, and knives, there was an advance of the first magnitude. Attention must now be drawn to the fact that humanity in the Stone Age took a fresh step towards freeing itself from regional isolation by the perfection of its techniques of making its tools.

In neolithic times man began making axes and adzes by the technique of grinding, which, needless to say, can be regarded as a progressive achievement. Students concentrating on this, however, and noticing improvements in the working of wood have overlooked a consequence of this. In reality this narrow technical achievement opened a new era in the history of humanity. Vast tracts of the globe hitherto uninhabitable became accessible for settlement and exploitation thanks to the ground axe and adze. The occupation of the forest areas of the northern hemisphere, the tropics and islands of the Pacific Ocean, was possible for two reasons. Firstly, ground axes were considerably more efficient than unground ones for chopping trees for houses, canoes, stake structures, and slash-and-burn agriculture; secondly, the grinding technique allowed these tools to be made of rocks which in earlier periods, because of the prevailing technique of flaking, had not and could not play a useful part in the economy, since techniques of splitting, flaking and retouch did not allow them to be worked.

The palaeolithic and mesolithic techniques of flaking, blade-making and retouch permitted the use only of flinty rocks of the quartz family, which are not abundant in nature, and in a whole group of countries are met only as small river pebbles, not suitable for the manufacture of such large implements as axes and adzes. The grinding technique allowed man to employ for this purpose different volcanic granular rocks and even the softer shales and slates.

It is well known that almost all the axes of the northern forest half of Europe are made of slate (*slanets*). The adzes with which the Melanesians and Polynesians dug out their outrigger and double canoes for settling the islands of the Pacific Ocean were made of basalt. Thanks to the ground axe, the earliest slash-and-burn agriculture became possible in the forested areas of the temperate and tropical zones, as well as the construction of pile-dwellings, which represents a great new step forward in the creative activity of man, in the development of society and the formation and strengthening of tribes.

Wood-working had a marked influence on the specialization of tools in neolithic times. In palaeolithic times an axe was a rare occurrence, in mesolithic an adze was added to the axe, although it was an exceptional object. In the neolithic period an axe, adze, and chisel were in use, and in some areas a whittling knife or even a plane (two-handled knife). In addition we can detect specialization in the adzes themselves, the most used tool at this time. There are adzes for rough trimming of wood, for surface work, for deep transverse hollowing-out, gouge and bevelled adzes and so on. Such profound specialization in neolithic wood-working tools is not found everywhere, for only where this branch of manufacture had reached a high degree of development did this become necessary. The same may be said about other forms of manufacture.

With regard to increase of force applied in tools in the neolithic period no major achievements are noticeable, only a fuller realization of striking tools mounted in handles. The latter covers chopping tools (axes, adzes, hoes, picks) as well as stone hammers. In neolithic stone-splitting the wedge and lever were widely employed. Levers were employed for moving great weights, as, for example, the stones used in building megaliths. It has to be recognized, however, that the wedge and lever had been employed in earlier periods, for example in splitting wood and bone and in digging the ground.

As a new achievement of this period at a higher level we must place the first attempt to make practical use of the moving forces of nature, for example the wind. This was the case with the adoption of a sail in some parts of the world (south-eastern Asia and the Mediterranean area). Evidently in neolithic times, particularly in southern Asia (India), the strength of domestic animals (horned cattle) was harnessed for transport.

As regards increasing the rapidity of movement of tools, this tendency in development found its expression in neolithic times in the application of the principle of rotation in some kinds of work. All bodies moving over a certain distance develop great force if they turn on their own axis. In its crudest form the principle of rotation was applied by prehistoric man in such throwing implements as a sling, boomerang, and bolas.

A more valuable application of the principle was found in the adoption of a very simple mechanical drill operated by bow and string. With this device a start was made with quicker and better-quality drilling of wood, bone, shell, stone, and also a swifter method of making fire. It has been mathematically calculated, and is supported by ethnography, that fire can be made in 12–15 seconds with a bow drill, assuming the *savoir faire* and all the rules observed. The bow drill is constructionally related to the archer's bow, but the disk drill, widely employed by tribes in America and the Pacific Ocean area, to the spindle.

The efficiency of drilling with a bow drill is relatively very great; if, for example, two-handed drilling (alternating spin between the palms) was two to three times more effective than one-handed drilling (half-turns), then bow drilling was twenty times more efficient than two-handed drilling.

Further development of the principle of rotation, which had found expression in neolithic times in the form of drilling tools, a little later (eneolithic times) led to the adoption of the potter's wheel and cart wheel, and so produced an exceptionally fruitful enhancement of the speed of movement in other sides of human activity and in the productivity of work.

However considerable may be the technical achievements of the Stone Age it is quite obvious that at the end of neolithic times the development of stone tools had reached a cul-de-sac with all possibilities of further improvement of technology on its existing material basis exhausted. Although cutting tools in the form of composite knives and daggers were a high achievement of stone technology, they were very complicated and laborious things to make and, more important, their efficiency was not great. They consisted of a set of flint blades in a bone haft which was considerably thicker than they were and which always impeded the cutting. In addition a combination of bone and stone did not give toughness and reliability in the more exacting requirements of the work. Flint inserts would break, splinter and fall out. As for stone drills, awls, spear- and arrowheads, they broke just as often as the palaeolithic ones. Man was powerless to alter the internal properties of stone in order to reduce its brittleness.

Especially important in the technology of this period were the chopping tools (axes, adzes, chisels, and picks), which had to retain a large angle of blade sharpness, otherwise they would have broken at the first blow. Some adzes had an edge angle of 45–50°, but the basic mass of chopping tools averaged 55–60° or even more. So in spite of grinding, in spite of bevelling on adzes the efficiency of which was greater, in spite of other improvements noticeable at the end of neolithic times (for example the manufacture of chopping tools of regular geometrical shapes by sawing out the rough-outs), the productivity of work had already ceased to increase. Furthermore, rotary movement, the positive qualities of which were described above, had little prospect of development while wood, stone or bone was employed for the axis.

An escape from the situation that had arisen was found in the extraction and working of metals. Metals are not distinguished by the hardness of some rocks and minerals, and the majority do not possess resistance to chemical reagents. All the same, metals had an incomparable advantage over stone; they possessed plastic qualities and were malleable without breaking, and did not splinter under a blow or pressure. The angle of sharpness on an axe or adze blade could be reduced to 15–20° and thus considerably raise the productivity of the implement.

The very process of making the tool achieved a reduction of friction without the necessity for grinding; casting and forging rendered this laborious process unnecessary and left only the sharpening to be done. The degree of hardness of metal was not consistently high, but fusing, forging, and quenching carried out at will could produce the requisite qualities. Forging and smelting could not only give any shape to a metal tool, but also employed it economically, not a scrap of the precious material being discarded.

The ability of metals to assume any shape and acquire a desired hardness gave man the opportunity to develop and perfect metal tools to an unlimited level of specialization. At the same time, due to its special mechanical quality, one metal tool could in case of necessity replace several stone ones. For example, a one-edged pointed knife of the early Bronze or Iron Age could equally satisfactorily be employed as a meat or whittling knife, but also as an awl, drill, burin or skin knife. The blending of such varied functions in a single stone tool would have been impossible.

In conclusion it should be observed that the study of the laws of development of material culture is an urgent task of archaeological science. A knowledge of these laws reveals the direction of the development of working tools, weapons, utensils, houses, clothing, of different manufactures and of transport, and sheds new rays of light on historical problems.

Index